GREAT WESTERN RAILWAY
STARS, CASTLES AND KINGS

GREAT WESTERN RAILWAY
STARS, CASTLES AND KINGS

ALLEN JACKSON

THE CROWOOD PRESS

First published in 2018 by
The Crowood Press Ltd
Ramsbury, Marlborough
Wiltshire SN8 2HR

www.crowood.com

British Library Cataloguing-in-Publication Data
A catalogue record for this book is available from the British
Library.

ISBN 978 1 78500 481 0

Typeset by Servis Filmsetting Ltd, Stockport, Cheshire

Printed and bound in India by Parksons Graphics

CONTENTS

PREFACE
AND ACKNOWLEDGEMENTS

By the turn of the nineteenth century the Great Western Railway had put behind it the enormous expense of the change from broad to standard gauge and the building of the Severn Tunnel, and was looking forward to a new era of prosperity and stability.

The Edwardian era was to continue the foundations established under Queen Victoria whose duration of reign was eclipsed by the GWR itself who preceded it.

Oher civil engineering projects included the South Wales line through Badminton, the Berks and Hants line and that connecting with Fishguard Harbour, as well as the harbour itself. In the depression of the 1930s improvements to infrastructure, carried out to alleviate unemployment, had a positive impact on GWR facilities.

In terms of locomotives, early work by Sir Daniel Gooch, Joseph Armstrong and later William Dean had provided steady if unspectacular progress. Dean's 4-4-0 express passenger locomotives were flyers and well capable of holding their own in a late nineteenth-century context of train loadings. His 27XX pannier tanks were the template for the enlarged 57XX panniers, which became the GWR's most numerous class. The Dean Goods, an example of which is preserved in STEAM – Museum of the Great Western Railway, Swindon, was to serve the nation in two World Wars as well as being a model for a free-steaming and reliable 0-6-0 freight locomotive, the nineteenth-century staple.

The other pre-grouping railways had established a formula for locomotive building that had not changed radically since the days of Stephenson's Rocket in 1830. Using that which had been tried and tested over sixty years or more was unlikely to get you sacked as a Locomotive Carriage and Wagon Superintendent.

During Dean's final years at Swindon, his failing health caused him to rely increasingly on the engineer who was to become his successor, George Jackson Churchward. Dean retired in 1902 to spend the last three years of his life by the seaside. Dean Street, Swindon, which runs along the south side of the GWR line, is named after him.

The original intention for this volume was to use previously unpublished photographs but this has proved impossible given the age of the subject matter. Where possible, however, locomotives are shown in unusual or notable circumstances and as much information is included as space permits.

Although personnel are generally referred to by the male gender, because in history that is what they were, it is recognized that not only men provide the many crews and operating staff on the heritage scene who are carrying out valuable work in helping to keep the railway history of this country alive.

I would like to thank the Great Western Trust team at Didcot, in particular the noted author Laurence Waters for his unstinting help with photographic research. The staff at STEAM – Museum of the Great Western Railway have also provided invaluable help.

CHAPTER ONE

GEORGE JACKSON CHURCHWARD

George Jackson Churchward (1957–1933) came from Stoke Gabriel, South Devon. He was blessed with the ability to recognize and implement the best features and practice of steam engineers from around the world. Steam technology had moved almost to its limits by the end of the nineteenth century, with the possible exception of superheating.

This commonsensical approach has to be viewed in the context of how an engineer would be promoted from a practical position on the shop floor to hidebound administrative responsibilities, divorced from the practicalities of the job and possibly mostly concerned with company politics. Churchward's common sense was derived from the acquisition of experience on the job.

Churchward was an eminently practical man who kept his engineering feet firmly on the ground, staying in touch with day-to-day practicalities. If there were any significant change to a locomotive he wanted tests and comparisons made with previous standards. The rolling test bed at Swindon and the GWR dynamometer car were testament to this measured approach. Churchward understood that the steam locomotive was principally a question of the boiler: from this all else could flow. The best valve gear and wheel arrangement were of no use if they could not be supplied with steam in abundance and at economical rates. In addition a poorly designed and constructed boiler could be ruinously expensive in maintenance costs and inconvenient in operational service.

Boilers

By the turn of the nineteenth century the GWR's locomotive practice might best be described as Dean's locomotives with Churchward's boilers. Churchward had adapted best practice in terms of a Belpaire firebox and coned taper boiler barrel and this was at variance with most other designers, except perhaps Samuel W. Johnson on the Midland Railway.

The Belpaire locomotive firebox is surrounded by a water jacket to enhance steam production and the

Churchward Family Locomotives – Star Class

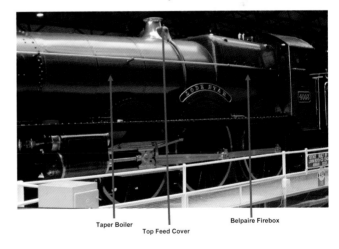

Taper Boiler   Top Feed Cover   Belpaire Firebox

Fig. 1. Star Class 4003 Lode Star at the National Railway Museum (NRM), York, illustrating the Belpaire firebox, coned boiler and top-feed boiler arrangements, June 2004.

actual firebox is constructed to the same shape suggested by the outside appearance, but is smaller to allow room for the water jacket on the outside. This allows the stays that support and keep the firebox apart from the water jacket to be simple straight pieces. However, the manufacturing cost was higher than that of the standard nineteenth-century round-topped firebox, which was basically two circular structures, one within the other. The advantage of the Belpaire type is that the enlarged space above the firebox contains more water, where most of the heat is. This was described at the time as having greater evaporative or steam-making potential.

The Belpaire firebox, as Churchward implemented it, had an enlarged area for water circulation at the front and at the point where it was farthest away from the hottest part of the fire.

The effect of this was to enhance water circulation in that area. As well as producing more steam, this led to a reduction in local overheating nearest the fire. The disproportionate effects resulting from the rear of the firebox being intensely hot, and the rest not so, produced distortion in the boiler plating and stays and consequently increased maintenance costs. Churchward's design avoided this pitfall. This meant that the Belpaire firebox of Churchward's manufacture was tapered towards the cab.

The propensity of steam production at the front of the firebox meant that there was no need for a dome to collect the steam as in a parallel round-topped boiler. Churchward always regarded the dome as a source of weakness in the structure that would obviously lead to additional cost. This would have an effect on the appearance of Churchward-boilered locomotives and

Fig. 2. Castle Class 5043 Earl of Mount Edgcumbe displays the Belpaire taper firebox, as adopted by Churchward and continued by his successor Charles Collett. Stratford-upon-Avon, August 2017.

make the other railways' domed engines seem stuck in the Victorian age and out of date. The appearance of Churchward's boilers, and subsequently the loco-motives, caused much criticism from frock-coated and bewhiskered traditionalists. Churchward took no notice and believed that appearance was not necessar-ily an attribute for efficiency.

The coned nature of the Belpaire firebox was mar-ried to a cone-tapered boiler barrel that accentuated the property for steam collection where the two com-ponents met. The greater surface area in this region meant that fewer bubbles formed: bubbles have a water component when what is required is a gas – pure steam.

Churchward, after typically trying one boiler with a dome and one without, found there was less foam-ing and priming and consequently more pure steam produced in the domeless type.

Priming is the means by which water is carried through the steam production process. This has a det-rimental effect on performance and damage can occur if water reaches the cylinders. Water is an uncom-pressible liquid and the force of a piston trying to compress the uncompressible will result in a damaged piston or cylinder.

In addition to the tapered Belpaire firebox, Church-ward found that the most efficient shape to assist water flow around the fire tubes on the boiler barrel was also tapered towards the smokebox, which itself was a parallel shape.

The boiler constantly uses the boiled water as steam and so must be replenished from time to time with a fresh cold supply. Churchward found that a top-feed arrangement through clack or check valves, the water supply of which was then distributed in droplets through the use of trays, was the most efficient means of getting water into a steaming boiler.

The check or clack valve is a non-return valve that is fed from steam-driven injectors to force water into a boiler that would naturally resist such an action from any source of a lower pressure than that in the boiler. It is usually the fireman's job to maintain a constant head of water in a boiler using the injectors. Gauge glasses are provided in the cab to enable levels to be observed.

In the view of the cab of 5043 Earl of Mount Edgcumbe (fig. 3), the gauge glass is the rectangular

Fig. 3. Inside the cab of 5043 Earl of Mount Edgcumbe. Stratford-upon-Avon, August 2017.

vertical polished steel object next to the two circular gauges. Other models had thick glass panels to enclose the glass tube that indicated the water content of the boiler. These have been known to break under the high pressure within, spraying the cab with scalding steam.

The tray distribution at the top of the boiler bar-rel minimizes the shock of cold water entering the boiler as this is where the temperature is the highest. To introduce water at the bottom of the boiler, where the temperature is the lowest, may reduce overall temperatures significantly and so drastically reduce steam production.

Churchward also propounded higher boiler pres-sures than had been used hitherto on British railways. He was able to prove in a series of tests that higher boiler pressures up to 225psi (pounds per square inch; 15.65 bar) produced more power and lower coal con-sumption for a given boiler size. There would be a price to pay in terms of a more robust and expensive construction than required for lower-pressure boil-ers, but Churchward believed that the Swindon works could easily engineer it and the directors would pay when they realized the benefits.

Churchward designed a standard set of boilers that would encompass the needs of most of the GWR's locomotives until the end of its existence, albeit with modifications en route.

Valves

With the boiler design settled, Churchward was able to concentrate on the subject of valves. Nearly all internal combustion cars in production in 2017 have four valves per cylinder whereas the twentieth-century standard was two valves per cylinder. This seeming extravagance in production costs can be explained in the efficiencies gained by getting fuel and air into the cylinder and exhaust gases out quickly in the cycle.

Churchward realized this in 1902, albeit in a steam engine context, and adopted large long-travel piston valves. However, it is first necessary to compare it with the slide valve, which had been the standard nineteenth-century design in extensive use, to see the benefits of Churchward's approach.

The principles of a slide or flat valve steam engine are shown in fig. 4. The long distance between the ports where steam is either admitted or exhausted can give rise to a lowering in temperature and efficiency. If the steam is superheated this kind of valve layout can lead to lubrication problems.

Churchward, however, used large-diameter valves with a long travel, as seen in the diagram illustrating the principles of a piston valve steam engine (fig. 5).

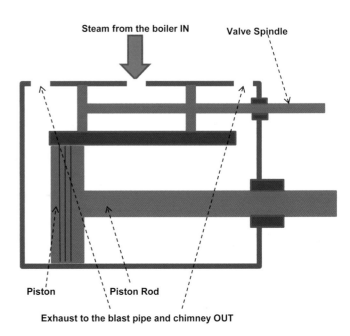

Parts coloured red are those that move

Steam from the boiler IN   Valve Spindle

Piston   Piston Rod

Exhaust to the blast pipe and chimney OUT

Fig. 5. Principles of a piston-valve steam engine.

In this design the steam has a shorter journey in order to do useful work, making more efficient use of the steam and reducing the tendency for the steam to cool along the way.

The longer travel piston valve enabled a larger diameter valve to be used, making it the Edwardian equivalent of the twenty-first-century's 4-valve per cylinder petrol car. The long travel and large valve size permitted efficient entry of steam and its consequent exhaust to get rid of the waste after the work had been done.

Churchward also adopted long lap valves. Lap is where the admission of steam is cut off by the valve's position while steam is already in the cylinder. This allows the steam to expand more and do useful work. So it is a delay, enforced by mechanical valve positioning that enables trapped steam to do more work.

The valve gear is a means of varying the amount by which the steam admitted to a cylinder is cut off or stopped or reversed. If steam is admitted to the cylinder throughout the time that a piston is moving in one direction, this is wasteful in terms of steam used. More efficient use of the steam is made the longer that the steam is cut off during the piston's stroke,

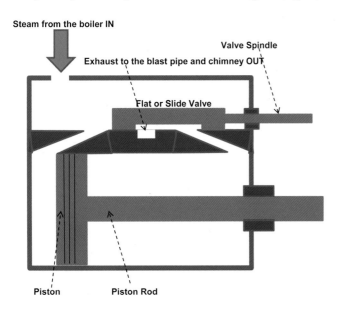

Steam from the boiler IN

Valve Spindle

Exhaust to the blast pipe and chimney OUT

Flat or Slide Valve

Piston   Piston Rod

Parts coloured red are those that move

Fig. 4. Principles of a slide- or flat-valve steam engine.

particularly when the locomotive is at speed. Starting off with a heavy load, the cut-off is eliminated or the locomotive is said to be in full forward (or reverse) gear.

A further refinement in terms of boiler and steam production was the superheater. Churchward was fully convinced by the theory of its advantages but by 1903 no one had managed to get one to work satisfactorily. The problem was to be solved in the following years.

The superheater provides a means of raising the temperature of the steam so that, by the time it reaches the relatively cold cylinders and valves, any reduction in the steam temperature does not significantly affect the locomotive's efficiency and eliminates priming.

The superheater is a set of pipes like a radiator placed in the way of the flue of hot gases on their way to the blast pipe and chimney. By this stage the gases have done their work of heating the water in the boiler and are now considered to be the waste products of combustion.

Now that he had addressed both the boiler and valves, Churchward set about introducing a standard set of locomotives equipped to meet the GWR's immediate and future needs.

The First GWR 4-6-0 Locomotives

Churchward introduced the first GWR 4-6-0 locomotive in February 1902. Although William Dean was still nominally in charge, the Board of Directors had listened to Churchward's ideas the previous year and given the go ahead to construct a batch of new 4-6-0 locomotives. Churchward's ultimate aim was to construct locomotives that could exert a drawbar pull of 2 tons force at 70mph (19.9kN at 112km/h) and maintain this with a long-distance passenger train.

The first was numbered 100 and given the name Dean in June 1902; this was changed to William Dean after his retirement in November 1902. Number 100 was a development engine and still retained the parallel boiler without a top feed, and the boiler was set low in the frames. The piston valves were fitted and the locomotive had an angular appearance that offended Victorian and GWR sensibilities accustomed to the flowing lines of the outside frame 4-4-0s that preceded it.

The piston valve diameter was a particular feature that Churchward concentrated on, understanding that valve events held the key to efficient use of steam, and hence power and speed. He rigged up an experimental single-cylinder stationary engine at Swindon as a test bed for experimenting with various piston valve diameters and found that the 6½in (15.24cm) valve, based on slide valve practice, was too small to get the steam in and out of the cylinders efficiently. The valves were holding back the capacity of the boiler to supply the steam and the cylinders to use it effectively. Their small size meant they were a bottleneck in the engine's running process.

Refinements to correct these deficiencies were introduced with number 98. It had 10in (25.4cm) piston valves and longer travel, which was subsequently increased to the final standard of 6¼in (15.86cm). The boiler was of the tapered short cone type and the firebox was also tapered. This form was to be considered as Churchward's Standard No. 1 boiler. Its pressure was only 200psi (13.79 bar). The piston valves would later be modified so that they formed a 'plug' in the valve chamber when under steam to effect a good seal, but they relaxed when not under pressure to provide the minimum resistance to motion. The LMS and SR later copied this idea.

The photograph of Castle 4-6-0 5043 Earl of Mount Edgcumbe amply demonstrates the size of the piston

Fig. 6. Piston valves belonging to King Class 6023 on display at Didcot Railway Centre. The piston and rod are behind. November 2017.

Fig. 7. Cylinder and valve chest covering of Castle 4-6-0 5043 Earl of Mount Edgcumbe. Stratford-upon-Avon, August 2017.

valve in relation to the piston (fig. 7). The housing on the upper left of the photo indicates the valve size. The three cylinder drain cocks at the bottom of the cylinder are used to evacuate condensed water from the cylinder, as mentioned above in the description of priming.

This locomotive was truly a step change in performance and efficiency compared with what had gone before. While there were to be many modifications over the years, number 98 was the template for thousands of locomotives to follow.

Engine number 171 named Albion, an ancient name for the islands of Great Britain, followed in February 1904. There was nothing ancient about its features, however, as it incorporated all Churchward's innovations at its introduction in December 1903. It had a higher pressure boiler of 225psi (15.51 bar) and the firebox and grate area were slightly increased to give a locomotive weighing in at 70 tons (71 tonnes).

These locomotives were to become the progenitors of the celebrated Saint class 4-6-0 and were a pivotal component of British steam locomotive history. They were originally intended as express passenger locomotives with 6ft 8½in (204.5cm) driving wheels with Stephenson's valve gear. They did all that could be asked of them at the time and more, and yet their adaption to the mixed traffic 6ft (1.85m) driving wheel Hall class 4-6-0 ensured a lasting place in railway history. The Great Western Society at Didcot has almost finished, in 2018, a Saint class locomotive, out of number and name sequence, 2999 Lady of Legend, which used parts of a Hall class. This reverse engineering seems appropriate.

Churchward had been impressed with the performance and smooth running of the de Glehn compound Atlantic 4-4-2 locomotives on the Nord Railway in France. These locomotives were 4-cylinder compounds in which the steam is used twice, first in a high-pressure cylinder and then in a lower pressure one. This design was extremely popular with marine engines but less so with railway locomotives in Britain. Marine engines would seem to have more constant working conditions and output than locomotives. The Midland Railway compound 4-4-0s were considered to be successful but only when compared with their Midland Railway predecessors, which were small and often not up to the job on their own, requiring two locomotives.

4-Cylinder de Glehn Compound Atlantic 4-4-2 Locomotives

Churchward persuaded the directors to pay for a de Glehn compound so he could compare it with his own locomotives. He wasn't convinced that the practicalities of compounding would live up to the theoretical advantages, but he was prepared to try it out.

The 4-4-2 was arranged so that the high-pressure cylinders drove the rear driving wheels, while the inside low-pressure cylinders drove the front axle through a crank. This is described as 'divided drive'. Although the LNWR Claughton class 4-6-0, which had all the cranks drive the front axle, was considered to be relatively successful, splitting the considerable forces over two axles instead of one would reduce the stress on the engine overall, leading to a more equitable division of wear on the bearing surfaces.

The locomotive, numbered 102 and named La France, was taken into GWR stock in October 1903. The locomotive was built by the Société Alsacienne de Constructions Mécaniques at its works in Belfort, which had remained French after most of Alsace was annexed by Germany in 1871. SACM's descendant company Alstom, which is renowned for its TGV, Eurostar and Pendolino designs, still has a factory in Belfort, close to the Swiss border, while the manufacturing headquarters of Peugeot cars is nearby at Sochaux.

Separate sets of Walschaerts valve gear were provided for the high- and low-pressure cylinders and they could be worked either together or separately, thanks to a catch on the compound screw reverser. In addition, the engine could be worked as a simple by routing the high-pressure exhaust to the chimney, instead of to the low-pressure cylinders, and by admitting ordinary boiler steam to the low-pressure cylinders via a pressure-reducing valve. This feature would help

Churchward in his comparison tests of simple versus compound.

Another novel feature was a variable blast pipe worked from the cab. It had long been a railwayman's tradition to secure a piece of flat steel bar across the blast pipe if an engine was not steaming well. This constriction caused the fire to draw more readily and increase steam production. Items like this were advertised as the 'Driver's Friend' and could be purchased for the sum of one shilling (5p).

Constriction of the blast pipe was not required, however, if the engine was at speed and working hard. This narrowing instead inhibited the exhaust flow, which was exactly what the larger piston valves had been designed to minimize. The variable blast pipe operated by the crew had the best of both worlds.

The problem with the crew-operated variable blast pipe was that the crew needed to operate it assiduously to take advantage of what it had to offer, and in the course of service the mechanism would become stuck in one position, requiring maintenance to keep it working.

Churchward designed a variable blast pipe with what was known as a jumper ring. Under the pressure of hard working from the locomotive, the ring would be raised inside the blast pipe and this would de-restrict the pipe opening. Upon reduction of the exhaust blast, the jumper ring would fall back and reduce the opening, enabling the fire to draw more readily.

Another of Churchward's concerns involved the balancing of reciprocating masses in particular, and any moving mass in general. Unbalanced masses will tend to shake the locomotive to pieces eventually. They cause rough riding and an uncomfortable experience for the engine crew, who may ease off the speed to make their own journey more bearable and less fatiguing. Unbalanced forces also promote rapid wear in bearing surfaces. An unbalanced locomotive can even leave the rails *in extremis*. As a result of unbalanced forces a locomotive possesses a 'hammer blow' on the track and it is not unknown for badly out-of-balance locomotives to crack rails.

The GWR continued with Churchward's balanced approach: as late as 1950 British Railways decided that, as the 2-cylinder 57XX Pannier Tanks had minimal hammer blow, they would be eased from Blue route to Yellow route availability, even though their weight indicated they should be allocated to the more restrictive Blue route.

The divided drive and four cylinders of the de Glehn compounds produced a much smoother-running machine that would be able to haul heavy trains at high speed with longer overhaul intervals. Although the initial cost of manufacture was higher, the ongoing costs over, say, a thirty-year life would be less. 102 La France remained in service until October 1926 and it ran a total of 728,031 miles (1,171,652km) before withdrawal. Not surprisingly the locomotive was nonstandard in an increasingly standardized Swindon and the cost of new cylinders would be thought excessive, although 102 and its two classmates, 103 and 104, all had Churchward Standard No. 1 boilers at some point.

The only downside that Churchward could see to the de Glehn locomotive was that compounds tend to work at higher cut-off values and therefore seemingly required more steam to do the same work. He could not produce any evidence that compounding, making use of the steam twice, gave any measurable benefit.

Churchward went the distance to make the comparison between his locos and La France a fair one. He converted no. 171, later 2971 Albion, into a 4-4-2 Atlantic. Albion had been produced with a boiler pressure of 225psi (15.51 bar) and so was on a par with the de Glehn at 227psi (15.65 bar). The comparative testing lasted a year. The only thing Churchward did not do was incorporate his own advances in valve design into the French locomotive.

Another feature of the de Glehn locomotives that was admired and incorporated into the GWR engines was the design of the bogie. The French locomotive had a side-springing arrangement instead of the more usual GWR swing links. Swing links are used in coaches and HST sets where the forces caused by piston thrusts and several large-diameter driving wheels are not present. Bogies of the traditional GWR design, although they were meant to alleviate flange wear on the leading driving wheels, were not as successful as the de Glehn type. The de Glehn type of bogie favoured the outside bearing axlebox, as with coaches, but the GWR resisted this feature until the

Fig. 8. The side-springing attachment on the locomotive bogie is seen here with the five nut-and-bolted angle bracket connecting the bogie to the locomotive frames. The inside cylinder piston rod is visible through the access hole cut in the frames. Stratford-upon-Avon, August 2017.

introduction of the King class more than twenty years later, and even then only in part. Some earlier 4-4-0s sported external axlebox leading bogies.

The de Glehn compounds first worked the arduous west of England expresses, but by 1907 were working Wolverhampton and Worcester expresses with some work on the Birmingham two-hour expresses. Finally they ended up on fast and semi-fast trains from Oxford to Birmingham and Paddington.

Their work done, the de Glehn compounds were to leave a lasting legacy on GWR practice, both from the point of view of what they contributed and what was missing from their design. After this valuable testing and comparison phase, Churchward moved forward with what was to be the last original design for an express passenger engine made during the GWR's existence, the Star class in 1906. All the GWR express passenger locomotives that followed were derived from the Stars.

Churchward's Ethos and Working Practices

The progress made was not just a matter of Churchward seeing the benefits of other technology and using it. An autocratic style of management was prevalent in the Edwardian era and rule by fear was the norm. Churchward was far-sighted enough to see that a consultative style would yield more from his staff. His unquestioned position as head of steam on the GWR meant he did not need to act as a martinet or bully, as some of his contemporaries had done.

He readily sought the opinions of foremen at the works on questions of manufacture, and of shed superintendents and locomotive inspectors on daily running of the engines. With all the information gathered, Churchward then had the depth of experience and general ability to see the way forward and decide how to proceed. His broad range of experience also enabled him to convince others that the chosen path was the right one. In this way GWR staff became involved in the process and aware that their contribution was valued and relevant. This was a great source of motivation for the company and a tie of loyalty that bound the workforce together at all levels.

Loco designers often complained that a sound design sometimes became lost in the detail left to a drawing by a junior draughtsman. For Churchward, however, the delight was in the detail and he would examine, and if necessary criticize, every detail before a drawing was signed off for manufacture.

A component for a locomotive would be assessed for the job it was to do and the following criteria had to be met before it was deemed to be successful in operation:

- Minimum cost of material.
- Efficiency of manufacture.
- Ease of maintenance in service.

Missing from the list is the need for designed items to appease Victorian aesthetic sensibilities and some of Churchward's work was criticized for not addressing them. Harry Holcroft, a senior designer at Swindon, often tidied up the outside appearance of Churchward's locomotives. After Churchward retired in 1922, Holcroft went to the South East and Chatham Railway, soon to become a constituent of the Southern Railway at grouping in 1923.

The downside to Churchward's holistic approach was that it was mostly inside his head: nobody in any department had access to every detail required for the design. Most of it was transferable though: when William Stanier left Swindon to go to the London, Midland and Scottish Railway (LMS) in 1932, he took with him enough knowledge to transform LMS locomotive performance and form the foundation for the standard class of British Railways locomotives after nationalization. Churchward's legacy lived on until the end of steam traction in Britain.

A couple of Stanier's ideas learned at the GWR, however, were not portable. The smokebox regulator and screwed-in piston rods were both adopted as LMS practice but were abandoned when they could not be got to work properly. There was an element of practical knowledge missing that Churchward, one feels, would have known.

The performance of Churchward's locomotives owed much to the following:

- Design that adopted and adapted the best practice of principles from around the world.

- Detail design of individual components, which, when put together, elevated the finished product beyond what could be that achieved by just adopting the first in the list.
- Economical use of the best materials.
- Superb quality of the workmanship and engineering at Swindon.
- Intelligence and enterprise of locomotive crews when driving Churchward's locomotives.
- High standards of maintenance and a channel to feed back any problems to the designer.

Churchward had control of all of the above and so his position was unsurpassed in terms of effectiveness.

The GWR was his life and he was honoured to become the first mayor of Swindon. He continued to live in a company house after his retirement in 1922, maintaining a strong interest in the company and its fortunes: on 19 December 1933 he was inspecting a defective sleeper on the down through main line near his house when, by an irony of ironies, he was struck and killed by Castle class locomotive 4085 Berkeley Castle, which was hauling a Paddington to Fishguard express. The locomotive was a direct descendant of Churchward's Star class locomotive, whose story is examined in Chapter 2.

It was commonplace, after the accession of a new Chief Mechanical Engineer, for the new broom to demonstrate that there was to be change, often for its own sake. There was no such activity on the GWR after Churchward retired. The succeeding CMEs sought to fine tune and adjust Churchward's work and produce locomotives that, while larger and more powerful, were enlarged versions of what had gone before. No radical policy was introduced, given the technology of the time, that would produce any meaningful improvements until the end of steam.

For technical details of the locomotive profiles that follow, please *see* the Appendices.

CHAPTER TWO

STAR CLASS LOCOMOTIVES: THE GAME CHANGER

Churchward was inspired to build a 4-cylinder Atlantic 4-4-2 locomotive after his experiences with the French de Glehn locomotives. The Saint class demonstrated the additional traction afforded by the extra set of coupled wheels of a 4-6-0 and yet Churchward was to persist with the Atlantic wheel arrangement, showing how his own simple expansion design could compare favourably with that by SACM. In addition the Atlantic was seen to run more smoothly than a 4-cylinder 4-6-0 at higher speeds.

North Star was turned out in 1906. The very name, bestowed some months after it was accepted into stock, was sufficient to evoke the history of one of the first locomotives on Brunel's broad-gauge GWR. Number 40 was to continue the legend and expand on it.

Churchward insisted that the connecting rods of the inside and outside cylinders should be the same length. This meant that, with divided drive, the inside cylinders had to be well forward of the frames, as they drove the front driving axle, and the outside cylinders had to be well to the rear of the smokebox, as they were to drive the rear coupled axle in Atlantic 4-4-2 configuration. This arrangement later caused issues with the inside and outside steam pipes that connected the boiler, cylinders and exhaust.

After he moved to the LMS, William Stanier continued with this arrangement on the Princess Elizabeth class.

Scissors Valve Gear, No. 40

The valve gear was effectively a Walschaerts design applied to the inside cylinders, with a connection to the outside cylinder on the opposite side to drive it. Churchward had devised this arrangement himself, but a similar idea had already been patented by R. M. Deeley of the Midland Railway, who objected to what he saw as an infringement of his patent. Thus no. 40 was to remain the only Star locomotive with what was referred to as 'scissors gear'. Churchward did not perpetuate the scissors gear on subsequent locomotives, although this was less in deference to Deeley but because the valve gear arrangement of cross connection meant that a failure of one cylinder automatically disabled an opposite cylinder, which totally immobilized the locomotive. In any case Churchward could prove that he had started work on the scissors gear before Deeley's patent had been granted.

All Star class locomotives were fitted with screw valve gear reversers.

It became apparent in service that a 4-6-0 would have greater adhesion and traction on the South Devon banks and so no. 40 was rebuilt as a 4-6-0 in 1909. In a short time forty similar 4-6-0s were built and formed the nucleus of the class that was eventually to number seventy-three locomotives.

Their power-to-weight ratio, economy of operation and smoothness of running remained unsurpassed by any British locomotive for about twenty years.

Star Class: Salient Features

After the scissors gear episode with no. 40, all subsequent class members, and indeed all succeeding 4-cylinder 4-6-0s, were fitted with Walschaerts valve gear. The Stephenson link gear used on the 2-cylinder locomotives was seen to be superior when starting off with a heavy train and under acceleration, and was thus ideal for freight and mixed traffic use, but the Walschaerts gave constant performance at all cut-off levels and was superior at higher sustained speeds. In any case the Stephenson gear was much bulkier and would not fit between the frames. The outside piston valves were actuated by rocking levers pivoted on the frames.

Design effort was required for even this seeming small detail. The outer arms of the levers were slightly longer and set back, so compensating for the angularity of the cranks at 180 degrees. The effect of this was to give more equal valve events between inside and outside cylinders, which could clearly be heard in the staccato bark of the exhaust of each side cylinder exhaust beat.

Churchward had justified the long 30in (76.2cm) stroke on the 2-cylinder Saint class by pointing out that the longer piston stroke enabled the steam to expand more readily and therefore do more useful work per cylinder event. The piston stroke on the Star class was reduced to 26in (66cm) to enable the whole valve gear to be better balanced. An even longer stroke would increase reciprocating forces and it is these types of forces that make the engine sway at speed. As the whole point of the 4-cylinder approach was the smooth running, the reduction in reciprocating out-of-balance forces was a welcome compromise.

The connection to the inside cylinders at the crank axle was known as the 'big end' and, in accordance with French practice, the big end was forked or split

so that the bearing surface could be examined or changed more easily. Conversely, where access was not so restricted, the big ends to the outside cylinders were not forked but solid.

The 8in piston valves were larger, relatively speaking, on the 14¼in (36.2cm) cylinders than the valves of the Saint class with 18in (45.7cm) cylinders. Coupled with this, the constant lead characteristics of the Walschaerts valve gear meant that it was not necessary to restrict the Stars to the 22 per cent minimum cut-off to which the Saints were limited, owing to their Stephenson valve gear and the relatively crude lever reverse. This made the Stars more economical when running fast, while the superior balanced layout of the four cylinders also gave a smoother ride. The cost of a Star was £3,700, which was seen as a great deal before World War I, but that investment was repaid with overhaul intervals of 120,000 to 130,000 miles (193,000–209,000km), compared to the Saints 70,000 to 80,000 miles (112,600–128,700km) initially. Later, the criteria centred on the axlebox wear, which meant that some Stars were shopped when the rest of the locomotive, excluding axleboxes, was in fine fettle. Therefore, they were overhauled somewhat needlessly just because there was wear in the axleboxes.

The coupled wheels and the trailing axle were fitted with spring compensation beams, the action of which was intended to ensure more even grip of the driving wheels on the track and consequently better adhesion.

Coupling rods had long been drop forged from a steel billet using a 4 ton (4.1 tonne) steam hammer in

Fig. 9. The rocking lever to the outside cylinder piston valve is connected to it by a universal joint to get through 90 degrees. The near inside cylinder piston rod is below. Castle Class 4073, STEAM, September 2017.

Swindon Works in the shape of a girder or 'I' section. This imparts a much stronger ability to resist deflection and is exactly what's required by civil engineers for bridges. The power output of the Stars, however, was such that it could bend the coupling rods. If the forces were extraordinarily severe, with 'I' section rods the bend would be permanent and the locomotive disabled or disastrously limited.

Churchward's solution was to use coupling rods with a rectangular section, which would flex or 'whip' without the deflection being permanent. Almost fifty years later someone who was not aware of Churchward's learned wisdom repeated these events with the British Railways Britannia Pacific locomotives, although the story was complicated by the locomotive being built with incorrect quartering of the driving wheels on the axles.

The leading four-wheeled bogie was carrying a substantial part of the locomotive's weight and it was thought that brake gear on the bogie would contribute to the overall effectiveness of the braking system. While undoubtedly correct, the differences were so small that they were not measurable and the bogie brakes were later removed. Stars would often be pulling a trailing load of 400 tons (406 tonnes), which would be vacuum braked on all passenger trains. The effect of bogie brakes acting on a carried weight of nearly 18 tons (18.3 tonnes) on a train that has an all-up weight of nearer 500 tons (508 tonnes) has to be minimal on braking efficiency as a whole. There may have been a measurable effect with Stars on unfitted goods trains, as they were to haul much later, but this was never regarded as a worthwhile issue to pursue.

Stars continued to be built in small batches until 1923, when the Castles were introduced.

Star Class: Illustrated Details

The inner workings of a steam locomotive, and particularly a 4-cylinder one built to the British loading gauge, is a complex tightly packed machine, which must have been extremely difficult to maintain in tip-top condition for regular high-speed express work.

There now follows an attempt to illustrate at least some of the workings, referring back to the reason they are there in the design process. All photographs in this section were taken by the author.

4003 Lode Star is preserved as part of the national collection at the National Railway Museum, York (fig. 10). None of the Star class survived to run in preservation and the last of the class left service in 1957. The locomotive displays a mixture of old features and newer ones introduced after World War I. Older features include no steam pipes, top lamp iron on top of smokebox, no whistle shield, a 3,500 gallon (15,911ltr) tender, polished smokebox hinges and other steel items. Newer features include no brass beading on the splashers, D-shaped and stowed front vacuum pipe, short safety valve bonnet, ejector pipe on other boiler side, 1927 livery and no bogie brakes.

Fig. 10. 4003 Lode Star at the National Railway Museum (NRM), York, October 2017. The detail views of Lode Star that follow (figs 11–25, 27–35) were all taken at the same time.

Fig. 11. Rear view.

Fig. 12. Front end.

The rear view of 4003 and the cab reveals the screw reverser in the typical GWR driving position on the right-hand side (fig. 11). The dome on the tender is to accommodate the curved water pickup scoop pipe. With only 3,500 gallons in the tender the locos depended heavily on water troughs to sustain longer non-stop runs. The Southern Railway was the only one of the big four companies that didn't have troughs and so needed some 5,000 gallon (22,730ltr) tenders. The parts of the buffers that crews used to step on are painted black. The brass tender works plate reads:

Great Western Railway
1726
Swindon Works
JAN 1907

This dovetails well with the loco's build date of February 1907 but it would be fanciful to suggest that the loco retained the same tender throughout its life.

On the front and left-hand side view of 4003 (fig. 12), the ejector pipe can be seen running from the cab to the smokebox. Note how the handrail is attached outside the pipe and along it. The D-shaped vacuum hose stowage no doubt assisted the positioning of the coupling on its hook below the left-hand buffer. Other railways attached the shackle to the coupling hook, but generally not the GWR. The lamp irons are at right angles to those on other railways' engines, as GWR lamps had side brackets and so the lamp irons are not symmetrically disposed on the bufferbeam. There is no steam heating connection on the front bufferbeam.

The close-up of some of the front end detail of Lode

Fig. 13. Front bufferbeam and fittings.

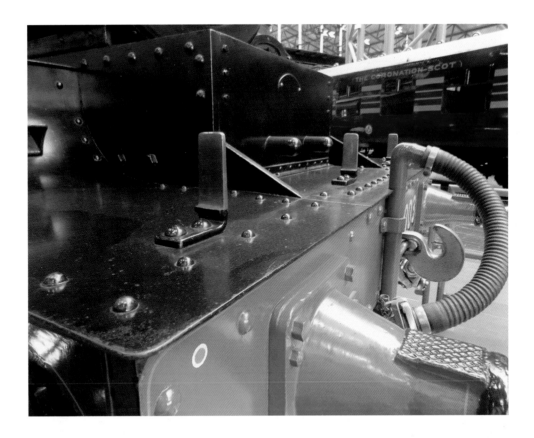

Fig. 14. Outside cylinders and smokebox.

Fig. 15. Cab side.

Star (fig. 13) shows that both the footplate valance and the buffer are lined in the same orange. The somewhat crude box that covers the inside cylinder piston valves is evident, confirming that this is an earlier built locomotive.

On the elegant front of Lode Star, as viewed from the side (fig. 14), the actuating lever to operate the large piston valves is clearly visible, as is its pivot point on the frames. Also shown is the bogie attachment to the frames and one of the following figures underneath the locomotive illustrates the side-springing arrangement copied from the de Glehn compounds. The shiny disc above the crosshead and on the footplate is the front sandbox filler and in front of it are the sandbox linkages. The GWR's lettering stating the engine's home depot is usually placed where the front bufferbeam meets the footplate valance, but in this case it is present in the cab.

The view of the cab's side (fig. 15) illustrates how

the lining is interrupted by the handrail. The red route availability disc signifies that the locomotive is too heavy for anything but main lines. The power classification letter D is only surpassed by the E class allocated to freight 2-8-0 tenders and some tanks, 2-8-2 tank engines and double red King class locos. However, the D letter is just a banding and it was also applied to more powerful locos than the Stars.

The route availability disc and power class letter would later be moved to just above the number plate during World War II and in BR days. The cab vertical handrail is at right angles to the cab side sheet.

On Lode Star's cab, fallplate and tender front (fig. 16) the letters CDF (Cardiff Canton) indicate the locomotive's home depot, although it actually started out at Old Oak Common and ended up at Landore, near Swansea. The steel upright sticking up from the tender side plate, with its mate on the opposite side, is there to support a weather sheet that the crew can rig up for extra protection or to enforce blackout regulations in wartime. On the left-hand side there is the brake T handle for the fireman to operate and opposite this is the water scoop lowering handle. The U-shaped stand is to support fire irons, with a built-in recess in the coal space to accommodate the longer irons.

In the view of the left-hand-side outside cylinders (fig. 17) there can just be seen, at the end of the slide-bars, a suggestion of the black massive motion bracket, attached to the frames, which braces the slidebars against the huge forces they withstand. Just behind the driving wheel is a brake block, with a sandpipe in front. The long lap piston valve spindle covers stick out on either side of the cylinder casing at the top. The orange valance lining is interrupted at the cylinder position.

Moving to the underside, the front bufferbeam can be seen (fig. 18). The two angled stays by the circular disc and large nut support the front coupling hook, as does the box section that makes up the bufferbeam. To the top left and right, although the right is here obscured by the vacuum pipe, are the snifting valves for the inside cylinders; above them are the valve chest covers with their spindle covers projecting through the rectangular box on the footplate, as seen in fig. 13.

From the bufferbeam, lined in orange, the vacuum pipe continues underneath the engine (fig. 19). When

Fig. 16. Loco and tender fallplate.

Fig. 17. Outside cylinder motion.

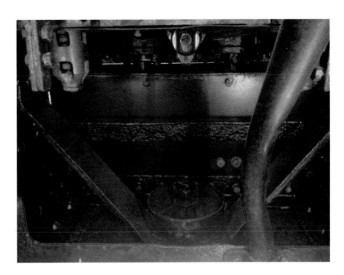

Fig. 18. Front bufferbeam and fittings below.

Fig. 19. Inside cylinders and vacuum pipe.

attached to the front bogie, which has to move up and down as well as sideways, the pipe has to go into flexible mode. The inside cylinder snifting valves are above the drain cock pipework and linkages.

The vacuum pipe continues its flexible way towards the rear of the engine, but in front is the first of the side springs that help keep the bogie centralized (fig. 20). There is another behind the bogie pivot pin. This was a de Glehn innovation that minimized flange wear on the leading driving wheels. The bogie equalizing bars are to the left and right of the side springs.

The end of the bogie equalizing bar bears down on the bogie axlebox (fig. 21). That movement is transmitted to the other bogie axlebox on the same side and acts as a compensating force. At this point there are similarities to the commonwealth bogie that BR used on some of its coaches many years later.

Fig. 20. Bogie side springing.

Fig. 21. Bogie equalizing beam.

Fig. 22. Inside cylinder slidebars.

As our journey progresses rearwards towards the tender, the next accessible items are the inside cylinder slidebars, which are the parallel large flat shiny pieces (fig. 22). The left-hand inside cylinder cross head is visible, but that on the right is out of shot nearer the cylinder face. The connecting rods for both inside cylinders are of T section. The two smaller forked rods are radius rods of the Walschaerts valve gear, which need the fork to articulate about the combination lever that drives the valves in and out.

There is definitely a lack of space around the inside cylinder valve gear with its connecting rods, radius rods, combination levers and linkage to the piston valves (fig. 23). The black rod across the picture is part of the brake rigging, which ensures that any brake application operates on all driving wheels.

The rearward journey continues with the smaller eccentric rods connected to the crank axle, from where they derive a rocking motion from the circular motion of the wheels (fig. 24). The large crank

axle balance weights are in view; that on the left is particularly prominent, while the right is 90 degrees out of phase and therefore partly out of shot. The device on the right-hand side, with the steel piston on one end and four bolts on the other, is the vacuum pump driven by the right-hand inside crosshead. This helps keep the brakes off while the engine is under way. On 2-cylinder locomotives the crosshead driven pump has an outside connection to the right crosshead. The lack of space is evident when you can see both frames. The large red shaft in the centre of the picture, between the connecting rods, is the vacuum brake actuating rod.

Going back slightly and outside the loco, the radius rod comes in from the right and parallel with the top of the picture (fig. 25). It articulates and moves the combination lever, which comes down at an angle that, depending on where the wheels are, can be a right angle. In the view shown it is diagonal. Attached to the combination lever is the rocking shaft for the outside cylinders, the large lever coming towards the camera and which pivots on the frames. The right-hand-side valve gear can just about be seen beyond these components. This is the point at which Churchward connected the rocking lever to the outside cylinder, as seen in the diagram illustrating the principles of Walschaerts valve gear, as used on the Star's inside cylinders (fig. 26).

Fig. 23. Inside cylinder connecting rods.

Fig. 24. Inside cylinder cranks and vacuum pump.

Fig. 25. Left-hand inside cylinder rocking shaft to outside cylinder.

Modified Walschearts Valve Gear

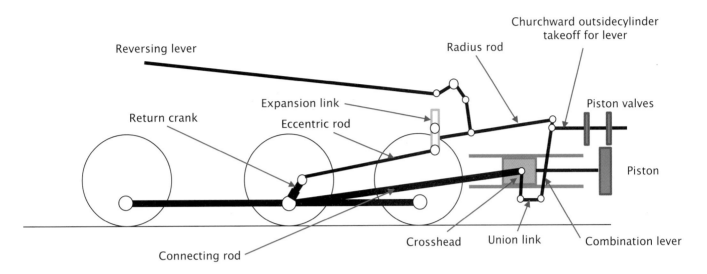

Fig. 26. Diagram of Walschaerts valve gear.

The next major component, further back towards the tender, is the locomotive vacuum brake cylinder (fig. 27), with the red shaft running off towards the front driving wheels (*see* fig. 24). It was partly the positioning of this unit that decided that the inside cylinder layout would be as forward as it is.

The driving wheel axle is seen towards the top of fig. 28. This can slide up and down and is contained by the hornblock, which is the black object that contains the axle. Its rectangular form enables it to slide up and down in a slot in the frames. The weight of part of the engine is on the leaf spring, shown towards the bottom of the picture, and the riding height and equality of weight carried by each wheel of the locomotive can be adjusted during an overhaul. Accurate achievement of this property is necessary for a smooth

Fig. 27. Vacuum cylinder.

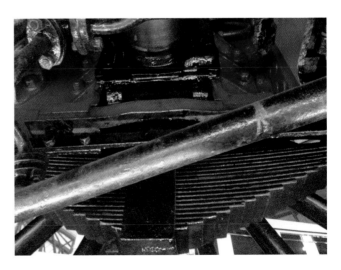

Fig. 28. Driving wheel hornblock and leaf spring.

Fig. 29. Ashpan.

running engine, as well as ensuring the balance of all rotating masses.

The large black rectangle in the centre of fig. 29 is the ashpan, with a flap that can be raised to rake out ashes and clinker. The larger pipe to the left is for water and will make its way up to the top feed on the boiler; the smaller on the right is the vacuum pipe. The brake gear rods dominate the rest of the layout.

The bronze coloured object behind the right-hand rear step of the engine is a live steam injector (fig. 30). This uses exhaust steam from the engine to force water

into the boiler against a possible boiler pressure of up to 225psi (15.51 bar). A property of thermodynamics known as the venturi effect enables high-pressure steam to convert to high-velocity steam at low pressure. A series of cones first lowers the pressure and drags along the water, before finally converting the water from high velocity to high pressure, enough to overcome the pressure in the boiler. It works better, however, when the hexagonal brass coupling is done up. The water overflow drain leaves the bottom of the unit to appear behind the right rear footstep of the engine.

The other option is to use a mechanical pump, which uses more energy to achieve the same result and is therefore less efficient. Injectors can be up to 98 per cent efficient, which is very high for any machine.

At the rear of the tender, the vacuum pipe is accompanied by a steam heating pipe on the right with its own brass tap, which is shown in the closed position (fig. 31). The pipes cross over as they proceed underneath the tender and the steam heating pipe is lagged. The coupling shackle has been secured on its own hook, despite there being a stowage hook on the left-hand buffer. The tender water scoop is the large black object at the bottom of the picture.

The bottom part of the tender water scoop is a curved pipe, which has its last section hinged at the top (fig. 32). In normal running the curve is broken as the hinged part is swung away towards the tender floor. When the fireman sees that the loco is

Fig. 30. Live steam injector.

Fig. 31. Rear bufferbeam of the tender, with vacuum and steam heating pipes.

Fig. 32. Tender water scoop apparatus.

Fig. 33. Tender tank drain.

approaching the troughs, the curved bottom section is lowered, which then makes contact with the rest of the pipe to form a seal. This avoids needing a flexible pipe between the fixed and lowered sections, which would be a maintenance issue and cause more load on the lowering linkages.

Looking towards the loco again, the circular black object between the steam heating and vacuum pipes

is the tender tank drain (fig. 33). Some 4,000 gallon (18,184ltr) tenders experimented with an aluminium tank that saved 3 tons (3.05 tonnes), a considerable weight, but probably encouraged dissimilar metal corrosion between the aluminium and the steel of the rest of the tender.

Illustrated in fig. 34 is the vacuum cylinder for the tender only. The proximity of the disconnected

Fig. 34. Tender vacuum brake cylinder.

injector at the bottom of the picture that this is near to the drag beam or the front of the tender. The cylinder is surrounded by brake rodding and linkages.

The 3,500 gallon tender is one of the later series with the extended coal side sheets, but with Churchward

taper buffer shanks (fig. 35). There are no 4003 numerals on the tender bufferbeam: tank engines had them at both ends.

Star Class in Production

The original Atlantic no. 40 had footplating that carried on where the cab was and the same at the front end. Subsequent Stars would have curved footplating to accommodate the cab and the locomotive would be similarly curved at the front end. These aesthetic issues also affected early Saint class 4-6-0 engines. The early Stars had a rectangular box-like structure to accommodate the piston rod ends of the inside cylinders. No. 40 as built did not have a superheater, although the issue was partly addressed in the next batch of engines.

After a few months in service no. 40 was named North Star, after a broad gauge precursor that had entered service in 1838. Within three years it had been converted to a 4-6-0. It was rebuilt as a Castle class locomotive in 1929.

Fig. 35. Tender's 1927 livery and shiny lamp irons.

Fig. 36. No. 4000 North Star after rebuilding to a 4-6-0. Old Oak Common, about 1914. GREAT WESTERN TRUST

No. 4000 North Star is shown here about 1914 after rebuilding to a 4-6-0 and with several modifications to the original Atlantic configuration (fig. 36). The ejector pipe runs from the cab to the smokebox; the top feed and superheater have been fitted. The tender has the longer coal plates and the centre splasher works plate has been removed. Bogie brakes and small cab windows above the firebox are still present. The locomotive is running in the World War I unlined livery and the splasher brass beading has been removed, but the cab side brass beading remains.

Star Batch Build Nos 4001 to 4010

4001	Dog Star	
4002	Evening Star*	
4003	Lode Star	
4004	Morning Star*	
4005	Polar Star	
4006	Red Star	
4007	Rising Star*	(renamed Swallowfield Park, May 1937)
4008	Royal Star*	
4009	Shooting Star*	(rebuilt as a Castle, April 1925)
4010	Western Star*	

Locomotives constructed as 4-6-0s from the outset were built in 1907. Their names continued the celestial theme that had been initiated with the broad-gauge engines of 1839 to 1841. Some of the names marked with an asterisk would be used again for Britannia locomotives constructed by British Railways to run on the Western Region or former GWR territory. The locomotives were constructed with the Standard No. 1 boiler, a feature that was shared with the Saint class.

All Stars from now on would have Walschaerts valve gear acting on the inside cylinders and rocking levers to actuate the outside cylinder valves. The cramped nature of the valve gear inside the frames was criticized for access, but the gear was so well designed and had such ample bearing surfaces that little maintenance was necessary.

The Holcroft beautifying process was applied to these engines from the start, so they all had curved front and cab ends, while the cab side sheets were extended to meet the now curved footplate.

The first two members of the batch, 4001 and 4002, had a visible peculiarity in that their slidebars were made of 'T' section steel instead of the usual 'I' section, and so appeared to have a slot cut into them. To complement this feature, these and other batch members had brackets that joined the upper and lower slidebars together. This device was subsequently fitted to all 4-cylinder 4-6-0 locomotives. There was also a wind deflector or capuchon attached to the leading surface of the chimney. The copper cap stopped at the chimney lip.

Fig. 37. 4001 Dog Star, probably at Old Oak Common, about 1920. GREAT WESTERN TRUST

In the view of 4001 Dog Star, believed to have been photographed at Old Oak Common about 1920, it retains bogie brakes and the rectangular box covering the inside cylinder valves and spindles (fig. 37). The engine has fluting on the slidebars and is coupled to a long coal-railed 3,500 gallon tender. An early feature is the smokebox lamp iron on top of the smokebox, instead of on the door as later. It also has the original slimline chimney and a rainstrip on the cab roof. It also has later features, however, including no works plate on the centre splasher and a boiler top feed. The brass piping removed from the splashers during World War I has not been replaced. The Churchward Mogul, 6332, in the background was also allocated to OOC at about that time.

Engines 4002, 4008 and 4009 were fitted with front steps forward of the cylinders and right in front of the access point to the inside slidebars and valve gear. These were later removed.

4005 Polar Star was photographed in early condition at Plymouth Millbay about 1910 (fig. 38). It has no top

Fig. 38. 4005 Polar Star in early condition at Plymouth Millbay, about 1910. GREAT WESTERN TRUST

feed, centre splasher works plate, a swan neck on the front vacuum pipe as opposed to the later D-shape and bufferbeam stowage, splasher as well as cab front brass beading and a chimney capuchon. The tender axlebox spring mounting points are in polished steel. Note the provision of three lamp stowage positions by the smokebox, whereas before there had been only two. This locomotive was to astonish the railway world with its performances on the London and North Western Railway exchanges of 1910. Plymouth Millbay and the nearby docks were used for ocean liner traffic.

It was a constant concern that the steam temperature was lowered by the journey it needed to take around a locomotive before it reached the cylinders to do useful work. This was one of the reasons why

Churchward had adopted piston valves. The steam entering the cylinders is cooled and condensation takes place. As the piston proceeds on its stroke and expansion occurs, some of the steam initially condensed will be re-evaporated. This is the principal source of thermal efficiency losses.

4001 Dog Star was photographed again about 1925, this time at Exeter motive power depot. Both types of wagon lettering may be seen, the 13 inch, which was not introduced until 1921, and the 25 inch. The ejector pipe is clearly visible and the loco appears to be unlined and generally in post-World War I condition.

The changing appearance of Star class locomotives is also illustrated in a view of 4007 Swallowfield Park in June 1937 (fig. 40). Until a name change the

Fig. 39. 4001 Dog Star, about 1925.
GREAT WESTERN TRUST

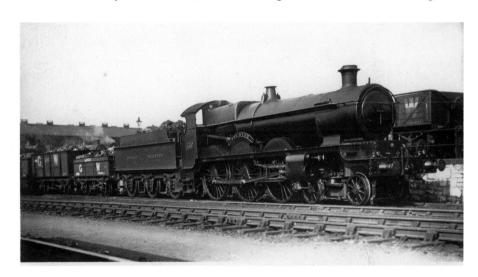

Fig. 40. 4007 Swallowfield Park (formerly Rising Star), June 1937. GREAT WESTERN TRUST

previous month this had been known as Rising Star. Despite being at Worcester shed and no longer carrying out top link duties, the loco appears well cared for in its lined green livery, which was applied from 1934 onwards.

The loco retains its top lamp iron on top of the smokebox; this would be lowered to the smokebox door before the outbreak of World War II. By this time bogie brakes were not fitted, but the engine retains its rectangular box inside cylinder valve casing. The swan neck vacuum pipe has given way to the D-shaped type with bufferbeam stowage.

It was about this time that the question of superheating came to the fore. If the steam was heated to a very high value, then any lowering of the temperature due to the steam's journey would be minimized or even trivialized. The first successful commercially available superheater device was patented by Wilhelm Schmidt. This raised the temperature of the steam from 250°C to 350°C, improving the thermal efficiency of a steam locomotive by up to 50 per cent. The Schmidt name lives on as a constituent of Alstom.

Churchward tried this on his locomotives, but he was not entirely happy with a situation where the GWR would have to pay licence fees for someone else's patent. The Schmidt superheater would also have to be accompanied by another patented device, 'wide' piston valve rings, to overcome problems with lubrication and superheated steam. In service the Schmidt superheater was found to be tricky to maintain due to its construction: access to one part was barred until another unrelated part had first been removed. It was also of complicated construction that made cleaning more difficult.

Churchward chose instead to develop his own superheater from one produced by the American Locomotive Company (Alco) at Schenectady in upstate New York. The Cole superheater was complicated but simpler to maintain and keep clean. Number 4010 was the first recipient of the Cole superheater.

Nevertheless, un-superheated engines performed well enough with the superb Welsh steam coal. In 1909, for example, 4004 Morning Star managed the Paddington to Exeter three-hour express. Although the load was only seven coaches as far as Westbury, the net time for the 173.7 miles was 171½ minutes and this included stops at Westbury and Taunton sta-

tions to detach coaches that could not be slipped due to adverse signals.

Of the original production series Stars, 4003 Lode Star was withdrawn for preservation in 1951 and spent some time in the converted Methodist Chapel that was the original Swindon railway museum. The building had originally been a lodging house for workers drawn to Swindon before about 300 cottages were erected to accommodate the workforce in what became New Swindon.

Star Batch Build Nos 4011 to 4020

4011	Knight of the Garter	
4012	Knight of the Thistle	
4013	Knight of the Patrick	
4014	Knight of the Bath	
4015	Knight of St. John	
4016	Knight of the Golden Fleece	(rebuilt as a Castle, October 1925)
4017	Knight of the Black Eagle	(renamed Knight of Liège, then Knight of Liége)
4018	Knight of the Grand Cross	
4019	Knight Templar	
4020	Knight Commander	

Until August 1914 No. 4017 was named Knight of the Black Eagle. Because of the name's association with Kaiser Wilhelm II of Germany, however, it was then changed to Knight of Liège, a somewhat less contentious name associated with allies in Belgium. Yet even this was controversial as the grave accent (è) is associated with the Flemish language in bilingual Belgium. About 1925 the nameplate was changed to Knight of Liége (with an acute accent), to associate the locomotive with French-speaking Belgium. Despite many protests, the French acute version was retained.

4017 Knight of the Black Eagle was seen at Hayes near West Drayton about 1912 in garter crest livery (fig. 41). The engine is in pre-war magnificence: the smokebox door hinges have been stripped down to bare metal and burnished with emery cloth. This was also often done on the buffers to create a four-segment pattern and front couplings were also polished; as were tender spring fixing points on some engines. Wolverhampton Stafford Road shed had the habit of engraving a cross of Lorraine shape on the smokebox

Fig. 41. 4017 Knight of the Black Eagle at Hayes, about 1912, before the World War I name change. GREAT WESTERN TRUST

door as their unique identifier, as well as the usual letters on bufferbeam and valance. The mixed rake of clerestory and toplight coaches appears to be in crimson lake livery. The engine has a tall safety valve bonnet and splasher works plate, but no boiler placed ejector.

Note the two distant signal arms in red with the fishtail painted motif. Both signals have a wheel mechanism for winding the signal lamp down and up the post for refilling.

This was the first series of locomotives to have Churchward's version of the de Glehn front bogie but without the original design's outside axleboxes. The usual swing link design was found to do a poor job of guiding the main driving wheels easily into a curve. The result was excess wear on the front driving wheels of 4-6-0 locomotives. In addition the extra springing provided by the de Glehn design tended to stop the locomotive swaying at speed from the front end. This made the Stars and its successors even more smooth runners. Churchward retained the American-inspired equalizing bar system of wheel springing. In that sense the bogie resembled an American coach bogie, although the equalizing bars were out of sight behind the wheels rather than in front with a coach.

Churchward's adaptation of the de Glehn bogie was immediately successful and all older 4-6-0 engines were retrofitted with the improved bogie on overhaul. This idea was copied by other railways until about 1942, when the London and North Eastern Railway's Thompson B1 4-6-0 mixed traffic engines were introduced.

The superheater story continued with the fitting of the Swindon 1 superheater to 4011, which appeared in March 1908. Churchward made sure the design included the ability to strip the unit down more readily than the Schmidt type, but in service it was found that steam leaked from the piping after reassembly. This model was superseded by the Swindon 2, which had a simpler layout, but the only recipient of this marque was a Saint class 2-cylinder 4-6-0 2922 Saint Gabriel.

4031 Queen Mary, seen here as out-shopped from Swindon Works in March 1936 (fig. 42), was a modernized Star with a Collett 4,000 gallon (18,184ltr) tender, no bogie brakes, top lamp iron on the smokebox, whistle shield and short safety valve bonnet.

One of the last batch to be built, 4062 Malmesbury Abbey, was also among the last to be scrapped. It is seen here at Swindon shed about 1947: the letters SDN can just about be discerned where the valance meets the front bufferbeam (fig. 43). It appears in post-war G crest W livery with the route availability disc and power classification letter above the cab side number plate, where it was to remain under BR. An Austerity Ministry of Supply WD 2-8-0 tender is lurking in the distance.

4020 Knight Commander, seen here at Swindon works about 1938 (fig. 44), is another ex-works loco. It retains the square box-type structure over the inside

Fig. 42. 4031 Queen Mary at Swindon Works, March 1936. GREAT WESTERN TRUST

Fig. 43. 4062 Malmesbury Abbey, about 1947. GREAT WESTERN TRUST

Fig. 44. 4020 Knight Commander, about 1938. GREAT WESTERN TRUST

valve spindle covers as an early marker. The small forward-facing windows that allowed crews to peer over the firebox have been plated over. The speedometer fitting on the rear driving wheel was then the acme of modernity.

Star Batch Build Nos 4021 to 4030

		Renamed in 1927	Names Removed
4021	King Edward	The British Monarch	
4022	King William	The Belgian Monarch	May 1940
4023	King George	The Danish Monarch	November 1940
4024	King James	The Dutch Monarch	Rebuilt as a Castle, February 1929
4025	King Charles	Italian Monarch	June 1940
4026	King Richard	The Japanese Monarch	January 1941
4027	King Henry	The Norwegian Monarch	
4028	King John	The Roumanian Monarch	November 1940
4029	King Stephen	The Spanish Monarch	
4030	King Harold	The Swedish Monarch	November 1940

All locomotives named with 'The' as the first word were modified to remove the definite article in October and November 1927. The engines with names removed had the words 'STAR CLASS' painted on the splasher below where the nameplate had been mounted. As a result of World War II hostilities some locomotives' names were removed and not replaced.

An example of this, clearly without the definite article and so after October 1927, is a view of 4022 Belgian Monarch pictured ex-works at Swindon in September 1935 (fig. 45). As a result of wartime austerity the locomotive sports a plain cast iron chimney. It has the shirt button monogram lined livery of 1934 and many later features, such as the D-shaped front vacuum hose, top lamp iron on smokebox, short safety valve bonnet and whistle shield, but the tender is of the earlier 3,500 gallon (15,911ltr) type.

This 1909 batch recorded names of kings of England but without their qualifying accession numbers. These were changed to national monarchs in 1927 at the introduction of the King class locomotives.

4021 received the Swindon 3 superheater in June 1909, while the other nine engines in the batch

Fig. 45. 4022 Belgian Monarch at Swindon, September 1935. GREAT WESTERN TRUST

37

initially received none. Some of the later engines had boiler detail variations.

Externally there was a change to the shape of the inside cylinder external casing. Previously it had been a rectangular box, but this was changed to curved sides and a shape more appropriate to the curve of the engine's footplate.

About the time of the introduction of the 'King' batch of engines, correspondence in the railway press was critical of the costs of maintaining the GWR's fleet, which was said to be £175 per engine for the year ending 1908. This compared with £100 for the same period paid by the Lancashire and Yorkshire, which had a main line of about 80 miles (129km), or the £157 paid by the Great Eastern and North Eastern, both of which had main lines of about 140 miles (225km).

This tirade against the GWR came to the attention of the directors and Churchward was summoned to account for the reason why the L&NWR could build three engines for the same cost of two on the GWR. Churchward's riposte is understood to be: 'because one of mine could pull two of those bloody things backwards!' This episode was thought to have instigated for the 1910 locomotive interchanges with the L&NWR, which is covered in detail later in this chapter.

The GWR's triumph over the LNWR in the 1910 exchanges was most appositely timed as the GWR was introducing its Paddington to Birmingham Snow Hill two-hour expresses in competition with the L&NWR's west coast main line route.

Star Batch Build Nos 4031 to 4040

4031	Queen Mary	
4032	Queen Alexandra	(rebuilt as a Castle, April 1926)
4033	Queen Victoria	
4034	Queen Adelaide	
4035	Queen Charlotte	
4036	Queen Elizabeth	
4037	Queen Philippa	(rebuilt as a Castle, June 1926)
4038	Queen Berengaria	
4039	Queen Matilda	
4040	Queen Boudicea	

The next batch to emerge in late 1910 and early 1911 were somewhat less troublesome than their male counterparts in that ambiguity was avoided and they retained their names at least until two members of the class were rebuilt as Castles.

This entire batch was fitted with the standard Swindon superheater and they were all issued with the standard 3,500 gallon (15,911ltr) tenders with the long coal rail, as had first been fitted to 4005 Polar Star.

The opportunity was then taken to retrofit all saturated engines with superheaters except for 4026 and 4030, which were adapted in 1913. The locomotives in this batch differed in boiler detail changes.

Star Batch Build Nos 4041 to 4045

4041	Prince of Wales
4042	Prince Albert
4043	Prince Henry
4044	Prince George
4045	Prince John

The next batch of only five locomotives is explained by the Saint class building programme. Until 1913 Saints had continued to be built in accompanying numbers to Stars, but when a further batch of ten Saints was ordered it was decided to truncate the order to five, The rest of the batch and all future batches would be built as 4-cylinder engines. So in 1913 five Saints and five Stars were constructed.

The Princes, who were named after the five sons of King George V, all incorporated a new feature: a top feed to the boiler. The 14¼in (36.2cm) cylinders of the usual Stars were bored out to 15in (38cm) on 4041, on the grounds that the superheated boiler was well capable of supplying the larger cylinders. This pushed the nominal tractive effort up to 27,800lb (124kN). However, this increase in cylinder size was not as large a change as it seemed: successive overhauls had seen cylinders that started out as 14¼in (36.2cm) bored out to 15in (38cm) and beyond. It did not occur to anyone to sleeve the cylinders and thereby retain the overall dimensions and cylinder hardware, as is routinely done on some cars.

In truth, however, this enlargement for more power was simply following the traffic demands of the time for heavier loads pulled at higher speeds.

While discussing royalty, this may be the place to mention the royal coat of arms that is now displayed above the visitors' entrance at STEAM – Museum of the Great Western Railway, Swindon (fig. 46). A former works apprentice has told me it was a Herculean task to mount the arms in this position: it was cast in one piece from iron.

An extremely heavy casting of the coat of arms may also be seen mounted on the footplate of 4006 Red Star, pictured in 1910 (fig. 47). The driver is standing to attention, oilcan in hand, next to the motion and driving wheels and the fireman is standing on the tender fall plate. The location is Old Oak

Fig. 46. The Royal Coat of Arms as applied to the side of Star class locomotives for Royal events such as the funeral of King Edward VII. STEAM, Swindon, September 2017.

Fig. 47. 4006 Red Star at Old Oak Common, 1910. GREAT WESTERN TRUST

Common, the only engine shed on the GWR with four roundhouses.

Star Batch Build Nos 4046 to 4060

4046	Princess Mary
4047	Princess Louise
4048	Princess Victoria
4049	Princess Maud
4050	Princess Alice
4051	Princess Helena
4052	Princess Beatrice
4053	Princess Alexandra
4054	Princess Charlotte
4055	Princess Sophia
4056	Princess Margaret
4057	Princess Elizabeth
4058	Princess Augusta
4059	Princess Patricia
4060	Princess Eugenie

The next and largest batch of fifteen Stars was constructed in the spring and early summer of 1914: the final working Star on British Railways was 4056 Princess Margaret, which survived until October 1957.

An experiment was made by reverting to fluted coupling rods made of special steel but these were all later substituted for the plain type. The vacuum brakes on the GWR worked in a different way to those used on other railways, with a higher vacuum needed to keep the brakes off. Vacuum brakes provide a fail safe in that a vacuum force is needed to keep the brakes from going on; without it the brakes are naturally on all the time. A steam ejector produced a high vacuum to release the brakes from rest initially or to cancel out a brake application when on the move. While the locomotive was moving a crosshead-driven vacuum pump maintained a level of vacuum to ensure the brakes did not leak on. With increasingly larger and longer trains, a large four-cone exhaust ejector to power the vacuum brakes' release was fitted to the right-hand side of the boiler and this was to become standard for all 4-cylinder engines. There was a refinement to this fitment in that a lever in the cab could select one, three or four cones, depending on the speed with which the brakes were to be released. There was a separate lever to actually operate the brakes.

Once again there were boiler variations that differed slightly from previous marques.

Star Batch Build Nos 4061 to 4072

4061	Glastonbury Abbey	Built with fluted coupling rods
4062	Malmesbury Abbey	Built with fluted coupling rods
4063	Bath Abbey	
4064	Reading Abbey	
4065	Evesham Abbey	
4066	Malvern Abbey	
4067	Tintern Abbey	Built with fluted coupling rods
4068	Llanthony Abbey	Built with fluted coupling rods
4069	Margam Abbey	Built with fluted coupling rods
4070	Neath Abbey	Built with fluted coupling rods
4071	Cleeve Abbey	Built with fluted coupling rods
4072	Tresco Abbey	Built with fluted coupling rods

This final batch was built in 1922 and 1923, a long gap after the hiatus of World War I, and employed improved balanced crank axles. They were all named after abbeys on GWR territory, although Margam Abbey was renamed Westminster Abbey in May 1923. 4066 was renamed Sir Robert Horne in May 1935, but in July the nameplates were removed and the name Viscount Horne substituted in August 1935.

The austerity of the war livery was retained. The engines had cast iron chimneys, but they lacked brass beading on the splashers.

The example shown here, 4061 Glastonbury Abbey, is as it was seen in Swindon works yard in September 1935 when fresh from the paint shop (fig. 48). The

Fig. 48. 4061 Glastonbury Abbey in Swindon Works yard, September 1935. GREAT WESTERN TRUST

aft mud-hole door has been displaced in the painting process and needs refitting.

Star Class: Detail Variations and Upgrades

The Star class was born of experimentation, Although the right recipe was found early on, Churchward could not resist the urge to experiment further to see if he could improve what were very competent engines.

In the listings a few of the engines were rebuilt as Castles, but retaining their original Star numbers. This early form of re-cycling, in which parts from the Stars were used in the new engines, was quite common on the GWR; the most notable occurrence was the withdrawal of 100 Moguls to form the basis of the Granges and Manor class locomotives. As well as saving on raw materials, this was also an accounting exercise.

While the photographs have depicted engines stripped of their splasher beading in World War I, the cab front beading was retained. The affected engines were numbers 4000 to 4060, inclusive, and it was never replaced except on those engines rebuilt as Castles.

As a further austerity measure that continued after World War I, numbers 4000, 4001, 4008, 4010, 4013, 4017, 4018, 4021, 4022, 4024, 4028, 4035, 4038, 4044, 4047, 4051, 4054, 4055 and 4057 were fitted with plain cast iron chimneys. 4021 and 4038 retained the plain chimney after the pre-war livery was restored for a short time.

In 1906 the GWR had developed a means of indicating to a driver in fog or falling snow the status of a distant signal arm. If the signal was 'off' or clear a bell would sound in the cab. If 'on' or at danger, a horn would sound. If the driver failed to cancel or acknowledge the warning, a valve would open to atmosphere, destroying the vacuum in the braking system and applying the train's brakes automatically.

Locos 4000 and 4003 were early recipients of this Automatic Train Control (ATC) equipment in 1908; 4006 followed soon afterwards. Hitherto the only source of fitment of the trackside equipment had been on the Fairford branch line, but the main line

out of Paddington between Slough and Reading in the Thames Valley, which was prone to fog, was fitted as a high-speed test track. The successor to the GWR system, Automatic Warning System (AWS) is in widespread use on Network Rail in 2018.

Bogie brakes were removed from about 1923 and the spring equalizing gear on the front bogie was substituted by more flexible springs from about 1930.

The frames, which were a source of weakness throughout the life of the Stars, were patched in the area by the outside cylinders and rear bogie wheels.

The class was at its most uniform from about 1925 to 1927, although there was some tinkering in the area of whistle shields. These were necessary to stop whispers of steam obscuring the forward-facing circular spectacle windows, which looked out over the top of the firebox. Their subsequent deployment among other classes was widespread.

As the years wore on some engines that needed new inside cylinders, but kept the outside pair, had to be fitted with 'elbow' type external steampipes, 4002 was the first to receive this treatment. After the advent of the Castles in 1923, those Stars that needed both inside and outside cylinders renewed were fitted with Castle-type external steampipes. Just such an upgrade was applied to 4024 in February 1929. Two engines, 4048 and 4060, carried both types eventually.

In the earlier years engine drivers judged the speed of their locomotives themselves or used the standard 60ft rail lengths, where these were fitted, to mentally calculate the speed by the beat of the wheels. No. 4050 had a speedometer fitted in 1914 as an experiment. It consisted of a rod from the right-hand rear driving wheel to drive a gearbox, causing an AC generator to turn. The generated voltage was calibrated in miles per hour and displayed on a moving coil meter in the cab, near the screw reverser on the right-hand side where the driver was placed. An early application of electronics was the provision of a rectifier (more modern term, diode) to convert the AC generated into DC (presumably half wave), so that the meter read the speed positively irrespective of its direction of travel.

The class was not widely fitted with this device until 1937. No. 4040, for example, never received one, although it was fitted to 4003, 4007, 4012, 4013, 4017 to 4023, 4025, 4026, 4030, 4031, 4033 to 4036,

4038, 4039, 4041 to 4043, and 4045 to 4062. This list excludes those engines rebuilt as Castles; the last series of Stars from 4063 onwards were not so fitted before they too were Castle rebuilds.

Throughout their long lives the Star class towed tenders of varying types. The Churchward 3,500 gallon (15,911ltr) tender and the Collett low-sided and high-sided tenders, both holding 4,000 gallons (18,184ltr), became standard for the class. In 1936 numbers 4045 and 4022 ran with the eight-wheeled bogie tender from The Great Bear, Churchward's experimental Pacific from 1908, and the 4,000 gallon, eight-wheeled tender made an appearance on 4043. Two class members even had Hawksworth flat-sided tenders.

The frequency of water troughs on the Great Western did not impel designers to consider tenders with a capacity greater than 4,000 gallons.

From 1932 onwards smokebox lamp irons were transferred to the smokebox door and this process continued until 1939. From 1939 the 'Grange' class chimneys were increasingly fitted to those locomotives that received new boilers.

The view of 4005 Polar Star at Euston in 1910 shows the class in all its pre-war magnificence and displaying early condition equipment (fig. 49). Its burnished steel fittings include smokebox door straps and hinges. There is no whistle shield or top lamp iron on top of the smokebox, but features that can be seen include three lamp irons to the left-hand side of the smokebox for spare lamps and a possible Royal train indicator, a splasher works plate, a swan-necked front vacuum pipe and bogie brakes. The loco is in garter crest livery. The L&NWR loco on the right looks old-fashioned and almost a nineteenth-century museum piece compared to the sleek Star.

Another early view shows 4038 Queen Berengaria on a down express at Old Oak Common in 1911 (fig. 50). The engine is in early condition with polished steel-ware, but without a top feed or whistle shield. It features an early short coal railed tender, bogie brakes and tall safety valve bonnet. The Churchward 'concertina' 70ft (21.3m) coaches are in crimson lake livery; the third one down from the engine is a 'dreadnought' coach.

4044 Prince George, seen here on a down express at Slough about 1914, came from the batch built in 1913 (fig. 51). The top feed was now an included feature with the tall safety valve bonnet. No splasher works plate is fitted, but there is splasher brass beading. The three spare lamp irons first seen on Polar Star are also here. The coaches are in the crimson lake livery and 5ft (1.5m) signal arms can be seen on the taller posts.

Fig. 49. 4005 Polar Star at Euston, 1910. GREAT WESTERN TRUST

Fig. 50. 4038 Queen Berengaria on a down express at Old Oak Common, 1911. GREAT WESTERN TRUST

Fig. 51. 4044 Prince George on a down express at Slough, about 1914. GREAT WESTERN TRUST

1910 Locomotive Interchanges with the L&NWR

As described above, Churchward met with the directors of the GWR to explain why it was his engines cost more than the London and North Western's to build and Churchward's reply was unequivocal.

It is thought that it was this interview that spurred Churchward into proving his assertion that his engines were far superior to the L&NWR's.

Charles Bowen Cooke, the Chief Mechanical Engineer of the L&NWR, was regarded as having advanced ideas about locomotive design and had written books on the subject. He had also been the first to employ superheating on a British locomotive. He was active in asking other CMEs to trial their engines on the 'Premier Line', but it is thought that on this occasion Churchward approached Cooke to affect the exchange.

The two locomotives involved in August 1910 were the GWR Star class 4005 Polar Star and the L&NWR's Experiment class 4-6-0 Worcestershire. The shed nearest to Euston that handled express passenger locos was Camden (BR code 1B), whose roundhouse is now a theatre. The shedmaster there was asked to release the locomotive he could most do without. Cooke was clearly more interested in what the Stars could do on the L&NWR than what an Experiment could do on the GWR.

Number 1471 Worcestershire was adjudged to be the locomotive to go to the GWR and it was in far from top link condition. Conversely 4005 Polar Star was in superb condition. Worcestershire found the work it had been allocated beyond its capabilities and lost time badly. In comparison, Polar Star played with the tasks it had been given.

The exchanges were carried out between 15 and 27 August 1910. In the first week Polar Star headed the 12:10 from Euston and it was allowed 175 minutes for the 158 miles to Crewe; this was carried out on the Monday, Tuesday and Wednesday. The load was eleven coaches, including two twelve-wheeler restaurant cars, to give an all-up weight of about 370 tons. The engine returned each day on the 17.02 from Crewe and it was allowed 188 minutes, as there was a five-minute stop at Rugby and a two-minute stop at Willesden.

Thursday was boiler washout day and time for other maintenance. Friday, Saturday and Sunday were taken up with the 10:00 down Glasgow and Edinburgh express and the 16.07 up from Crewe.

In the second week Polar Star worked the 10:00 to Crewe on Monday and Tuesday, with shed maintenance on Wednesday, and then the 12:10 down on Thursday, Friday and Saturday. The L&NWR Experiment Herefordshire worked the opposite turns for each of the weeks.

The celebrated writer Cecil J. Allen noted an up run on which the entire run was made in 168¾ minutes and clearly well within the schedule.

The authenticated run below does not show Polar Star in a particularly favourable light, however, and

Polar Star LNWR Exchanges – August 1910
L&NWR EUSTON to CREWE locomotive: 4005 Polar Star
Driver: J Springthorpe OOC
Load 338 tons (343 tonnes) tare, 410 tons (417 tonnes) full
(RED Actual Time denotes behind schedule, GREEN on time or in front)

Distance miles (km)	Place on Journey	Schedule time mins	Actual time mins.s	Average speeds mph	(km/h)
0.0 (0.0)	EUSTON	0	0.0		
1.3 (2.1)	Chalk Farm		3.35		
2.4 (3.9)	Loudon Road		5.20		
5.4 (8.7)	WILLESDEN JUNCTION	9	9.15	46.0	(74.0)
11.4 (18.3)	Harrow		16.35	49.2	(79.2)
13.3 (21.4)	Pinner		19.05	45.6	(73.4)
17.5 (28.1)	WATFORD JUNCTION	23	24.10	49.2	(79.2)
21.0 (33.8)	King's Langley		27.55	56.0	(90.1)
28.0 (45.1)	Berkhamsted		35.55	54.8	(88.2)
31.7 (51.0)	Tring	40	39.40	54.4	(87.5)
46.7 (75.1)	BLETCHLEY	55	54.20	61.5	(98.9)
52.4 (84.3)	Wolverton		59.35	65.2	(104.9)
59.9 (96.4)	Roade	69	67.40	55.7	(89.6)
62.8 (101)	BLISWORTH		71.05	50.9	(81.9)
--------------	Permanent Way Slack				
69.7 (112)	Weedon		79.20	50.2	(80.8)
75.3 (121)	Welton		86.25	47.5	(76.4)
82.5 (133)	RUGBY	93	94.55	51.6	(83.0)
88.0 (142)	Brinklow		101.45	48.4	(77.9)
91.4 (147)	Shilton		105.15	56.5	(90.9)
93.5 (150)	Bulkington		107.45	52.8	(85.0)
97.1 (156)	NUNEATON	109	111.50	61.7	(99.3)
102.3 (165)	Atherstone		115.55	66.8	(107.5)
106.5 (171)	Polesworth		119.35	68.7	(110.6)
110.0 (177)	TAMWORTH	122	122.40	68.0	(109.4)
116.3 (187)	Lichfield		128.30	64.8	(104.3)
121.0 (195)	Armitage		133.45	53.7	(86.4)
--------------	Adverse Signals				
124.3 (200)	Rugeley	137	138.40	40.3	(64.9)
--------------	Adverse Signals				
127.2 (205)	Colwich		145.15	26.4	(42.5)
133.6 (215)	STAFFORD	147	155.15	38.4	(61.8)
138.9 (224)	Norton Bridge	154	161.40	49.5	(79.7)
143.4 (231)	Standon Bridge		166.50	52.4	(84.3)
147.6 (238)	Whitmore		171.35	53.0	(85.3)
150.1 (242)	Madeley		174.25	53.0	(85.3)
153.3 (247)	Betley Road		177.25	64.0	(103.0)
158.0 (254)	CREWE	175	183.25		

it was thought at the time that the driver was trying to conserve coal to demonstrate economy of operation. The almost continual climb to Tring was within time and the speed increased once the summit had been breasted. After Wolverton the line climbs again and the speed fell slightly to the summit past Welton.

It is interesting to note that when Polar Star was falling behind time only slightly, the driver opened her out and she recovered the time, except for that lost due to the signals checks around Armitage and Rugeley. Although no concerted effort was made to recoup time lost to external checks, the net time was well within the scheduled value.

Recordings of similar runs on the GWR with the L&NWR engine have not surfaced, but it is accepted that the L&NWR engine lost time consistently.

Nevertheless the overall results were enough to convince Bowen Cooke of the L&NWR that his engines needed modification, if not rebuilding, and Churchward was completely vindicated.

The timing of the L&NWR trouncing was just right as the GWR was to introduce its London to Birmingham two-hour expresses in direct competition with the L&NWR's own Euston to Birmingham New Street services.

Bowen Cooke subsequently introduced the Claughton class 4-6-0 with four cylinders acting on the leading driving wheels but with a Belpaire firebox. Despite superficial resemblances to Churchward's Stars, there were none of the innovative details to do with valves and piston stroke that Churchward championed and consequently the Claughtons never approached the success of the Stars in service.

CHAPTER THREE

STAR CLASS LOCOMOTIVES: ALLOCATION AND WORK

The Stars were designed from the outset as the crack express locomotives of their day. On their introduction they would be among the fastest and most powerful land-based machinery in Britain. Their early existence was characterized by their class name. They were the stars of the railway.

At first they toyed with their allocated tasks, but gradually trains became heavier and the schedules tighter until the Stars could no longer inhabit the top link they were given and had to make way for the Castles, which themselves made way for King class engines on the heaviest trains.

A typical working about 1930 is seen in this view of 4030 Swedish Monarch, with plenty of steam on board, coasting down Hatton Bank with an up express from Birmingham Snow Hill (fig. 52). The Hatton Junction station and signal box are visible in the background. The furthest track away from the train is an extended loop that ends up at the Stratford-bound platform of the junction. The locomotive would have had the definite article 'The' removed in late 1927 and the tender carries the Great crest Western livery of 1927.

The Stars would still turn in remarkable performances when pressed in their declining years. Some class members would notch up more than forty years in service, but it must be admitted that World War II would have extended some of their lives.

Fig. 52. 4030 Swedish Monarch coasts down Hatton Bank with an up express from Birmingham Snow Hill, about 1930.
GREAT WESTERN TRUST

The story begins with a preponderance of the class at Old Oak Common shed near Paddington, and a balancing number at Plymouth for the West of England expresses, with some representation for the Birmingham and South Wales expresses. In 1923 there was a large increase at Wolverhampton Stafford Road for the two-hour expresses.

By the 1930s dispersion of the class meant that Stars could be seen on stopping passenger and cross-country services, and even on freight trains. This trend was to continue after World War II. The class distinguished themselves on the West to North expresses, which were usually very heavily loaded trains running over a switchback route on the Welsh marches to and from Plymouth, Liverpool and Manchester. They also starred on the Birkenhead to Kent Coast resorts expresses, which had destinations such as Margate, Ramsgate, Hastings, Deal, Sandwich and Eastbourne: the Stars would work as far as Reading, where the South East and Chatham Railway, later the Southern, had a connection.

These West Country services are typified by 4054 Princess Charlotte, seen in later condition in 1934 livery, with the top lamp iron moved to the smokebox door and a whistle shield, but retaining the 3,500 gallon (15,911ltr) tender (fig. 53). The train is on white class B lamps (stopping train) at Exeter St. David's about 1938, headed for the West Country. The locomotive crew standing on the walkway at the end of the platform look as though they are making their way to the engine shed, which was behind and to the left of the camera. The depot is still accessed that way today. The coaches are a mixture of clerestories and toplights, with a white-roofed ex-works clerestory just visible.

Further along the line, 4010 Western Star was photographed at Torquay station about 1930 (fig. 54). The next stop is Paignton. This early engine, still with the

Fig. 53. 4054 Princess Charlotte and train on class B lamps at Exeter St. David's, about 1938. GREAT WESTERN TRUST

Fig. 54. 4010 Western Star at Torquay station, about 1930. GREAT WESTERN TRUST

box over the inside cylinders, has its front coupling unusually hooked back over the coupling hook, rather than stowed on the left-hand buffer hook. This may indicate that the engine was attached at the front to another locomotive. The signal box behind the locomotive was still there in 2016 and is now a tourist information centre.

Allocation by Individual Locomotive

For a complete list of GWR locomotive depots and their British Railways equivalents, *see* Appendix III.

January 1910

Old Oak Common
40, 4003, 4004, 4005, 4006, 4007, 4016, 4018, 4021, 4022, 4023, 4024, 4025, 4026, 4027, 4028, 4029, 4030

Bristol
4010, 4015, 4017, 4020

Newton Abbot
4009

Plymouth
4002, 4004, 4011, 4012

Cardiff
4008, 4014

Swindon Factory
4001 to Cardiff, 4019 to Cardiff

August 1914

Old Oak Common
4002, 4003, 4005, 4006, 4007, 4008, 4010, 4012, 4013, 4014, 4015, 4019, 4021, 4022, 4023, 4025, 4027, 4030, 4031, 4033, 4035, 4040, 4043, 4044, 4045, 4046, 4048, 4049, 4053, 4055, 4059, 4060

Exeter
4037

Plymouth
4009, 4011, 4016, 4018, 4020, 4024, 4028, 4029, 4032, 4038, 4041, 4042, 4047, 4051, 4052, 4054

Goodwick (for Fishguard Harbour boat trains)
4000, 4001, 4017, 4026, 4039

Wolverhampton
4004, 4036, 4050, 4056, 4057, 4058

Swindon Factory
4034 to Old Oak Common

January 1920

Old Oak Common
4000, 4001, 4002, 4003, 4007, 4008, 4010, 4012,
4013, 4014, 4019, 4021, 4023, 4026, 4027, 4029,
4031, 4032, 4033, 4034, 4036, 4037, 4043, 4047,
4046, 4048, 4055, 4056, 4059

Exeter
4052

Newton Abbot
4035, 4046

Plymouth Laira
4004, 4005, 4006, 4009, 4017, 4018, 4020, 4024, 4025,
4028, 4038, 4040, 4041, 4044, 4045, 4051, 4058, 4060

Wolverhampton
4008, 4015, 4016, 4043, 4049, 4050, 4054

Swindon Factory
4022 to Laira, 4030 to Laira, 4039 to Laira, 4053 to
Exeter, 4057 to Old Oak Common

January 1929

By now the class had been completed and after the
introduction of the Castles in 1923 there was a mass
clear out at Old Oak Common. Bristol, Wolverhampton and Worcester were the main recipients and the
Oxley freight shed saw its first Star.

Old Oak Common
4001, 4026, 4045, 4047, 4049, 4050, 4052, 4054,
4064, 4072

Bristol
4000, 4004, 4005, 4010, 4012, 4015, 4018, 4020,
4023, 4025, 4027, 4028, 4029, 4041, 4044, 4051,
4056, 4059, 4063

Exeter
4008, 4011, 4014, 4021, 4061, 4068, 4069

Newton Abbot
4039

Cardiff Canton
4003, 4006, 4036, 4067, 4070

Wolverhampton Stafford Road (Passenger Shed)
4002, 4030, 4034, 4040, 4046, 4048, 4053, 4065,
4071

Wolverhampton Oxley (Freight Shed)
4016

Worcester
4017, 4022, 4024, 4031, 4042, 4058, 4060, 4066

Swindon Factory
4007 to Old Oak Common, 4019 to Worcester, 4035
to Bristol, 4038 to Old Oak Common, 4055 to Old
Oak Common

December 1938

The decline in top class work for the Stars continued
after the 1929 clear out and they found themselves on
secondary passenger trains, postal, parcels and freight
work. Castles had established themselves as the standard GWR express passenger engine and their number multiplied accordingly. By this time Star numbers
have reduced to 52 engines from 73, following withdrawals and Castle rebuilds.

Oxford
4004, 4021, 4052

Bristol Bath Road
4015, 4017, 4019, 4022, 4033, 4035, 4038, 4041,
4043, 4045, 4055, 4057, 4062, 4069

Swindon
4020, 4028, 4030, 4042

Westbury
4034

Weymouth
4036, 4047

Taunton
4012, 4026, 4054, 4056

Wolverhampton Stafford Road
4018, 4025, 4065, 4067

Shrewsbury
4013, 4031, 4044, 4046, 4053, 4061

Worcester
4007, 4049, 4051

Gloucester
4070

Landore
4003, 4023, 4039, 4040, 4048, 4050

Swindon Factory
4014 to Wolverhampton Stafford Road, 4058 to Tyseley, 4059 to Gloucester, 4060 to Tyseley

January 1942

Oxford
4004, 4021, 4052

Bristol Bath Road
4019, 4020, 4028, 4030, 4033, 4034, 4036, 4042

Weston-super-Mare
4047

Swindon
4015, 4017, 4022, 4057, 4062

Westbury
4038, 4041

Weymouth
4035, 4043, 4055

Taunton
4026, 4054, 4056

Newton Abbot
4012

Wolverhampton Stafford Road
4013, 4014, 4018, 4031

Shrewsbury
4044, 4046, 4061

Chester
4025, 4053

Worcester
4007, 4040, 4049, 4051

Gloucester
4059

Landore
4003, 4023, 4039, 4048, 4050

Swindon Factory
4045 to Bristol Bath Road

The Stars at Work, 1906–17

The period before World War I has often been described as the railway's heyday. Competition between the railway companies was fierce but road traffic was negligible in comparison. The railways made healthy profits and some of it was ploughed back in as investment in the public's demand for more railway travel. This period coincided with the Stars asserting themselves as the foremost express passenger locomotives in Britain, particularly over longer distances and with increasingly heavier trains.

Fig. 55. 4033 Queen Victoria on the L&NWR Royal Train on the Shrewsbury and Hereford joint line, about 1911. GREAT WESTERN TRUST

The high regard in which the Stars were held is demonstrated by their service on the Royal Train. Here 4033 Queen Victoria is seen hauling the L&NWR Royal Train on the Shrewsbury and Hereford joint line (fig. 55). The L&NWR distant signal has a red arm and a band rather than the GWR fishtail. The train does not seem to be carrying any members of the Royal Family despite the attentive, loyal and patriotic spectators. The loco needs three lamps, including the top one, for lesser royals and four, including the lower centre one, for the reigning monarch. This suggests the train was one its way to pick up a family member or has deposited one, possibly connected with the funeral of King Edward VII (1910) or the coronation of King George V (1911).

An early measured exploit of an un-superheated Star occurred on 28 April 1908 with the locomotive 4013 Knight of St. Patrick pulling a gross trailing load of 390 tons (396 tonnes) on the up Torquay Diner. The dynamometer car recorded all relevant criteria, including the Star's production of 2.2 tons (21.9kN) drawbar pull at 69mph (111km/h). This was almost spot on with Churchward's design aim of 2 tons (19.92kN) at 70mph (113km/h). It should be noted that this was an early locomotive: with future developments performances would comfortably eclipse the design ideal.

The almost continuous climb to Whiteball tunnel from St. David's station saw speeds ranging from 47 to 77½mph (77–125km/h) with the lower figure at the summit and the higher once the train was over it. The train was more than a minute to the good at Taunton and more than two minutes at Castle Cary, by which time the speed was 64mph (103km/h) after the climb. Despite a pair of slacks, Westbury was passed over two minutes early. A significant permanent way slack was encountered where a two-minute credit became a four-minute deficit and the train spent the rest of the journey trying to retrieve the situation. By Southall 4013 had cut the arrears to less than two minutes. A signal stop outside Paddington restored the deficit to nearer four minutes, but the net time of 183 minutes was against the schedule of 185 minutes.

The dynamometer car produced the following readings:

Location	Speed mph	Speed km/h	Drawbar tons	Drawbar tonnes
Tiverton Junction	63	101	2.8	27.9kN
Keinton Mandeville	69	111	2.1	20.9kN
Patney	51	82	2.4	23.9kN
Taplow	69	111	2.2	21.9kN

The first timed run involved the down Cornish Riviera Express, which had been introduced in 1904;

The Down Cornish Riviera Express
Locomotive: 4045 Prince John
Load 13 Coaches 441 tons (448 tonnes) tare,
470 tons (477 tonnes) full
(RED Actual Time denotes behind schedule, GREEN on time
or in front)

Distance miles (km)	Place on journey	Schedule time mins	Actual time mins.s	Average speeds mph	(km/h)
0.0 (00.0)	PADDINGTON	0	0.0		
			22.38	67 max	(107.8)
24.2 (38.9)	Maidenhead				
31.0 (49.9)	Twyford				
35.0 (56.3)	Milepost 35		37.35		
36.0 (57.9)	READING	37	38.40		
44.8 (72.1)	Aldermaston				
53.1 (85.5)	NEWBURY	56	57.41		
61.5 (99.0)	Hungerford				
70.1 (113)	Savernake	73.5	76.23	42.5	(68.4)
81.1 (130)	Patney				
82.0 (131)	Milepost 82		87.05		
91.4 (147)	Edington				
94.0 (151)	Milepost 94		96.30	80.5	(129.5)
95.6 (154)	WESTBURY	97.5	98.17	Slack	
101.3 (163)	FROME			Slack	
106.6 (172)	Witham			48.4	(77.9)
108.5 (175)	Milepost 122¾		116.23	39.5	(63.6)
115.3 (186)	CASTLE CARY	120	122.17	79.5	(127.9)
125.7 (202)	Somerton				
137.9 (222)	Cogload Junction	144	141.10		
142.9 (230)	TAUNTON	149	145.38	63.4	(102.0)
150.0 (241)	Wellington (Somerset)		153.03	51.0	(82.1)
150.8 (243)	Milepost 171		155.03	51.0	(82.1)
151.8 (244)	Milepost 172		154.01	42.5	(68.4)
152.8 (246)	Milepost 173		157.15	32.8	(52.8)
153.8 (248)	Whiteball Signal Box		159.31	26.5	(42.6)
158.8 (256)	Tiverton Junction				
166.5 (268)	Silverton				
173.7 (280)	EXETER ST. DAVIDS	179	177.41		

the load was thirteen coaches right through to Exeter. Usually, of the fourteen- or fifteen-coach rake, three coaches would be slipped at Westbury for Weymouth, two at Taunton for Minehead and branches and the

train would usually arrive at Exeter with only nine coaches or around 300 tons (320 tonnes).

For the Star to take the best part of 500 tons to Exeter and bring it in before time, when the locomotive could have expected the load to lessen as the journey wore on, was a startling achievement.

Note: The milepost figures are at variance with the distance travelled from Paddington via the Berks and Hants line through Westbury as the mileposts were and are calculated from Paddington via Swindon.

The journey was taken over the newly formed Berks and Hants line and some of the cuttings and other earthworks were still settling in. One of the greatest challenges in keeping a heavy train to time is the question of the initial inertia of the load when setting off and the requirement of starting off with a thick fire. 4045 Prince John lost some time at the start of the run, although the line is almost level as far as Reading. The first 70 miles (112km) to Savernake saw a loss of almost three minutes, but in the next 70 miles that deficit was turned around to be a surplus of almost three minutes. At no point did the speed exceed 80.5mph (129.5km), so it was a testament to sustained running at speed with no sudden bursts. The schedule permitted an allowance of twenty-four minutes for the 22.6 miles (36.4km) from Castle Cary to Cogload Junction, where the Berks and Hants line meets with the Bristol to Exeter tracks. This scheduled average of 56.5mph (91km/h) was resoundingly hammered by Prince John's average over the same distance of 71.8mph (116km/h), and this with a load approaching 500 tons (508 tonnes).

The next journey was more conventional in terms of train makeup and the slipping of coaches en route. June 1916 was well into World War I, but this was before schedules would be eased in January 1917 and generally speeds lowered. The aim of this policy was not only to conserve coal but to allow for the increase in unfitted goods trains that would characterize running during the later war periods on the GWR. Their presence would inevitably slow down a fast-approaching express, particularly if goods loops or sidings could not be found as a safe enclave away from the main line due to their numbers and sheer volume of traffic. In addition much of the quadrupling of busy lines was not carried out until the depression

The Down Cornish Riviera Express
Date: 10 June 1916
Locomotive: 4018 Knight of the Grand Cross
Load to Westbury 15 Coaches 494 tons (501 tonnes) tare, 535 tons (543 tonnes) full
Load to Taunton 12 Coaches 402 tons (408 tonnes) tare, 435 tons (441 tonnes) full
Load to Exeter 9 Coaches 314 tons (319 tonnes) tare, 340 tons (345 tonnes) full
Load to Plymouth 7 Coaches 244 tons (247 tonnes) tare, 265 tons (269 tonnes) full
(RED Actual Time denotes behind schedule, GREEN in front)

Distance miles (km)	Place on journey	Schedule time mins	Actual time mins	Average speeds mph	(km/h)
0.0 (00.0)	PADDINGTON	0	0.0		
18.5 (29.8)	SLOUGH	20	23	47.3	(76.1)
36.0 (57.9)	READING	37	41	60.0	(96.6)
	Permanent Way Slack				
53.1 (86)	NEWBURY	56	62	48.8	(78.5)
70.1 (113)	Savernake	73.5	81	42.5	(68.4)
95.6 (154)	WESTBURY	97.5	104	66.6	(107.1)
115.3 (186)	CASTLE CARY	120	127	51.4	(82.7)
137.9 (222)	Cogload Junction	144	146.5	69.5	(111.8)
142.9 (230)	TAUNTON	149	151	66.7	(107.3)
153.8 (248)	Whiteball Signal Box		162.5	56.9	(91.6)
173.7 (280)	EXETER ST. DAVIDS	180	180	68.3	(109.9)
193.9 (312)	NEWTON ABBOT	203	202.5	53.8	(86.6)
202.5 (326)	Totnes	215.5	214.5	43.0	(69.2)
209.4 (337)	Brent	225	227.5	31.9	(51.3)
225.7 (363)	PLYMOUTH NORTH ROAD	247	246	52.9	(85.1)

era of the early 1930s. At this point, however, wartime austerity was six months away.

The guards on passenger trains were notionally in charge of the train and it was their duty to log the journey times. For this purpose they were provided with quality pocket watches, originally supplied by Kay's of Worcester, with which to record the journey times accurately. Lateness of any train was sometimes investigated and action taken against the perceived guilty parties, usually with a fine. The publicity-minded GWR occasionally published the guard's log of the journey, like this example.

A prodigious load of 535 tons (543 tonnes) saw 4018 Knight of the Grand Cross lose the struggle to keep time with the deficit being recorded as 3 minutes, 4 minutes and 6 minutes by Slough, Reading and Newbury respectively. A permanent way slack between Reading and Newbury, however, accounted for three and a half minutes of lost time.

By Castle Cary the deficit had widened to seven minutes, despite the slip at Westbury of three coaches

for Weymouth. With about 100 tons less behind the drawbar, 4018 was able to bring the arrears down to just over two minutes by Taunton. This effort was continued with even time at Exeter and improved on through South Devon, despite Dainton and Rattery banks, to reach Plymouth North Road one minute early. This was a very creditable achievement when it is realized that the train was behind time for about two-thirds of the journey.

The next run concerns the 15:30 Paddington to Exeter three-hour express and an early non-superheated locomotive 4004 Morning Star, which wasn't upgraded to a superheater until January 1911; this places the run firmly in the Edwardian era.

The journey was scheduled to slip a coach each at Westbury and Taunton, but in the event it wasn't possible to do so at either way point. Instead the train had to make an unscheduled stop to detach the coach. The intention had been to release it at speed and either bring it to a stand outside the station, so it could be drawn in by a pilot locomotive, or halted at

Paddington to Exeter 3 hr Express
Locomotive: 4004 Morning Star
Load 9 Coaches 287 tons (291 tonnes) tare, 305 tons (309 tonnes) full – Westbury
Load 8 Coaches 262 tons (266 tonnes) tare, 277 tons (281 tonnes) full – Taunton
Load 7 Coaches 237 tons (240 tonnes) tare, 250 tons (254 tonnes) full – Exeter
(RED Actual Time denotes behind schedule, GREEN in front or on time)

Distance miles (km)	Place on journey	Schedule time mins	Actual time mins.s	Average speeds mph	(km/h)
0.0 (00.0)	PADDINGTON	0	0.0		
9.1 (14.6)	Southall	12	11.32	67	(107.8)
18.5 (29.8)	SLOUGH	21		75	(120.7)
	Adverse signals			30	(48.3)
24.2 (38.9)	Maidenhead	26		45	(72.4)
31.0 (49.9)	Twyford				
34.0 (54.7)	Milepost 34		36.07	69	(111.0)
36.0 (57.9)	READING	38	38.10	20	(32.2)
44.8 (72.1)	Aldermaston			64	(103.0)
53.1 (85.5)	NEWBURY	57	55.50	66	(106.2)
58.5 (94.1)	Kintbury			68	(109.4)
61.5 (99.0)	Hungerford			62	(99.8)
66.4 (107)	Bedwyn			66	(106.2)
70.1 (113)	Savernake	74	71.27	51	(82.1)
81.1 (130)	Patney				
86.9 (140)	Lavington		86.47	73	(117.5)
91.4 (147)	Edington			48	(77.9)
94.0 (151)	Milepost 94			80	(129.5)
95.6 (154)	WESTBURY	97	96.44	Arrived	
			98.26	Departed	
101.3 (163)	FROME	104	107.18	30	(48.3)
106.6 (172)	Witham				
108.5 (175)	Milepost 122¾	114	115.59	47	(75.6)
115.3 (186)	CASTLE CARY	121	122.14	62	(99.8)
125.7 (202)	Somerton		131.32	69	(111.0)
137.9 (222)	Cogload Junction	144	146.04	68	(109.4)
142.9 (230)	TAUNTON	149	152.04	Arrived	
			153.12	Departed	
144.9 (233)	Norton Fitzwarren		156.52	46	(74.0)
150.0 (241)	Wellington (Somerset)		162.08	61	(98.2)
153.8 (248)	Whiteball Signal Box	161	166.42	41	(42.6)
158.8 (256)	Tiverton Junction		171.12	77	(123.9)
170.2 (274)	Stoke Canon		180.54		
	Permanent Way Slack			30	(48.3)
173.7 (280)	EXETER ST. DAVIDS	180	186.50		

Net Time, exclusive of unscheduled stops, 171.5 minutes

the platform by the slip guard using the special vacuum reservoir cylinders attached to every slip coach. The vacuum brake connections self-sealed after the coach had been detached or else the train's brakes would come on. As well as the GWR and BR Western Region, the tried and tested system was used by other railways until 1960.

A minor deficit by Reading was made up and surpassed by Newbury, and by Savernake the train was about two and a half minutes ahead of time.

At Westbury sterling work by the station staff managed to detach the first coach in under four minutes, but this still left the train more than three minutes in arrears at Frome.

Some speedy running to Cogload Junction lowered the deficit to nearer two minutes, but slowing down for the stop at Taunton increased the lateness. This was despite an astonishingly brief stop of just over one minute at Taunton station.

A permanent way slack at Stoke Canon brought the speed tumbling to 30mph (49km/h) and on arrival at Exeter St. David's it was nearly seven minutes adrift.

When the unscheduled stops and other delays are taken into account the train's net time was 171½ minutes, as against the booked time of 180 minutes.

All in all this was a very good performance from a locomotive in early condition, a testament to the locomotive's crew and what could be achieved with an un-superheated engine using what was probably Welsh steam coal.

This run from Taunton to Paddington is notable for the difficulties imposed on the train by outside events and the efforts of the locomotive and crew to overcome them. The train had encountered a severe

Taunton to Paddington
16:11 Date: 1913
Locomotive: 4030 King Harold
Load 15 Coaches 473 tons (481 tonnes) tare, 520 tons (528 tonnes) full
(RED Actual Time denotes behind schedule, GREEN in front or on time)

Distance miles (km)	Place on journey	Schedule time mins	Actual time mins.s	Average speeds mph	(km/h)
0.0 (0.0)	TAUNTON	0	0.0		
5.0 (8.0)	Cogload Junction		7.55	51/63.5	(82/102)
17.2 (27.7)	Somerton		21.05	48.5	(78)
27.6 (44.4)	CASTLE CARY		32.20	61.5	(99)
34.4 (55.4)	Milepost 122¾		41.40	30.5/68	(49/116)
41.6 (66.9)	FROME		49.20	67 Slack	(108)
47.3 (76.1)	WESTBURY		56.20	60 Slack	(97)
56.0 (90.1)	Lavington		66.25	45	(72)
61.8 (99.5)	Patney		73.45	59	(95)
67.1 (109)	Pewsey		80.20		
72.8 (117)	Savernake		86.25	48	(77)
	Bedwyn			71.5	(115)
81.4 (131)	Hungerford		94.15	74	(119)
89.8 (145)	NEWBURY		101.30		
	Thatcham			70.5	(113)
	Aldermaston			68	(109)
101.7 (164)	Theale		111.55	67	(108)
	Reading West	Severe		Checks	
106.9 (172)	READING	Checks	119.20	Checks	
111.9 (180)	Twyford		125.35	58	(99.8)
118.8 (191)	Maidenhead		132.10	62.5	(75.6)
	Taplow			64	(102)
124.4 (200)	SLOUGH		137.30	67	(108)
133.8 (215)	Southall		146.35	62.5	(101)
	Acton		151.30	Eased	
142.9 (230)	PADDINGTON	154	160.20		

Net Time 154 minutes

slack due to a bridge replacement, and the throng of passengers on the platform upon arrival at Taunton station meant that an extra coach had to be added to the fourteen that had arrived there. When the two factors were taken into account, the train was about half an hour late leaving Taunton and had therefore lost its pre-planned path.

Freight trains and especially pick-up goods would normally be kept well clear of speeding passenger trains and would be shunted into goods loops in good time before the arrival of an express that was to overtake them. A passenger train that had set off late would be likely to be held up at signals or at least slowed while freight trains, and perhaps local passenger trains, were shunted out of the way.

Yet despite all these difficulties the train's net time was 154 minutes – right time.

After the generally favourable gradients leaving Taunton on the 'up', King Harold was managing nearly 50mph (80km/h) on the climb through Somerton. Once over the top at Brewham Signal Box the 520 ton (528 tonnes) train accelerated to the mid-sixties after a slack at Frome. Similarly, after the continuous drag from Westbury to Savernake, 4030 achieved 71.5mph (115km/h) at Bedwyn and 74mph (119km/h) at Hungerford. This is from a locomotive that was classified by British Railways as power class 5P! The drawbar pull after Westbury was rated at about 1,200hp (894.8kW).

From Savernake the run is almost all downhill, although by the Thames Valley at Reading the track is more level than anything else. By Reading, however, the train was quite severely delayed by signal checks, no doubt a result of encountering services

	Paddington to Bath Express 11:05 Date: 1916 Locomotive: 4005 Polar Star Load 11 Coaches 358 tons (364 tonnes) tare, 380 tons (386 tonnes) full – Westbury (RED Actual Time denotes behind schedule, GREEN in front or on time)				
Distance miles (km)	Place on journey	Schedule time mins	Actual time mins.s	Average speeds mph	(km/h)
0.0 (00.0)	PADDINGTON	0	0.0		
	Adverse signals				
	Permanent Way Slack				
9.1 (14.6)	SOUTHALL	11	13.30		
18.5 (29.8)	SLOUGH	20	22.24	63.4	(102)
24.2 (38.9)	Maidenhead	26		66.3	(106)
31.0 (49.9)	Twyford			66.8	(104)
36.0 (57.9)	READING	37	38.10	66.7	(107)
44.8 (72.1)	Goring-on-Thames			70	(113)
53.1 (85.5)	DIDCOT	53.5	53.00	68.3	(110)
60.4 (94.1)	Wantage Road		59.38	66	(106)
66.5 (99.0)	Uffington		65.22	63.7	(103)
71.5 (107)	Shrivenham		70.06	64.5	(104)
77.3 (113)	SWINDON	77	75.30	63.3	(102)
82.9 (130)	Wootton Bassett		80.46	63.9	(103)
87.7 (140)	Dauntsey		84.45	72.1	(116)
	Adverse signals				
94.0 (151)	CHIPPENHAM	93	89.41	76.5	(123)
98.3 (154)	Corsham		93.41	64.5	(104)
101.9 (163)	Box		97.04	63.9	(103)
102 (172)	Milepost 102				
104.6 (175)	Bathampton		99.29	67	(108)
106.9 (186)	BATH	105	101.53	57.5	(93)

that would normally be out of the way if the train had set off on time. A spirited recovery saw the train achieve 67mph (108km/h) by Slough, but at Acton the train was eased and finally held at the approach to Paddington.

The star of the LNWR locomotive exchanges of 1911 was the Star of the next run from Paddington to Bath, though with a moderate load of eleven coaches of 380 tons (386 tonnes) full.

A fire that was initially thick had not burned through enough to produce the harder work the engine needed, so there was a minor deficit at Southall, but by Didcot 4005 Polar Star was half a minute to the good. From Maidenhead to Swindon the average speed was 66.5mph (107km/h). This steady performance saw Swindon passed 1.5 minutes early. The 1 in 100 down Dauntsey Bank saw the speed rise to 72.1mph (116km/h) and 76.5mph (123km/h) by Chippenham.

Paddington to Birmingham Snow Hill
Locomotive: 4048 Princess Victoria
Load 12 Coaches 348 tons (354 tonnes) tare, 370 tons (376 tonnes) full
(RED Actual Time denotes behind schedule, GREEN in front)

Distance miles (km)	Place on journey	Schedule time mins	Actual time mins.s	Average speeds mph	(km/h)
0.0 (00.0)	PADDINGTON	0	0.0		
3.3 (5.31)	Old Oak Common West		6.10	35	(56)
7.8 (12.5)	Greenford		11.25	59	(95)
10.3 (16.6)	Northolt Junction	15.5	14.05	60	(97)
14.1 (22.7)	Milepost 3¾				
14.8 (23.8)	Denham		18.30	60	(97)
21.1 (33.9)	Milepost 10¾				
21.7 (34.9)	Beaconsfield		26.15	51.5	(83)
26.5 (42.6)	HIGH WYCOMBE	32		Adverse Signal	
28.8 (46.3)	West Wycombe		31.2	35	(56)
31.5 (50.7)	Saunderton		37.5	47	(76)
33.0 (53.1)	Milepost 22¾			45	(72)
34.7 (55.8)	PRINCES RISBOROUGH	42	41.30	62	(100)
40.1 (64.5)	Haddenham		45.50	82	(132)
44.1 (71.0)	Ashendon Junction		48.12	Slack	
50.4 (81.1)	Blackthorn		54.30	70	(117)
51.6 (83.0)	Milepost 7½ (from Ashendon Junction)				
53.4 (85.9)	BICESTER		57.10	65	(105)
57.1 (91.9)	Milepost 13			48	(77)
57.2 (92.0)	Ardley		61.14	51.5	(83)
62.4 (100)	Aynho Junction	69	66.25	60	(97)
67.5 (109)	BANBURY	74	71.30	63.5	(102)
73.4 (118)	Milepost 92				
76.3 (123)	Fenny Compton		80.52	50/70.5	(88/113)
81.2 (131)	Southam Road		85.15	69/72.5	(111/117)
87.3 (140)	LEAMINGTON SPA	93	90.50	40	(64)
89.2 (144)	Warwick		93		
93.5 (150)	Hatton		99.58		
100.2 (161)	Knowle and Dorridge		106.55		
103.6 (167)	Solihull		110.25		
107.4 (173)	Tyseley		114.02		
109.5 (176)	Bordesley		116.50	Permanent Way Slack	
110.6 (178)	BIRMINGHAM SNOW HILL	120	119.05		

Net Time 117.5 minutes

Brisk running was maintained into Bath Spa station to arrive more than three minutes early.

This run, to what was Britain's third city at the time, was some way into the Birmingham two-hour expresses. These had hitherto worked with trains of only 300 tons (305 tonnes) or so, which were well within the capacity of Saints and early un-superheated Stars. The 11:05 am from Paddington in August 1915 slipped two coaches at Leamington Spa. The terrain between Paddington and Birmingham is very much up and down where the Chiltern Hills have to be surmounted between Saunderton and Princes Risborough. The north Oxfordshire ironstone hills between Bicester and Banbury present another summit.

After the downhill slip of two coaches for Leamington Spa, the gradient becomes uphill by Warwick and continues in this vein until Birmingham Snow Hill.

4048 Princess Victoria made a spirited departure from the terminus and was up on the schedule by one and a half minutes, but the climb from Denham saw this lead pegged back to 40 seconds at High Wycombe and the right time by Princes Risborough, with a creditable 45mph (72km/h) at Saunderton summit. The summit at Ardley was passed at 51½mph (83km/h) after a strenuous climb. The train was two and a half minutes ahead of time by Tyseley and this early showing was checked by signalling and a permanent way slack at Bordesley, which cut the lead to one minute over the schedule but more than that when the external checks were taken into account.

The early runs were made with coaches with a high rolling resistance and it was to be some years before innovations such as roller bearing axleboxes made a significant difference to the power needed to pull the train at speed.

The four tables of Star workings that follow in this chapter are taken from depot returns and records of trains worked with their loadings. Although they may resemble timetable extracts, they are a part record of what some of the engines did for a job of work on particular days.

Stars were still being built in this period so their full application to all express services had not yet taken place. They were mostly confined to West of England

			Star Class Workings, 1910–11			
DD/MM/YY	Loco	From	To	Descriptor	Details	
		Bristol Bath Road				
26/3/10	4010	8.18 Bath	Exeter	Passenger	From Bristol	
29/7/10	4017	4/15 Paddington	Plymouth	Passenger	15 coaches	
25/12/10	4010	10.20 Kingswear	Paddington	Passenger	From Plymouth	
		Cardiff Canton				
8/10/10	4001	8/45 Paddington	Fishguard	Mail		
3/6/10	4001	11.30 Paddington	Neyland	Passenger	13 coaches	
28/9/10	4014	8/45 Paddington	Fishguard	Passenger	From Cardiff	
29/9/10	4014	8.41 Swansea	Paddington	Passenger		
8/11/10	4001	8/45 Paddington	Fishguard	Passenger	From Cardiff	
11/12/10	4014	8/45 Paddington	Fishguard	Passenger	From Cardiff	
		Exeter				
3/6/10	4012	11.00 Paddington	Penzance	Passenger	14 coaches	
		Plymouth Laira				
11/1/10	4009	14.15 Paddington	Penzance	Newspapers	From Bristol	
12/2/10	4009	6/45 Plymouth	Bristol	Passenger		
12/2/10	4012	10.00 Penzance	Paddington	Passenger	From Plymouth	
19/3/10	4002	10.30 Paddington	Penzance	Passenger		
28/7/10	4004	11.50 Paddington	Kingswear	Passenger	14 coaches	
28/7/10	4009	11.10 Paddington	Penzance	Passenger	17 coaches	

DD/MM/YY	Loco	From	To	Descriptor	Details
28/7/10	4012	3/30 Paddington	Penzance	Passenger	13 coaches
30/7/10	4009	10.30 Paddington	Penzance	Passenger	13 coaches
17/8/10	4004	9.25 Plymouth	Exeter	Passenger	
27/8/10	4011	10.30 Paddington	Penzance	Passenger	
10/11/10	4012	10.30 Paddington	Penzance	Passenger	
16/11/10	4032	10.20 Kingswear	Paddington	Passenger	From Plymouth
18/11/10	4012	1.05 Plymouth	Paddington	Special	Boat train
22/12/10	4002	10.30 Paddington	Penzance	Passenger	14 coaches
24/12/10	4002	3/30 Paddington	Penzance	Passenger	14 coaches
24/12/10	4033	11.50 Paddington	Kingswear	Passenger	14 coaches
6/1/11	4035	10.20 Kingswear	Paddington	Passenger	From Newton Abbot
8/2/11	4035	10.00 Penzance	Paddington	Passenger	From Plymouth
13/4/11	4032	10.30 Paddington	Penzance	Passenger	13 coaches
13/4/11	4033	11.50 Paddington	Kingswear	Passenger	17 coaches
13/4/11	4037	3.30 Paddington	Penzance	Passenger	13 coaches 2nd Part
3/6/11	4035	11.50 Paddington	Kingswear	Passenger	14 coaches
3/6/11	4037	3/30 Paddington	Penzance	Passenger	14 coaches
25/7/11	4011	3/30 Paddington	Penzance	Passenger	
		Old Oak Common			
3/5/10	4022	8.30 Plymouth	Paddington	Passenger	
19/5/10	4027	10.00 Penzance	Paddington	Passenger	From Plymouth
20/7/10	4023	6/0 Penzance	Paddington	Postal	From Bristol
26/7/10	4030	10.20 Kingswear	Paddington	Passenger	From Exeter
27/7/10	4028	11.50 Paddington	Kingswear	Passenger	17 coaches
28/7/10	4026	1/0 Paddington	Penzance	Passenger	15 coaches
29/7/10	4023	1/0 Paddington	Penzance	Passenger	16 coaches
29/7/10	4028	11.50 Paddington	Kingswear	Passenger	14 coaches
29/7/10	4029	11.10 Paddington	Penzance	Passenger	13 coaches 2nd Part
30/7/10	4007	6/30 Paddington	Plymouth	Passenger	15 coaches
16/8/10	4024	8.30 Plymouth	Paddington	Passenger	
27/8/10	40	12.20 Paddington	Cardiff	Passenger	
3/11/10	40	8.30 Plymouth	Paddington	Passenger	
14/10/10	4027	11.50 Paddington	Kingswear	Passenger	
15/11/10	4027	8.20 Paddington	Plymouth	Passenger	
21/12/10	4003	8.30 Plymouth	Paddington	Passenger	
23/12/10	4003	11.50 Paddington	Kingswear	Passenger	14 coaches
23/12/10	4007	7/5 Paddington	Penzance	Excursion	13 coaches
23/12/10	4026	9/50 Paddington	Penzance	Passenger	15 coaches
23/12/10	4027	1/0 Paddington	Penzance	Passenger	14 coaches
23/12/10	4030	10.30 Paddington	Penzance	Passenger	13 coaches
23/12/10	4031	6/34 Kensington	Penzance	Excursion	13 coaches
23/12/10	4034	3/30 Paddington	Penzance	Passenger	13 coaches
01/01/11	4034	2/10 Paddington	Bristol	Excursion	
14/1/11	4007	4/0 Fishguard	Paddington	Passenger	From Cardiff
16/1/11	4006	10.30 Paddington	Penzance	Passenger	
17/1/11	4006	10.20 Kingswear	Paddington	Passenger	From Newton Abbot
11/2/11	4030	8.30 Plymouth	Paddington	Passenger	
17/2/11	4026	4/0 Fishguard	Paddington	Passenger	From Cardiff
18/2/11	4007	8/5 Paddington	Bristol	Passenger	
18/2/11	4028	3/30 Paddington	Penzance	Passenger	

(continued)

DD/MM/YY	Loco	From	To	Descriptor	Details
9/3/11	4025	10.00 Penzance	Paddington	Passenger	From Plymouth
16/3/11	4021	8/5 Bristol	Paddington	Passenger	
18/3/11	4038	10.00 Penzance	Paddington	Passenger	From Plymouth
23/3/11	4040	10.00 Penzance	Paddington	Passenger	From Plymouth
12/4/11	4024	11.00 Paddington	Penzance	Passenger	15 coaches
12/4/11	4031	1/0 Paddington	Penzance	Passenger	16 coaches
12/4/11	4039	3/30 Paddington	Penzance	Passenger	15 coaches
13/4/11	40	8.38 Paddington	Penzance	Excursion	13 coaches
13/4/11	4005	9/50 Paddington	Penzance	Passenger	17 coaches
13/4/11	4018	6/30 Paddington	Plymouth	Passenger	13 coaches
13/4/11	4022	6/30 Paddington	Plymouth	Passenger	15 coaches 3rd Pt
2/6/11	4005	1/0 Paddington	Penzance	Passenger	14 coaches
2/6/11	4022	11.00 Paddington	Penzance	Passenger	16 coaches
2/6/11	4028	11.50 Paddington	Kingswear	Passenger	13 coaches
2/6/11	4038	10.30 Paddington	Penzance	Passenger	14 coaches
2/6/11	4013	1/0 Paddington	Penzance	Passenger	15 coaches
29/6/11	4024	1/0 Paddington	Penzance	Passenger	
10/7/11	4003	9/50 Paddington	Penzance	Passenger	
25/7/11	4025	10.15 Paddington	Ilfracombe	Passenger	
22/8/11	4024	4/0 Fishguard	Paddington	Passenger	From Cardiff
7/9/11	4018	3/30 Paddington	Penzance	Passenger	
20/9/11	4021	8/45 Paddington	Fishguard	Mail	
11/11/11	4018	4/35 Birkenhead	Paddington	Passenger	
15/12/11	4038	4/0 Fishguard	Paddington	Passenger	From Cardiff
21/12/11	4021	6/0 Penzance	Paddington	Postal	From Bristol
23/12/11	4029	8.30 Plymouth	Paddington	Passenger	
28/12/11	4021	2/35 Birkenhead	Paddington	Passenger	From Wolverhampton

Notes: Workings by Depot, 4/15 indicates 4.15 pm or 16:15 hrs. From/to Bristol indicates the engine worked from that point onwards or to that point. 2nd Part means the train was run in multiple parts because of passenger demand.

expresses. The table indicates that some of the trains were up to seventeen coaches, with a tare weight of well over 500 tons (508 tonnes). The West of England expresses also served Reading, Weymouth and Taunton through the medium of slip coaches. The Cornish Riviera Express was a 10.30am departure from platform 1 at Paddington and 10am at Penzance.

A Cardiff Star, 4001, was recorded working the Paddington 8.45pm (20:45hrs) mail train to Fishguard and a return trip the next morning on a boat train.

At this time Plymouth depot provided the engines for Penzance and Kingswear services. It would be some years before Newton Abbot would get Stars to service Torbay and Kingswear trains. Some of the trains required multiple parts for trains to be run to keep up with passenger demand. Holidays with pay would not be introduced for another twenty-five

years, so clearly the trains were mostly for the better off of the time.

Old Oak Common engines worked occasional turns far and wide to Penzance, Ilfracombe, Kingswear, Fishguard, Cardiff, Bristol and, latterly, Birkenhead trains as far as Wolverhampton Low Level. Cardiff, Bristol and Wolverhampton were often worked there and back in a day by Old Oak crews, depending on departure time, but longer trips needed an overnight lodging turn. Records show that in 1912 Saint 2-cylinder 4-6-0 engines shared the work on the West of England expresses, with Laira's 2943 Hampton Court making 25 trips and Old Oak's 2941 Easton Court 21 journeys.

This situation continued until 1916, after which schedules were eased considerably. By then loading was down as the general public was encouraged to travel only if they thought their journey was really necessary. This is reflected in only five occurrences of fourteen coaches, whereas nine coaches accounted for seventeen trips in a sample of about forty journeys.

Stars Between the Wars

By 1920 The Torbay Express was either 11.30am or 12 noon from Paddington or 11.30am from King-swear for the return journey. Outbound, passengers for Dartmouth had to take the ferry across the river to reach their destination, and similarly at Birkenhead Woodside for Liverpool Landing Stage.

Star services in the 1920s are illustrated by a view of 4030 The Swedish Monarch passing Kensal Green gasworks with an express for South Wales (fig. 56). The name shows that this was before July 1927. Kensal Green is between Westbourne Park and Old Oak Common. The train has three modern coaches, which appear to be of the 57ft (17.4m) type, followed by a 70ft (21.3m) Dreadnought coach. The loco is in a transition to modernity but retains older features, such as a swan-necked vacuum pipe, firebox overview portholes and a tall safety valve bonnet. The left-hand injector is dumping water from the overflow.

A Star was involved in an accident on 15 April 1923 at Curry Rivel Junction, where the Taunton to Frome line met the line coming in from Yeovil. 4048 Princess Victoria was hauling sixty-eight loaded coal and mixed freight wagons, weighing around 800 tons (813 tonnes). The train had averaged 12mph (19km/h) on its journey when it was involved in a collision caused by a signaller's error. There were injuries but no loss of life. This incident demonstrated the use of a Star on a freight train and its ability to cope with the unexpected.

In 1915 this loco had put up a spirited performance on the Birmingham two-hour express (see above). Eight years later the railway had just gone through World War I and everywhere was in turmoil. Trains were backed up and congestion was rife. The use of such an engine would help this situation as well as work the loco back to its next regular work.

As well as Somerset, Stars were to be found on freight trains in Cornwall, where they would be employed to work the engine to its next primary task on occasions when they had no other duty; light engine running was considered wasteful by the GWR.

An example of this working was the record of 4022 King William, from Laira, heading west at St. Austell on 15 August 1921 running under class F headcode lamps (express cattle or goods train).

Fig. 56. 4030 The Swedish Monarch passing Kensal Green gasworks with an express for South Wales. The definite article in the name means this was taken before July 1927. GREAT WESTERN TRUST

Double heading was also used for the same purpose as well as to assist an overloaded train.

Another loco from the same 1909 batch as King William, 4021 King Edward is seen here about 1912 in garter crest livery at Twyford with a Bristol express of coaches in crimson lake (fig. 57). Note the firebox porthole rims are polished brass. The loco had worked the funeral train of King Edward VII in May 1910 and was depicted then with no top feed and splasher works plate, so this photograph clearly post-dates that occasion, but it still has the splasher brass beading that would be removed in World War I.

By 1926 the building of Castle class engines had reached a total of thirty. This meant that Stars were moved out of Old Oak Common to make way for Castles, but they remained in force at Laira and Exeter. This clear-out saw Cardiff Canton with six engines: these held sway on the Pembroke Dock and Milford Haven services, which were both dining car trains.

Carmarthen also received an allocation. These were used on the Carmarthen to Paddington service, with trains consisting of four coaches for Swansea and five for Carmarthen itself.

A regular on the West Country services, operating out of Taunton, was 4054 Princess Charlotte, seen here on a Bristol to Taunton stopper about 1939 (fig. 58). A change since this loco was previously seen (*see* fig. 53) is that it now has a 4,000 gallon (18,184ltr)

tender. The outside framed SIPHON G van next to the engine was commonly used for parcels; such vans were known as 'brown vehicles', meaning they were suitable for use on passenger trains. The train would also consist of four to five coaches.

Newton Abbot Stars regularly performed on Paddington, Bristol, Plymouth and Kingswear duties, and branched out onto West to North expresses working as far as Shrewsbury.

The West to North expresses comprised of GWR and LMSR coaches working to and from destinations such as Penzance, Newquay, Plymouth, Paignton, Ilfracombe, Cardiff, Manchester, Liverpool, Birkenhead, Leeds and Bradford. The LMSR engines would work north of Shrewsbury, where there was a separate engine shed for the LMSR (formerly LNWR), co-located with the GWR depot at Coleham.

The introduction of the Kings in 1927 and the building of yet more Castles saw Worcester receive an allocation in this period. These engines worked Worcester and other services in the West Midlands, all of which were out and back in a day.

The remaining Old Oak Common Stars worked secondary expresses to Fishguard, Wolverhampton, Oxford and Swindon, as well as race specials to Newbury.

Excursions to and from the capital made more work for the class. The 1930 FA Cup Final, for example, had

Fig. 57. 4021 King Edward at Twyford with the Bristol express, about 1910.
GREAT WESTERN TRUST

Star Class Workings, 1926–8

DD/MM/YY	Loco	From	To	Descriptor	Details
		Bristol Bath Road			
6/8/27	4051	5.30 Paddington	Penzance	Passenger	4 coaches
6/8/27	4051	10.45 Penzance	Wolverhampton	Passenger	8 coaches from Ply
22/2/28	4063	1/15 Paddington	Weston-super-Mare	Passenger	
11/8/28	4059	5.30 Paddington	Penzance	Passenger	9 coaches to Ply
11/8/28	4059	10.45 Penzance	Wolverhampton	Passenger	9 coaches from Ply
8/9/28	4004	10.45 Penzance	Wolverhampton	Passenger	9 coaches from Ply
8/9/28	4010	8.20 Penzance	Cardiff	Passenger	8 coaches from Ply
8/9/28	4004	5.30 Paddington	Penzance	Passenger	8 coaches
17/9/28	4023	5.30 Paddington	Penzance	Passenger	to Plymouth
17/9/28	4014	8/45 Paddington	Fishguard	Passenger	From Cardiff
		Carmarthen			
05/27/27	4056	3/55 Paddington	Carmarthen	Passenger	
		Cardiff Canton			
11/1/26	4064	7.30 Cardiff	Paddington	Excursion	11 coaches
1/5/27	4036	11.10 Paddington	Cardiff	Excursion	14 coaches
8/6/27	4064	7.55 Pembroke Dock	Paddington	Passenger	10 coaches
8/6/27	4006	1/18 Paddington	Neyland	Passenger	11 Crdf 5 Swindon
9/6/27	4036	11.55 Paddington	Milford Haven	Passenger	11 coaches
7/10/28	4003	7/15 Cardiff	Paddington	Excursion	13 coaches 1st Part
		Exeter			
3/4/26	4008	10.10 Bath Spa	Plymouth Millbay	Passenger	10 coaches
3/4/26	4008	4/20 Plymouth Millbay	Taunton	Passenger	6 coaches
3/4/26	4018	10.35 Wolverhampton	Penzance	Passenger	9 coaches to Plymh
19/6/26	4011	10.30 Penzance	Wolverhampton	Passenger	10 fm Exeter 2nd Pt
31/7/26	4011	10.30 Paddington	Penzance	Passenger	3rd Part
7/8/26	4010	10.10 Penzance	Crewe	Passenger	7 from Plymouth
7/8/26	4011	10.10 Bath Spa	Plymouth North R	Passenger	
28/8/26	4057	11.0 Paddington	Penzance	Passenger	8 coaches 2nd Pt
1/8/27	4001	6/45 Penzance	Paddington	Postal	
1/8/27	4018	1/30 Paddington	Penzance	Passenger	7 + 2 coaches
2/8/27	4018	9.15 Falmouth	Paddington	Passenger	
6/8/27	4014	8.05 Carmarthen	Truro	Passenger	4 coaches to Plymh
11/8/27	4008	10.30 Paddington	Penzance	Passenger	11 to Plym 2nd
		Plymouth Laira			
3/4/26	4044	2/40 Newton Abbot	Plymouth Millbay	Passenger	8 coaches
3/4/26	4052	11.00 Penzance	Paddington	Passenger	8 coaches to Plymh
3/4/26	4064	11.10 Exeter	Plymouth Millbay	Passenger	8 coaches
3/4/26	4064	10.30 Paddington	Penzance	Passenger	6 from Plymouth
3/4/26	4064	1/0 Plymouth Millbay	Liverpool	Passenger	8 coaches
19/6/26	4067	10.30 Penzance	Wolverhampton	Passenger	8 to Plymouth
31/7/26	4009	10.30 Paddington	Penzance	Passenger	10 1st Part
2/8/26	4009	7.50 Truro	Plymouth Millbay	Passenger	
2/8/26	4030	0.00 Paddington	Penzance	Passenger	
2/8/26	4009	11.50 Paddington	Penzance	Passenger	10 coaches
9/8/26	4009	12/0 Paddington	Penzance	Passenger	5 + 2 coaches

(continued)

DD/MM/YY	Loco	From	To	Descriptor	Details
27/8/26	4009	9.00 Penzance	Paddington	Excursion	10 from Plymouth
28/8/26	4067	10.30 Paddington	Penzance	Passenger	12 coaches 1st Part
28/8/26	4009	10.30 Paddington	Penzance	Passenger	14 coaches 2nd Part
30/7/26	4007	6/30 Paddington	Plymouth	Passenger	15 coaches
16/8/26	4024	8.30 Plymouth	Paddington	Passenger	
27/12/26	4038	11.00 Penzance	Paddington	Passenger	6 to Plymouth
14/4/27	4070	11.00 Penzance	Paddington	Excursion	13 coaches
16/4/27	4052	10.00 Penzance	Paddington	Passenger	6 coaches
16/4/27	4038	11.00 Penzance	Paddington	Passenger	
17/4/27	4009	8.30 Plymouth	Paddington	Passenger	
18/4/27	4014	10.00 Penzance	Paddington	Passenger	6 coaches
18/4/27	4052	10.30 Penzance	Wolverhampton	Passenger	
18/4/27	4014	1/15 Plymouth Millbay	Truro	Passenger	
6/8/27	4020	10.00 Plymouth Millbay	Crewe	Passenger	6 coaches
11/8/27	4014	11.00 Paddington	Newquay	Passenger	11 coaches
		Newton Abbot			
1/4/26	4025	10.30 Paddington	Penzance	Passenger	7 coaches to Truro
1/4/26	4025	4/25 Penzance	Crewe	Passenger	10 coaches
28/4/26	4062	11.20 Kingswear	Paddington	Passenger	11 coaches
31/7/26	4062	10.30 Paddington	Penzance	Passenger	10 from Plym 2nd
2/8/26	4025	12/0 Paddington	Kingswear	Passenger	1st Part
2/8/26	4026	4/0 Fishguard	Paddington	Passenger	From Cardiff
27/12/26	4044	11.00 Penzance	Paddington	Passenger	7 fm Ply 10 fm NAb
18/4/27	4066	10.30 Paddington	Penzance	Passenger	6 coaches
6/8/27	4067	10.10 Bath Spa	Plymouth Millbay	Passenger	
6/8/27	4067	10.30 Paddington	Penzance	Passenger	8 from Plym 2nd
11/8/27	4060	10.05 Bath Spa	Plymouth N Road	Passenger	
11/8/27	4060	10.30 Paddington	Penzance	Passenger	10 from Plymouth
		Old Oak Common			
19/1/26	4021	11.20 Kingswear	Paddington	Passenger	9 coaches
14/2/26	4063	11.50 Paddington	Wolverhampton	Excursion	14 coaches
1/4/26	4004	10.30 Paddington	Penzance	Passenger	11 coaches 3rd Part
1/4/26	4026	10.30 Paddington	Penzance	Passenger	14 coaches 2nd Part
3/4/26	4051	11.0 Penzance	Paddington	Passenger	8 from Plymouth
3/4/26	4056	11.0 Penzance	Paddington	Passenger	9 from Plymouth
21/5/26	4071	5/55 Paddington	Fishguard Harbour	Passenger	11 coaches
31/7/26	4056	10.30 Paddington	Penzance	Passenger	5th Part
7/8/26	4022	10.0 Penzance	Paddington	Passenger	5 coaches 1st Part
15/8/26	4013	1/0 Paddington	Penzance	Passenger	15 coaches
19/9/26	4015	Weymouth	High Wycombe	Excursion	
26/9/26	4022	11.50 Paddington	Snow Hill	Excursion	12 coaches
2/10/26	4055	1/45 Paddington	Wolverhampton	Passenger	14 coaches
22/8/27	4024	4/0 Fishguard	Paddington	Passenger	From Cardiff
27/3/27	4029	11.18 Paddington	Worcester	Excursion	13 f Pad 12 f Ox 1st
27/3/27	4049	Wor Foregate Street	Paddington	Excursion	8 coaches 1st Part
8/6/27	4022	12/20 Bristol T Meads	Paddington	Passenger	From Swindon
8/6/27	4051	10.15 Paddington	Swindon	Milk Empty	
8/6/27	4051	2/30 Cheltenham	Paddington	Passenger	9 from Swindon
8/6/27	4051	2/30 Cheltenham	Paddington	Passenger	9

DD/MM/YY	Loco	From	To	Descriptor	Details
6/8/27	4054	11.10 Penzance	Paddington	Passenger	9 from Plymouth
7/9/28	4050	10.30 Paddington	Penzance	Passenger	9 coaches
		Swindon Stock Shed			
8/6/27	4035	11.30 Cheltenham	Paddington	Passenger	
9/6/27	4035	11.30 Cheltenham	Paddington	Passenger	
		Stafford Road, Wolverhampton			
13/8/26	4065	7/10 Paddington	Shrewsbury	Passenger	10 coaches
28/8/26	4048	11.10 Paddington	Birkenhead	Passenger	14 coaches
26/9/26	4058	8/5 Snow Hill Bir'ham	Paddington	Excursion	12 coaches
8/8/27	4027	2/35 Oxford	Paddington	Passenger	
		Taunton			
6/8/27	4038	1/45 Bristol	Plymouth Millbay	Passenger	5 coaches
6/8/27	4038	1/50 Penzance	Taunton	Passenger	from Plymouth
		Worcester			
5/11/27	4017	12/50 Hereford	Paddington	Passenger	

Notes: Workings by Depot, 4/15 indicates 4.15 pm or 16:15 hrs. From/to Bristol indicates the engine worked from that point onwards or to that point. 2nd Part means the train was run in multiple parts because of passenger demand. Red destinations, other than GWR including joint lines.

Fig. 58. 4054 *Princess Charlotte* on a Bristol to Taunton stopper, about 1939.
GREAT WESTERN TRUST

Fig. 59. 4028 Roumanian Monarch on class B lamps with a stopper near Pangbourne, west of Reading, about 1938.
GREAT WESTERN TRUST

three Stars working in from South Wales on excursions, with six more from Bristol and the Midlands, despite the match being between Huddersfield and Arsenal.

Day-to-day services were typified by this view, taken about 1938, of 4028 Roumanian Monarch on class B lamps with a stopper near Pangbourne, west of Reading in the Thames Valley. The locomotive has the full set of modern items except the larger tender, which is in 1934 livery. The clerestory coach is succeeded by three modern coaches, followed by what appears to be, judging by its low-profile roof, a 40ft (12.2m) passenger luggage van.

Moving to the 1930s and the approach to World War II, the decline from top link work continued and some were withdrawn, mostly the older engines that would be about twenty-five years old by now. The Stars would frequently be called upon to deputize for a failed locomotive or run an excursion or a further part of a named express, giving a good account of themselves with heavy loadings at high speeds.

The Stars at Exeter were particularly used on postal services, which would run at a typical average speed of 40 to 45mph (64–72km/h), similar to that of passenger trains but not at the top link velocities. The engines used on these services include the following:

Date	Number
14 June 1930	4018
6 August 1930	4071
8 August 1931	4070
13 July 1931	4063
23 July 1932	4015
25 July 1932	4063
30 July 1932	4012

Mid-1930s workings included trains to holiday resorts such as Weston-super-Mare, Minehead (pre-Butlin's days), Porthcawl, Newquay, St. Erth for St. Ives and Clifton Down for Bristol Zoo.

Star class 4017 has been illustrated before (see fig. 41). When photographed on express duty about 1928, it was now in 1927 livery and called Knight of Liége (fig. 60). For the evolving story of this loco's name changes, see Chapter 2.

The first appearance in these tables of '+ 1' to indicate the addition of a non-passenger vehicle is on a 1937 Minehead train to Paddington. This is a symptom of a slower stopping passenger train where vehicles not suitable for running at express passenger speeds can be added to a slower train. An example of the mixed

Star Class Workings, 1935–7

DD/MM/YY	Loco	From	To	Descriptor	Details
		Bristol Bath Road			
2/1/35	4021	9/50 Paddington	Penzance	Passenger	To Bristol
17/1/35	4028	10/45 Paddington	Bristol	Parcels	
13/3/35	4022	11.00 Bristol	Paddington	Excursion	
22/6/35	4023	11.45 Bristol	Paddington	Passenger	9 coaches
10/8/35	4023	10.35 St Erth	Porthcawl	Passenger	11 from Plymouth
20/5/36	4043	2/39 Dr. Day's Jun Br	Swindon	Passenger	Light engine return
1/8/36	4015	2.35 Shrewsbury	Penzance	Passenger	10 to Ply 1st Part
1/8/36	4042	6.41 Clifton Down Br	Plymouth North R	Excursion	10 to Ply
1/8/36	4042	10.37 St Erth	Porthcawl	Passenger	11 from Plymouth
1/8/36	4043	10.10 Penzance	Crewe	Passenger	7 from Plymouth
1/8/36	4064	10.40 Wolverhampton	Penzance	Passenger	9 coaches to Plymh
16/8/36	4022	5/20 Bristol	Paddington	Relief Pas	8 relief to 1/20 Plym
22/8/36	4057	11.00 Minehead	Paddington	Passenger	11 coaches
12/9/36	4064	11.22 Bristol	Paddington	Passenger	11 coch via Devizes
12/9/36	4069	3/15 Paddington	Cheltenham	Passenger	11 coaches
12/3/37	4043	9.50 Plymouth	Paddington	Passenger	From Bristol
22/7/37	4022	7.45 Penzance	Crewe	Passenger	15 – Ply 13 Exet–Br
31/7/37	4015	10.15 Penzance	Crewe	Assist	From Plymouth
31/7/37	4022	12/32 Newquay	Paddington	Passenger	To Plymouth
31/7/37	4055	3/20 Totnes	Plymouth Millbay	Passenger	9 coaches
1/8/37	4022	10.50 Penzance	Paddington	Passenger	8 coaches
14/8/37	4071	6/30 Paddington	Plymouth	Passenger	
28/8/37	4042	11.00 Minehead	Paddington	Passenger	10 + 1 coaches
9/10/37	4033	11.45 Bristol	Paddington	Passenger	9 coaches
		Gloucester			
22/8/36	4066	5/0 Paddington	Cheltenham	Passenger	
22/8/36	4066	1/55 Swindon	Paddington	Passenger	6 coaches
12/9/36	4066	1/55 Swindon	Paddington	Passenger	11 coaches
14/8/37	4007	1/55 Swindon	Paddington	Passenger	
14/8/37	4007	5/0 Paddington	Cheltenham	Passenger	8 coaches
28/8/37	4007	1/55 Swindon	Paddington	Passenger	8 + 4 coaches
28/8/37	4007	5/0 Paddington	Cheltenham	Passenger	8 coaches
		Landore (Swansea)			
13/10/35	4040	1.23 Paddington	Swansea	Excursion	
30/5/36	4047	1/55 Paddington	Neyland	Passenger	
30/5/36	4050	3/55 Paddington	Carmarthen	Passenger	
30/5/36	4059	9/13 Cardiff	Swansea	Passenger	
30/5/36	4023	7/55 Paddington	Fishguard Harbour	Passenger	8 coaches from Swan
13/9/36	4040	3.55 Fishguard Harbour	Paddington	Assist	
12/12/36	4003	7/55 Paddington	Plymouth N Rd	Passenger	13 fm Pad 9 fm Slou 6 fm Read 6 + 2 Didc
1/4/37	4036	12/25 Swansea	Carmarthen	Passenger	
7/8/37	4036	10.30 Paddington	Kingswear	Passenger	7 coaches
7/8/37	4036	11.40 Cheltenham	Paddington	Passenger	13 coaches
28/8/37	4050	8.50 Pembroke Dock	Paddington	Passenger	10 coaches 1st Part
28/8/37	4036	5/30 Paddington	Swansea	Passenger	13 coaches

(continued)

DD/MM/YY	Loco	From	To	Descriptor	Details
		Old Oak Common			
13/1/35	4038	7/0 Swindon	Paddington	Excursion	9 coaches
24/2/35	4038	10.00 Paddington	Snow Hill	Excursion	12 coaches
24/2/35	4038	7/35 Snow Hill	Paddington	Excursion	12 coaches
22/8/36	4021	2/38 Oxford	Paddington	Passenger	5 coaches
		Oxford			
13/9/36	4052	10.15 Paddington	Wolverhampton	Passenger	
6/6/37	4021	12.30 Paddington	Weston-super-Mare	Passenger	16 coaches
		Swindon			
21/2/37	4014	11.00 Paddington	Didcot	Passenger	
15/5/37	4045	3/15 Kingswear	Plymouth Millbay	Passenger	4 coaches
31/7/37	4015	8.5 Manchester	Penzance	Passenger	6 to Plym 1st Part
		Shrewsbury			
15/4/35	4065	7.45 Penzance	Liverpool	Passenger	
23/6/35	4065	2/15 Shrewsbury	Pontypool Road	Passenger	
10/8/35	4030	10.15 Penzance	Crewe	Passenger	13 from Plymouth
22/9/35	4025	2/15 Shrewsbury	Cardiff	Passenger	
2/6/36	4013	11.00 Shrewsbury	Paddington	Passenger and Parcels	
27/8/37	4025	5/18 Westbury (SLP)	Bristol Temple M	Passenger	5 coaches + 5
13/7/37	4067	11.10 St Erth	York	Passenger	12 + 1 from Plymouth
		Stafford Road, Wolverhampton			
10/8/35	4004	9.55 Plymouth Millbay	Manchester	Passenger	9 coaches
4/8/36	4031	6/8 Portsmouth	Wolverhampton	Passenger	
28/3/37	4065	9.50 Paddington	Stourbridge Jun	Excursion	11 coaches
28/3/37	4065	7/10 Stourbridge Jun	Penzance	Excursion	11 coaches
18/5/37	4065	10.45 Penzance	Wolverhampton	Passenger	10 from Exeter
28/8/37	4065	4/5 Paddington	Birkenhead	Passenger	14 coaches
		Taunton			
12/10/35	4056	4/20 Taunton	Paddington	Passenger	
12/12/35	4054	12/5 Paddington	Penzance	Passenger	9 to Newton A 2nd Pt
12/9/36	4054	12/20 Minehead	Paddington	Passenger	9 coaches 2nd Part
		Westbury			
22/8/36	4041	1/50 Weymouth	Paddington	Passenger	7 coaches 1st Part
		Worcester			
18/7/36	4051	1/44 Henwick Worc	Snow Hill Birm	Passenger	
22/8/36	4007	12/50 Hereford	Paddington	Passenger	11 coaches
14/8/37	4049	12/55 Ruabon	Paddington	Passenger	11 coaches 1st Part

Notes: Workings by Depot, 4/15 indicates 4.15 pm or 16:15 hrs. From/to Bristol, Br indicates the engine worked from that point onwards or to that point. 2nd Part means the train was run in multiple parts because of passenger demand. Red destinations, other than GWR including joint lines. The + designation in some of the workings means that extra non-passenger vehicles have been added to the train. These were of the types: 6-wheel milk tanker empty, Syphons C, D, F,G,H, J for milk churns or parcels, passenger brake vans, horseboxes and other vehicles for parcels type traffic.

Fig. 60. 4017 Knight of Liége on express duty, about 1930. GREAT WESTERN TRUST

nature of slower passenger trains was 4045 Prince John of Bristol Bath Road on the 5.20pm Swindon to Bristol stopping passenger train. This comprised five assorted vehicles (an empty six-wheeled milk tank, Siphon D, Monster, another Siphon D and a further unidentifiable van) plus two passenger coaches, running under class B lamps. This motley collection was at Hullavington in Wiltshire on 8 August 1935.

A further example was 4069 Westminster Abbey with 4,000 gallon tender in 1927 livery hauling a clerestory brake, three toplight coaches and a Siphon C from Salisbury to Bristol Temple Meads under class B lamps, reported near Bathampton in March 1936.

For the first time in these tables the locomotives were rostered to 'Assist' another engine with a train.

Unlikely starting points for Stars, mindful of their celestial past, were Westbury in Shropshire, Henwick (a suburb of Worcester), Stourbridge Junction in Worcestershire and Ruabon, near Wrexham in the former Denbighshire.

Among the rural byways was a sixteen-coach train from Paddington to Weston-super-Mare in June 1937.

One photograph that can be dated to within a couple of months is that of 4028 The Roumanian Monarch, seen at Paddington in July 1927 (fig. 61). The locomotive had been named King John up until this date, whereupon the King class 6026 took the name. The engine retained the definite article in its name for only two or three months before it was altered to how it appears in fig. 59.

One locomotive that had a particularly long career was 4015 Knight of St. John, seen here at Exeter running shed yard about 1936. This locomotive was involved in the running of postal services in 1932. The engine appears in fine condition, with all modern features except a speedometer, which did not become a general fit until 1937. 4015 would carry on for about another fifteen years, giving almost forty-three years' service.

World War II and Nationalization

Any thoughts of continuing, much less accelerating, the programme of withdrawals was dispelled at the outbreak of World War II. All available resources were pressed into service and remained there for the duration.

Stars were recorded on freight trains more than before, but they had been doing those duties since the 1920s with their work in Cornwall and the example in Somerset.

Depots would continue to roster Stars on passenger trains, however, and the engines were well liked by their crews. Some, it is said, preferred them to Castles.

The evacuation of Dunkirk mainly involved the Southern Railway but the GWR lent locos and coaches to assist. The mass evacuation of children from the cities generated much traffic and the subsequent specials run in December 1939 to enable estranged parents to see their children added to the workload. By the summer of 1942

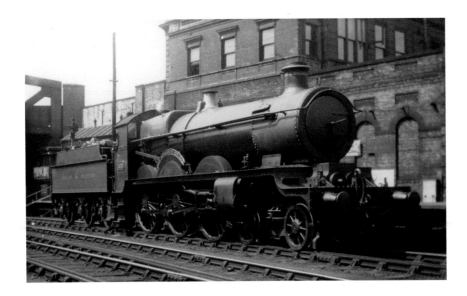

Fig. 61. 4028 The Roumanian Monarch at Paddington in July 1927. GREAT WESTERN TRUST

Fig. 62. 4015 Knight of St. John at Exeter running shed yard, about 1936. GREAT WESTERN TRUST

there were 5,000 extra trains a month running. This number increased as D-Day approached in June 1944.

Rather than reproduce another table from loco depot work-cards, the following table is a construct of locomotive workings from other publications. These are listed chronologically by year of publication in the Bibliography sub-section 'Star Class Workings References' (for example 1978b). Many of the publications listed are out of print but readily available on the second-hand market and internet auction sites, should you wish to acquire the images to further research a particular locomotive.

Expresses to Weymouth, Kingswear and Birkenhead feature in the above table. The two entries in 1951 for 4007 Swallowfield Park are particularly poignant; the first has the gleaming loco at the head of a named express, and yet two months later it is awaiting the cutter's torch on a stopping train. The last of the Castles came into service in 1950 and they may have been the final straw for some of the remaining Stars.

Harold Gasson recounts in *Firing Days* how 4045 Prince John and ten coaches of empty stock from Gloucester to Westbury was re-routed because of a derailment at Chippenham in 1944. The overall

Star Class Workings, 1939–57

Date	Loco	Location	Notes	Ref.
14/2/1939	4038	West Ealing dn (WEY)	Weymouth express	1977
24/2/1939	4038	Newbury (WEY)	Weymouth express, stationary	1989
1939	4041	Swindon shed (SDN)	Paddington, Bristol & South Wales turns	1978b
3/6/1939	4017	Dawlish	Penzance–Liverpool Expr 11 coaches+	1976b
15/8/1939	4015	Taunton stn	A lamps Bristol–Taunton stopper	1989
Jan 1941	4047	Weymouth shed	Air raid damaged	1970b
1945	4059	nr Kemble	Piloting 2913 B lamps c11 coaches	1977
26/8/1946	4036	Cowley Bridge Junctn	A lamps 8 coaches mixed – to Exeter	1977
Oct 1947	4060	Leamington Spa (SRD)	Up express Paddington, final G crest W livery	2000a
6/11/1947	4039	Hereford Shed	Prepared for Cardiff express	1984
1948	4026	Swindon Works	BRITISH RAILWAYS on tender	2006
Jul 1948	4046	Leamington Spa (SLP)	Vacuum freight C lamps	2000a
Aug 1948	4053	Hatton Bank (SRD)	Birkenhead–Paddington relief – 1934 livery	2000a
1949	4041	Bristol Bath Road	Elbow steam pipes	1970a
Apr 1949	4018	Balderton crossing	Bournemouth West to Birkenhead Expr	1981a
30/7/1949	4028	Newbury station (WES	Paddington–Kingswear Express	1989
Dec 1949	4049	West Ruislip	E lamps vacuum freight GW post-war livery	1991
1950	4061	Shrewsbury stn	B lamps stopper Platform 4 to Chester	1986
May 1950	4044	Goring Troughs (SLP)	B lamps stopper Paddington–Oxford	2000a
8/7/1950	4051	Abergavenny Monmouth Road	Paignton–Manchester Victoria – 10 LMR coaches ex-LMS	2011
Jul 1950	4028	Salisbury shed (WES)	B lamps BR cycling lion	2000a
12/8/1950	4049	Salisbury stn sbox	Portsmouth to Cardiff Exp	1977
1951	4036	Reading east platform 5	A lamps Reading East Main signal box	2000b
1/06/1951	4007	Kingswear platform	Torbay Express – 8 coaches Hawksworth	1981a
Aug 1951	4007	Hereford stn (WOS)	B class lamps, just before withdrawal	1983
Oct 1951	4049	Swindon shed (SRD)	Ex-works BR cycling lion	1976c
Feb 1952	4036	Reading shed (RDG)	Stored – red nameplate Staffrd Rd Wks?	2000a
5/7/1952	4062	Wantage on the up	Late tender and weather sheet	1985
Aug 1952	4056	Bath Road Shed	BR cycling lion tender	2006
May 1952	4056	Wootton Bassett (BRD)	B lamps elbow steam pipes	1976c
15/6/1952	4062	Swindon shed	Castle type screw reverse lever housing	1976c
1952	4053	Oldfield Park, Bath	Swindon–Bristol B lamps 5 coaches 1 vn	1973c
Feb 1953	4053	Solihull stn	BR cycling lion 5ft signal arm	1978a
28/2/1953	4053	Warwick power station	Snow Hill–Oxford semi-fast	1973a
7/4/1953	4053	Cholsey & Moulsford	Paddington–Wolves Express 9 coaches plus	1973a
Sep 1953	4056	Bedminster Park stn	Nottingham–Paignton Saturday Expr	1975
June 1954	4056	Bristol Temple Meads	Taunton stopper B lamps mixed coach	1973c
10/9/1955	4061	Tyseley shed	Ex-works – Stephensons LS special	1973a
11/9/1955	4062	Swindon roundhouse (SDN)	Light steam, Hawksworth tender	1977
11/9/1955	4061	Swindon Works (SRD)	SLS Special BR front number removed	1977
24/9/1955	4061	Hatton Bank	TRPS Special A lamps, 4061 bufferbeam	1970b
May 1956	4061	Shrewsbury	D lamps ECS for local to Chester	1981b
14/7/1956	4056	Aller Junction	Swindon Trip returning excursion	1996
9/9/1956	4056	Pass Hereford shed	SLS Special Hereford to Swindon	1973a
9/9/1956	4056	Snow Hill platform	SLS Special to Swindon Works	1984
10/8/1957	4056	Southall	Paddington–Kingswear GWR 4056 bufferbeam	1970b

Notes: Aug date indicates around that date, similarly other information.
Depot where known thus: (SRD) Wolverhampton Stafford Road
Workings also include locos on shed but exclude any photo where the loco is not identifiable.
For source details, see 'Star Class Workings References' in the Bibliography.

75mph (121km/h) speed limit was still in force, but the fireman was able to monitor the speeds recorded as this loco had a speedometer fitted.

He tells with glee of a 'forty in good nick'. The speeds at first were around a sedate 45mph (72km/h), but by Shrivenham, with good Welsh steam coal and full pressure, the speed reached 70 to 75mph (113–121km/h). Between Uffington and Challow the speed reached 80mph (129km/h) and finally 85 to 90mph (137–145km/h) through Steventon. They were going for 100mph (160km/h), but eased off before Didcot lest they be reported for speeding. The engine was more than thirty years old at this point.

Gasson, in *Footplate Days*, also describes 4038 Queen Berengaria in 1949, but the story here was of a locomotive well overdue a major overhaul and in bad condition. The engine had a leaking superheater and blocked tubes, so would not steam well. There was no opportunity to 'clear her throat' with fast running as the turn was a stopping passenger train.

To illustrate the last days of the Star class, here are two late photographs. The first is of 4012 Knight of

Fig. 64. 4028 Roumanian Monarch on the Merchant Venturer express at Bristol Temple Meads, 1951. GREAT WESTERN TRUST

the Thistle at Bristol Bath Road motive power depot in August 1949 (fig. 63). This was another engine that hauled the postal trains in 1932.

Finally we reach 4028 Roumanian Monarch on the Merchant Venturer express arriving at Temple Meads, underneath Bristol Bath Road bridge, in August 1951 (fig. 64). The train of BR Mark 1 coaches had been worked from Weston-super-Mare and either a King or Castle would usually take the train forward to Paddington from Bristol. There are, however, recorded occurrences of 4062 Malmesbury Abbey completing the entire journey as late as 1952. 4028 would be withdrawn three months later.

There are further mentions in the tables of specials that rang down the curtain on the Star story, at least in terms of main-line operation. But the story continued in the best family tradition, since the engines' successors would earn a lasting place in railway history and continue in operation to this day.

Fig. 63. 4012 Knight of the Thistle at Bristol Bath Road motive power depot, August 1949. GREAT WESTERN TRUST

CHAPTER FOUR

CASTLE CLASS LOCOMOTIVES

The civil engineering department on the GWR had an inordinate effect on the development of the railway's locomotive size: it was they who vetoed Churchward's idea of putting a larger boiler on the Stars and were only made to relent on the question of the even heavier King class in 1927. This would involve putting the No. 7 Standard boiler of the 1919-designed 47XX mixed traffic 2-8-0 on a Star.

Over the course of twenty years Churchward had developed the standardized designs that were to be the blueprint for the company's motive power to its end. Charles Benjamin Collett had been on board with the whole process and carried on Churchward's work after the latter's retirement in January 1922. Although he was a student of Churchward, he had modernizing ideas of his own and took GWR locomotive development almost to its ultimate within a short period of time.

Collett produced the Standard No. 8 boiler by using the same firebox as the 47XX but reduced the boiler diameter by 3in (7.5cm), which gave the weight reduction needed to satisfy the civil engineers. The resulting locomotive, the Castle, was something of a compromise but was still touted as the most powerful express engine in Britain in 1923: what is more, the class was to prove it. Castles became a byword for power and speed and the company standard when comparing other types of engine. The 2-cylinder Saint class at Hereford, because of their sterling performances, were described as 'Hereford Castles'.

The GWR was only the third largest of the big four but replicated the Castle class to 171 engines, which were built over a period from 1923 to 1950, into the days of British Railways.

An example of a Castle class in almost original condition, in terms of livery, is 4073 Caerphilly Castle at STEAM, Swindon (fig. 65). It has a 3,500 gallon (15,911ltr) tender but not the diagonal rain strip on the cab roof, which has been removed as they had been on the Stars. Similarly the first Castles came out with bogie brakes, but these were soon removed as here. Stars had pulled the Cheltenham Flyer in 1925 but Castles were to be record breakers. Castles at this date resembled pre-World War I Stars with their splasher brass beading. The number 4073 followed on from the last Star: this was unusual in GWR history as new locomotive classes usually merited a new number series in either the hundreds or thousands numbers.

Another fine preserved Castle that we will turn to when illustrating the features of the class is 5043 Earl of Mount Edgcumbe, which was originally named Barbury Castle. Work during restoration revealed that the left-hand coupling rod, seen here with the rear driving wheel (fig. 66), had been fitted to at least two Star class engines, 4033 Queen Victoria and 4069 Westminster Abbey. Tyseley October 2017.

Boiler apart, Castles owed much to their Star forebears and features such as the motion were a direct engineering drawing copy.

The most significant external visual features that distinguished the engines from the Stars were the curved steam pipes and the side window cab. The inside steam pipes on Stars had always been a maintenance problem in that they restricted access to some of the boiler tubes and there had been issues with maintaining a steam-tight connection. Flexible external steam pipes were that much more accessible and less prone to leakage in the first place.

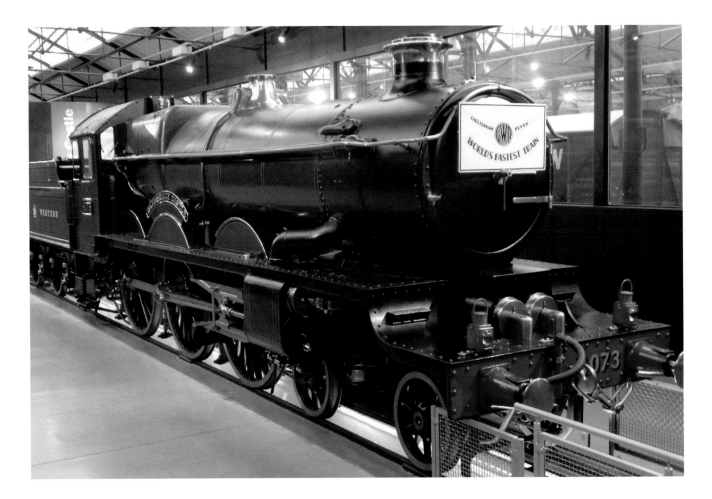

Fig. 65. 4073 Caerphilly Castle at STEAM, Swindon, October 2017. AUTHOR

Fig. 66. 5043 Earl of Mount Edgcumbe, left-hand coupling rod and rear driving wheel, Tyseley, October 2017. AUTHOR

The side window cab updated the crew's facilities to those of the other big three railway companies, but seating was limited to a tip-up wooden bench-type seat (see fig. 99). The LNER, in comparison, had something akin to a sports car upholstered bucket seat on the A3 Pacifics and later engines.

The cab side cut-outs meant that for the first time crews could look out forward while seated, typically for signals, although many preferred to stand.

The headline tractive effort was a record for a British locomotive at the time. The GWR's publicity department made full use of the figure and managed to irritate other railway companies into a series of challenges to compare the Castles with their own products. Caerphilly Castle herself merited a book of her own and the initial print run of 10,000 copies

Fig. 67. 4073 Caerphilly Castle at Weymouth, 1928. GREAT WESTERN TRUST

was expanded to 40,000 copies within one month of publication. Unprecedented crowds gathered on platform 1 at Paddington to salute the putative conquering hero of the GWR.

Caerphilly Castle is seen here at Weymouth in 1928, minus the adoring crowds and away from the glamour routes (fig. 67). At some point the small step on the front bogie that can be seen was removed and the superheater header blister on the smokebox varies from how it is now. The chimney is longer in the older photograph, whereas now the 'Grange' chimney seems to have been substituted. About a year after the change to twin city heraldry, Caerphilly Castle still bears its garter crest livery. The engine looks in good condition but has been working hard.

Caerphilly Castle cost £5,565 to build in 1923. It was withdrawn from Cardiff Canton in 1960 with 1,910,730 miles on the clock (3,075,022km). The budget for its cosmetic restoration was £3,500. The works manager, however, authorized spending £11,000 for a full works overhaul, although it was commonly believed the engine would never run again. The works manager was hauled before top brass to explain and it is accepted that he was lucky to keep his job as this was now public money.

Castle on Display

The British Empire Exhibition of 1924, held at Wembley Park and Wembley Stadium, was so successful that its run was extended until October 1925. One of the many buildings intended to house and showcase British achievements in engineering and construction was the Palace of Engineering, which brought together 4073 Caerphilly Castle and 4472 Flying Scotsman. The latter was yet to become a metaphor for speed and power, but set against the much smaller GWR Castle it seemed triumphantly overwhelming. Nonetheless the GWR was able to claim the more powerful engine, even if it was only based on theoretical tractive effort. In 1925 Caerphilly Castle was rested and 4079 Pendennis Castle took its place in the exhibition.

The initial Welsh theme of Castles was extended to include 4082 as Windsor Castle, the Royal Family's actual home when not at their ceremonial residences or at Balmoral. This was a publicity masterstroke creation as King George V and Queen Mary accepted an invitation to visit Swindon Works on 28 April 1924. 4082 Windsor Castle was in attendance and King George V drove 4082 from the works to Swindon station. A brass plaque was affixed to the cab of 4082 and the inscription read as follows:

G	R

This engine No. 4082 "Windsor Castle" was built at Swindon in 1924 and was driven from the works to the station by His Majesty King George V accompanied by Queen Mary on the occasion of the visit by their Majesties to the Great Western Railway Works at Swindon on April 28th 1924. With their Majesties on the footplate were

Viscount Churchill	Chairman
Sir Felix Pole	General Manager
Mr. C. B. Collett	Chief Mechanical Engineer
G. H. Flewellyn	Locomotive Inspector
E. R. B. Rowe	Engine Driver
A. W. Cook	Fireman

Collett had provided a more roomy cab and extended roof compared with the Stars and no doubt the assembled gathering on the footplate were glad of such facilities.

The following year 4082 Windsor Castle was seen heading a down passenger train past Aldermaston (fig. 68). Some of the modern Collett coaches have white roofs. The tender is in garter crest livery and the swan-necked vacuum pipe and bogie brakes are early features. The Star-like firebox porthole circular windows have polished brass rims, as have the brass cab forward-facing windows.

Castle on Test

The third part of the strategy to establish the reputation of the Castles was a series of dynamometer car test runs between Swindon and Plymouth. The dynamometer car, housed in an elderly clerestory coach, held all the latest means of recording the performance of a locomotive while it was pulling a load and behaving as it would in service. The train was headed by 4074 Caldicot Castle and loaded up to the maximum then allowed for a single engine over the route.

Down Journey	
Swindon to Taunton	485 tons (493 tonnes)
Taunton to Newton Abbot	390 tons (396 tonnes)
Newton Abbot to Plymouth	288 tons (293 tonnes)
Up Journey	
Plymouth to Newton Abbot	288 tons (293 tonnes)
Newton Abbot to Swindon	485 tons (493 tonnes)

The running and speeds achieved were in the best traditions of the Star class and the train was competently able to manage the 485-ton (493 tonnes) train of

Fig. 68. 4082 Windsor Castle heads a down express train past Aldermaston, about 1925. GREAT WESTERN TRUST

fourteen coaches on the occasion of the runs during March 1924. So why all the subsequent fuss?

For the first time the results of the trials were made public by the very open vehicle of the World Power Conference, where most of the railway-related papers presented were on the subject of electrification. Before 1923 some experiments and small systems had been tried on the North Eastern Railway and others, but it was to be some years before the Southern Railway was to make a large-scale investment in a suburban context.

Collett, however, presented a paper on the subject of 'Testing of Locomotives of the Great Western Railway'. This included revelations about how testing had been carried out at Swindon, but among the detail was a figure that was to cause shockwaves throughout the railway engineering domestic scene: the weight of coal per drawbar horsepower hour was extremely low, low enough to bring accusations of incredulity. The following table attempts to illustrate this effect.

Source	Value, lb (kg)
Typical for other railways	4.5–6 (2–2.7)
Hughes 4-6-0 Lanc & York Railway (LMS from 1923)	5 (2.3)
GWR non-superheated Star	3.5 (1.6)
GWR superheated Castle	2.83 (1.3)

The result was nothing less than astonishing – and this with a locomotive pulling getting on for 500 tons (508 tonnes). The Castle 3,500 gallon (15,911ltr) tender had a coal capacity of only 6 tons (6.1 tonnes), but with these figures the engine wouldn't seem to need more. There are tales of engines on other routes where the prodigious appetite for coal of their locos has meant that especially large lumps of coal had to be placed vertically by the coal rails to build up a wall to increase the coal capacity of the engine to get it to its destination. Other accounts tell of firemen using a brush to sweep the last vestiges of fuel forward to feed the hungry firebox. The soubriquet 'black pig' was commonly applied to black-painted Great Central engines that had a ravenous appetite for the dark fuel.

This figure is more than that, though, as it demonstrates how comfortably and competently the engine was working even when heavily loaded and running a tight schedule. Their fuel consumption revealed an economic and efficient engine. The burning question was, 'What would these engines do when really extended?'

The calorific value of the fuels used must be taken into account. Calorific value is the energy contained within the fuel when it is completely burnt. Welsh steam coal, as used by the GWR, was always noted for its high calorific value. Blidworth coal, often quoted as 'northern' hard coal (although Blidworth is near Mansfield in Nottinghamshire), did not have as high a calorific value as that of the Welsh coal. Blidworth was used by the LNER, among others, but even when that is taken into account the figures are still remarkable. Indeed, further developments with superheating on the GWR in later years were to extend its lead even more.

Castle in Contest: 1. LNER

Sir Felix Pole, the GWR's general manager, and one of the participants on the crowded footplate at Swindon with their Majesties, was ever keen to seek out the maximum good publicity for the railway. He proposed to Alexander Wilson, the LNER's Southern Area (that is, ex-Great Northern territory) General Manager, that there should be an exchange of engines with the LNER. It is also said that Sir Felix Pole broached this matter with Sir Ralph Wedgwood, Chief General Manager of the LNER, at a private luncheon: perhaps he asked the one after an unenthusiastic reply from the other.

The GWR engine would work from King's Cross to Grantham, Doncaster, Leeds and Bradford, and the LNER from Paddington to Plymouth on the Cornish Riviera Express.

Sir Nigel Gresley was not entirely satisfied with the performance of his A3 Pacifics and was curious to see if any technical data could be gleaned that would point the way to improvements. He was to be rewarded.

The locomotives involved were 4073 Pendennis Castle and the LNER's 4474 Victor Wild (later BR No. 60105). The engine 4475 Flying Fox (BR No. 60106) had originally been selected to represent the LNER, but ran a hot tender axlebox and was withdrawn from the trials.

They were used on ordinary service trains, so although both companies possessed dynamometer cars they were not used.

On the GWR Victor Wild had to cope with trains of between 530 tons (539 tonnes) leaving Paddington to 310 tons (315 tonnes) from Exeter to Plymouth on the down, and between 310 and 385 tons (315–391 tonnes) on the up towards Paddington. On the LNER loads were typically 480 tons (488 tonnes).

In general 4079 Pendennis Castle was able to equal anything the LNER Pacific could muster. In some cases the timing and performance were without parallel by the LNER. In particular, the start from King's Cross is level and then is up a gradient of 1 in 107 through the tricky and often wet Gas Works and Copenhagen tunnels. A3 Pacifics were notoriously prone to slipping and special techniques had to be evolved, particularly at York station, which is on a sharp curve, to get a train started from Platform 9 (as it then was) to head north.

All eyes were therefore on Pendennis Castle as it set off for Leeds with 480 tons (488 tonnes) behind the drawbar. On this and every run the Castle beat the Pacific's time to Finsbury Park by between one and six minutes and on only one run was the slightest trace of slipping detected. It seemed the GWR had mastered the notion of traction control in 1925 before it became a standard for the car industry ninety years later.

The rest of 4079's running was as exemplary: on many of the runs the engine was eased to avoid being too far ahead of time and encountering adverse signals as a result. On 30 April 1925 4079 took sixteen coaches weighing 475 tons (483 tonnes) from King's Cross to Peterborough in a shade over 80 minutes when the schedule was 83 minutes for the 76.4 miles (123km). The engine was eased at Biggleswade as it was running up too much of a surplus to time. The maximum speed was 83.5mph (134km/h) and the engine sustained an average of 71.2mph (115km/h) over a distance of 27 miles (43.4km) from Hitchin to Huntingdon.

Times for some of the other runs over the same course were 78 minutes 39 seconds, 80 minutes 5 seconds, 80 minutes 37 seconds and 80 minutes 45 seconds against the scheduled 83 minutes.

The LNER's engine Victor Wild found the severe curvature and south Devon banks not to its liking. On the first down run shavings of white metal from the coupling rod bearings were found by the driving wheels. Drivers were also thought to be 'coal dodging', by trying to economize on coal consumption to the detriment of timekeeping and overall performance.

The GWR ran service trains in competition with the LNER's trials engine and 4074 Caldicot Castle brought the down Cornish Riviera express into Plymouth North Road in 231 minutes and 58 seconds, against a schedule of 247 minutes. The LNER engine was just about able to keep to the schedule.

The LNER had sent E. D. Trask, one of their ablest engineers, to supervise the preparation of Victor Wild and monitor its performance. Sir Nigel Gresley met Trask on platform 1 at Paddington when the up Cornish Riviera Express was due. Gresley asked Trask how it was going. Trask replied, 'Oh all right, but not as well as the G W.'

Gresley's reply was, 'Oh but you must!', to which Trask's answer was, 'I don't see how we can. They got a better valve gear than we have.'

Gresley replied, 'Mr Winter's getting out an improved gear for us.'

Trask was not one to mince words and retorted, 'Well that won't be much use to us this week.'

Gresley was not best pleased and stormed off. Trask remained at the LNER but did not progress to the highest level.

If this were not enough evidence of the GWR's superiority, then the clincher was the coal consumption. The GWR engine showed itself to have 12½ per cent lower coal consumption with Welsh steam coal and 6½ per cent lower coal consumption with 'northern hards' on the LNER. Even the oft quoted jibe that the GWR's engines could only perform with superior Welsh coal was disproved.

Sir Felix Pole trumpeted the results in the *GWR Magazine* of June 1925, although some of the runs by the A3 Pacific were shown up to be late because of factors other than the engine, and in some cases the engine inherited a late-running train for which no allowance was made. The LNER had expected, naively, that the running data would be private between the two companies, but should have realized that the only thing the GWR wanted was publicity.

The LNER wrote to Sir Felix Pole to complain but Pole rebutted the complaint by pointing out that Cecil

J. Allen, an LNER employee, had tried to spin the situation at 180 degrees to reality. This issue was to cause rancour between the two companies, but whatever interpretation was put on events it did not mask the fact that the exchanges were a complete triumph for the GWR.

Gresley and the LNER learned this lesson and modified the A3 Pacifics with a series of changes carried out from 1926 on No. 4477 Gay Crusader (BR 60108). The valve gear was changed to include increased lap and longer travel of the piston valves, in accordance with Great Western practice. Increasing the boiler pressure from the low 180psi (12.4 bar) and improvements to the superheater made the engines into flyers capable of hauling heavy trains over long distances at moderate coal consumption.

Although the eminent engineer W. A. Tuplin maintained that boiler pressure had no effect on performance, there are plenty of anecdotes relating to engines fitted with wrongly calibrated safety valves, resulting in the boiler running at increased pressures that their drivers always regarded as more powerful than the usual for their class of engine.

4095 Harlech Castle came from the third batch of locomotives from May 1926. When seen at Newton Abbot about 1930 it was teamed with Collett's improved 4,000 gallon (18,184ltr) tender in the 1927 livery (fig. 69). The bogie step first seen on 4073 is present (see fig. 67), but not the bogie brakes. The rear sandpipe by the cab steps is a curiosity in that it can hardly have been necessary for an engine running in reverse, although it could be that an engine setting off with a heavy train would first lay down a layer of sand when backing on to the load, so as to be ready when forward motion was necessary. Note the oil painted pattern on the front bogie wheel.

The preceding engine in this batch was 4094 Dynevor Castle, pictured in 1927 livery among the weeds at Old Oak Common in 1928 (fig. 70). This was an early recipient of a whistle shield, which did not become standard across the rest of the class until 1936. The top lamp bracket is in front of the chimney; it would be 1935 before nearly all the class had it moved to the smokebox door.

Castle in Contest: 2. LMSR

The board of the newly formed LMS Railway was strongly influenced by one of its constituent companies, the Midland Railway. While every other company was moving on to larger engines, they had a policy of double heading almost every express passenger train with typically small 4-4-0 engines that were firmly rooted in the nineteenth century. Sir Henry Fowler, himself a Midland man, was the Chief Mechanical

Fig. 69. 4095 Harlech Castle at Newton Abbot, about 1930. GREAT WESTERN TRUST

Fig. 70. 4094 Dynevor Castle at Old Oak Common, 1928. GREAT WESTERN TRUST

Engineer of the LMS. The lesson taught to the LNWR by 4005 Polar Star in 1910 (*see* Chapter 3) seems to have been disregarded. Fowler was working on a large compound and memories lingered at Crewe of the Webb compounds of the LNWR.

Questions were being asked about the cost of the Midland small engine policy. Fowler was seen as an obstacle to progress, so he was bypassed when the GWR was approached. Sir Guy Granet, the LMSR chairman, contacted Sir Felix Pole about the supply of a Castle class locomotive to work on the West Coast Main Line (WCML) for some weeks with a view to seeing if this engine would be suitable to work the line. Driver Young, who had participated in the LNER exchanges the year before, was a natural choice and he took 5000 Launceston Castle to the LMS for the trials in October

1926. The engine worked first between Euston and Crewe and then between Crewe and Carlisle.

Earlier that year 5000 Launceston Castle had been recorded in the yard at Old Oak Common in as-built condition (fig. 71). It has the first of the 4,000 gallon (18,184ltr) tenders (*see* below) and the garter crest livery, which was to give way to two cities heraldic shields months later. The water cranes were later modified to have an angle crank to enable the larger tenders to be filled easily. There are two types of manual point lever with bullhead rail acting as the safety rail on the smaller type.

An example of the work of 5000 Launceston Castle was a run made from Crewe to Carlisle on 16 November 1926. The train was of 57 axles of 400 tons tare and 415 tons full (406 and 422 tonnes). The train

Fig. 71. 5000 Launceston Castle in the yard at Old Oak Common, 1926. GREAT WESTERN TRUST

set off from Crewe across the Cheshire plain, By Winsford it was two minutes behind schedule, but by Warrington, despite a permanent way slack, it was over 1½ minutes up. By Preston the credit in the time account had risen to 5½ minutes and by Lancaster it was almost 6 minutes. The last of the mostly flat running came to an end at Carnforth where the train was almost 6½ minutes up. The 1 in 134 gradient out of Carnforth was a prelude to sterner tests as gradients of 1 in 111, 1 in 131 and 1 in 106 had to be tackled before reaching a plateau at Grayrigg. The engine was still about 5½ minutes up and rushed past Dillicar Troughs and on to Tebay at 66mph (106km/h). The long slog up the 1 in 75 gradient to Shap Summit, where the train could only manage 20mph (32km/h), was rewarded by the run's maximum speed down the other side of 79mph (127km/h) at Clifton. By Penrith the train was 7 minutes 20 seconds to the good and, despite a permanent way slack just before Carlisle, it reached Citadel station seven minutes before time. The net time when delays due to other factors were taken into account was 154½ minutes, against a schedule of 165 minutes for the 141 miles (227km). 5000 Launceston Castle and Driver Young, not to mention the unnamed fireman, brought in trains weighing up to 100 tons more than this before time. This was not all, for the LMS men made a comparison between the quiet efficiency of the Castle, which clearly had power in reserve, and the all-out thrashing of the ex-LNWR Claughton class engines that were needed to perform the same duties but not to the same effect.

The result was that the Castle made a stunning impression on the diehard Midland men at the LMS. J.E. Anderson, Superintendent of Motive Power on the LMS, who was never known to praise anything GWR, said he wouldn't mind having twenty-four Castles for the West Coast Main Line for 1927. The GWR was approached for fifty but declined; the request was modified to a full set of drawings and was still declined. Sir Henry Fowler hurriedly produced a set of drawings for a 4-6-0 and commissioned the North British Locomotive Co. in Glasgow to turn out the Royal Scot class.

These were larger 4-6-0 engines but not Castles. After William Stanier, who was Swindon Works General Manager, had been headhunted to take over as CME of the LMS in 1932, he set about 'Swindonizing'

the LMS. The indifferently steaming Royal Scots were later modified to have GWR-type features, including taper boilers and Belpaire fireboxes.

One unusual feature was that during the trials the engine, 5000 Launceston Castle, was photographed at Carlisle Durran Hill depot, which served the former Midland Railway and the Settle and Carlisle route. It was almost as if the LMS were trying to keep quiet the presence of the GWR 4-6-0 by keeping it away from the LMS (LNWR) main steam passenger shed of Upperby.

Once again the Castle had proved to be superior to the competition, but the Southern Railway was to muddy the waters with their announcement of an engine that was theoretically more powerful than a Castle: the Lord Nelsons.

Castles in Production

The introduction of Caerphilly Castle in August 1923 was followed by nine more from December 1923 to April 1924:

4074	Caldicot Castle
4075	Cardiff Castle
4076	Carmarthen Castle
4077	Chepstow Castle
4078	Pembroke Castle
4079	Pendennis Castle
4080	Powderham Castle
4081	Warwick Castle
4082	Windsor Castle

Powderham Castle was to run the highest mileage of any Castle at 1,974,461 miles (3,177,587km) in forty years and five months of service.

The pride that its crew took in 5003 Lulworth Castle is evident as they posed with it at Old Oak Common about 1928 (fig. 72). Note the decorative pattern on the front bogie wheel, most probably done in oil. Unlike 4073 and 4095 (see above), there is no sign of the bogie step. Castles had been the top-line express engines on the GWR for only about four years before the Kings came along: one may be seen buffered up to the Castle behind it. Lulworth Castle was

to distinguish itself on the Cheltenham Flyer a few years later.

As well as trumpeting the most powerful engine in the land, the GWR was able to cite Royal approval for its creation, which was then an invaluable attribute in publicity and public relations. It was as if the locomotives and coaches of the GWR carried the 'By appointment to their Majesties […]' royal endorsement, which suppliers to the Royal Family can proudly display on their wares.

The GWR had long been a favourite of the Royal Family as that was how they travelled to Windsor, initially via Slough and then later by their own branch line and station.

The next batch of engines followed in May 1925:

4083	Abbotsbury Castle
4084	Aberystwyth Castle
4085	Berkeley Castle
4086	Builth Castle
4087	Cardigan Castle
4088	Dartmouth Castle
4089	Donnington Castle
4090	Dorchester Castle
4091	Dudley Castle
4092	Dunraven Castle

This second lot differed from the first batch in the omission of bogie brakes, as the later Stars had. The

frames were set inwards or 'joggled' to clear the bogie wheels as had been the case with the Stars.

The rebuilding of Stars to Castles started about this time in April 1925. This mainly consisted of extending the frames at the back by 1ft (30.5cm) to accommodate the larger side windowed cab, the provision of new cylinders and the standard Castle boiler. The Great Bear rebuild was more involved with the frames needing extensive modifications to fit their new identity. This meant a new junction of the frames between the middle and trailing driving wheels, as this distance was shorter on the Pacific than on the Stars and Castles.

The third batch followed a year later in May 1926 and consisted of the following engines:

4093	Dunster Castle
4094	Dynevor Castle
4095	Harlech Castle
4096	Highclere Castle
4097	Kenilworth Castle
4098	Kidwelly Castle
4099	Kilgerran Castle
5000	Launceston Castle
5001	Llandovery Castle
5002	Ludlow Castle

These engines had the frames dished or shaven to clear the bogie wheels rather than joggling. This addressed a weakness manifested as cracking to the front of the frames caused by the inside cylinder piston thrusts working on the bend in the joggling of the frames. Dished frames were standard for all subsequent Castles except the Star rebuilds.

From 1926 onwards Collett introduced a 4,000 gallon (18,184ltr) tender that retained the 6 ton (6.1 tonne) coal capacity of the Churchward tender, but had the tank wholly above the footplate, while the coal space had more of a slope downwards towards the footplate. Under way this meant that the tender was largely self-trimming with a procession of coal onto the footplate. 5000 Launceston Castle was the first recipient of the new tender in September 1926 and this was timely as the engine was soon to be dispatched to the LMS for its stint on the WCML. The pattern of updating engines built with smaller tenders was somewhat sporadic: 5002 and 5003 were built with the larger tender, but 5004 to 5012 built had the smaller type, but all engines had the larger tenders by 1930. Engine number 5001 ran with 6ft 6in (1.98m) driving wheels from December 1926 to March 1928 in connection with the introduction of the King class and their adoption of the smaller diameter driving wheel. The trial report stated that there was no discernible difference between the performances with larger or smaller driving wheels. It would have been remarkable had the trials found otherwise as the smaller diameter was within the tolerances of wheel tyres that Castles ran with in ordinary service.

The fourth batch of ten engines came out in May 1927:

5003	Lulworth Castle
5004	Llanstephan Castle
5005	Manorbier Castle
5006	Tregenna Castle
5007	Rougemont Castle
5008	Raglan Castle
5009	Shrewsbury Castle
5010	Restormel Castle
5011	Tintagel Castle
5012	Berry Pomeroy Castle

This batch, together with engine numbers 4084–95 from the two previous batches, was fitted with Automatic Train Control (ATC) apparatus from the outset.

After the 1927 building programme had been completed in the July of that year there was to be no more Castle building until almost five years later in June 1932.

In the years 1932, 1934 and 1935 a total of ten engines were built for each year: in the difficult years of the Great Depression, following the Wall Street Crash of 1929, it seemed an extravagance that the company could ill afford.

In the company accounts there were two separate funds for locomotives. Maintenance and Depreciation was basically intended to keep the fleet going, while Renewals was for the construction of new engines. The Maintenance and Depreciation fund had become run down and as a result some of the oldest Saints and Stars had become neglected or had their maintenance intervals increased. As was discussed in Chapter 1, the Saints were more affected. Their neglect was to run up a large potential deficit for the Maintenance and Depreciation fund, but the Renewals fund was relatively healthy. It was decided therefore to build new engines. The next thirty Castles could then be thought of as being paid for by an accounting exercise. Between 1931 and 1935 twenty Saints and ten Stars were withdrawn.

A similar process in reverse happened in later years with the withdrawal of one hundred 43XX class Mogul 2-6-0s and their use to build the Granges and Manor class 4-6-0 engines.

These next batches, totalling thirty engines in all, had sufficient detail differences, and therefore different engineering drawings sets, from the previous engines as to merit a different Swindon works designation as the 5013 class, by which name all the drawings would be marked up.

5013	Abergavenny Castle
5014	Goodrich Castle
5015	Kingswear Castle
5016	Montgomery Castle
5017	St. Donat's Castle
5018	St. Mawes Castle
5019	Treago Castle
5020	Trematon Castle
5021	Whittington Castle
5022	Wigmore Castle
5023	Brecon Castle
5024	Carew Castle
5025	Chirk Castle
5026	Criccieth Castle

5027	Farleigh Castle
5028	Llantilio Castle
5029	Nunney Castle
5030	Shirburn Castle
5031	Totnes Castle
5032	Usk Castle
5033	Broughton Castle
5034	Corfe Castle
5035	Coity Castle
5036	Lyonshall Castle
5037	Monmouth Castle
5038	Morlais Castle
5039	Rhuddlan Castle
5040	Stokesay Castle
5041	Tiverton Castle
5042	Winchester Castle

Visually the most striking differences were the reshaping of the inside cylinder valve chests to give a more rounded appearance and the provision of an enclosed chamber on the fireman's (left hand) side for the stowage of fire irons.

The front end of 5043 Earl of Mount Edgcumbe has been restored as it would have appeared in its later British Railways days (fig. 73). As a member of the 5013 class, it displays the rounded inside cylinder valve covers. The 84E shed plate for Tyseley is part of the engine's British Railways identity, so there are no GWR letters on the bufferbeam valence and no front number on the bufferbeam, although the inside cab roof retains the GWR TYS. Note also the Collett parallel buffers rather than the earlier Churchward taper type.

The fireiron tunnel, which emerges from the cab in a Y shape and proceeds behind the trailing and centre driving wheel splashers, ending behind the nameplate, is another 5013 class detail (fig. 74). The manually operated windscreen wiper on the front window is a later addition.

In the twenty-first century the laser has been accepted as an accurate light source used for all sorts of physical alignment tasks, such as surveying, DIY work, DVD players and fibre optic communications. High-powered lasers are used for cutting sheet steel.

In the 1930s the Deutsche Reichsbahn (German National Railways) pioneered the use of an extremely accurate optical system to line up and assemble the

Fig. 73. 5043 Earl of Mount Edgcumbe front end, Stratford-upon-Avon, September 2017.

Fig. 74. 5043 Earl of Mount Edgcumbe fire-iron tunnel, Stratford-upon-Avon, September 2017.

major components of the cylinders and hornblock guides for the driving wheels. It used a system of telescopes and sighting scales that could be adjusted to give hitherto unparalleled accuracy. A collimator or light tube was needed to concentrate the light into a parallel beam. (One of the convenient properties of a laser is that the light is already collimated.) It was as if the fanned-out light of a torch was persuaded to produce a pinpoint parallel beam of light. To complement the extremely accurate properties of collimated light, Vernier scales were used to give plus or minus values, to increase the level of accuracy.

The optical alignment system, devised by Carl Zeiss of Germany, which remains a byword for optical excellence, was sold with the claim that it reduced the time needed to set up a locomotive frame and cylinders by three-quarters. This was an astonishing benefit to any organization for which time is money, but the almost overlooked benefit was in how the finished locomotive performed and lasted in service.

From 5023 Brecon Castle in 1934, the engines were said to run like sewing machines and were immensely strong on steep gradients when working hard. If a locomotive is not built and assembled accurately, part of its energy is spent fighting itself with out of balance forces causing the engine to ride roughly as a protest at extra effort. The corollary is that when all the forces act in concert they produce a fast and free-running engine. The other benefit was that the

interval between overhauls could be increased, which was also a cost benefit.

This movement away from the tape measure, wire and centre punch school of nineteenth-century engineering was to put Swindon at the forefront of British locomotive construction until nationalization.

With frames and cylinders accurately set up the valve gear components could be made extremely accurately in the certain knowledge that they would fit with only minor fettling when offered up to the larger assemblies. Extremely close tolerances are now commonplace in the car industry with computerized monitoring of production standards and CNC machines, but what Swindon was doing in the 1930s was a groundbreaking development for the British railway industry.

Previously the accepted standard for manufacture had been 0.010 inches or ten thousandths of an inch (0.254mm); with the Zeiss system it became 0.002 inches or two thousandths of an inch (0.051mm).

During World War II Lord Beaverbrook, Minister of Aircraft Production, declared that Swindon was the finest workshop outside the aircraft industry. A Swindon engineer at nationalization was amazed at the engineering practices of other railways and was reputed to have said, 'We scrap at the clearances they start with.'

One of the early optical alignment engines, 5030 Shirburn Castle, went for an unprecedented 420,000 miles (675,294km) before the boiler was lifted from the frames.

Collett's fine tuning of an already capable class of locomotives, continuing the Churchward tradition of using best practice wherever it was to be found, was to lead to operational fireworks on the road.

5028 Llantilio Castle of the 5013 sub-class is seen here on 28 May 1936 at Newton Abbot, where it spent all of its life, apart from six years at Laira (fig. 75). The ATC shoe is positioned by the front bogie wheels. The engine was scrapped prematurely after it collided in December 1959 with a diesel loco that had failed in service.

The first thirty-five engines occupied the years thus: 1936 – 15 new engines, 1937 – 10 new engines, 1938 – 10 new engines. The rest of the build were a mixture of rebuilt Stars and new engines, with only 5087 and 5089 actually built during World War II. There was then a hiatus during which no new engines were constructed until the end of the war.

Fig. 75. 5028 Llantilio Castle at Newton Abbot, 28 May 1936. GREAT WESTERN TRUST

5043	Barbury Castle		5071	Clifford Castle
5044	Beverston Castle		5072	Compton Castle
5045	Bridgwater Castle		5073	Cranbrook Castle
5046	Clifford Castle		5074	Denbigh Castle
5047	Compton Castle		5075	Devizes Castle
5048	Cranbrook Castle		5076	Drysllwyn Castle
5049	Denbigh Castle		5077	Eastnor Castle
5050	Devizes Castle		5078	Lamphey Castle
5051	Drysllwyn Castle		5079	Lydford Castle
5052	Eastnor Castle		5080	Ogmore Castle
5053	Bishop's Castle		5081	Penrice Castle
5054	Lamphey Castle		5082	Powis Castle
5055	Lydford Castle		5083	Bath Abbey
5056	Ogmore Castle		5084	Reading Abbey
5057	Penrice Castle		5085	Evesham Abbey
5058	Newport Castle		5086	Viscount Horne
5059	Powis Castle		5087	Tintern Abbey
5060	Sarum Castle		5088	Llanthony Abbey
5061	Sudeley Castle		5089	Westminster Abbey
5062	Tenby Castle		5090	Neath Abbey
5063	Thornbury Castle		5091	Cleeve Abbey
5064	Tretower Castle		5092	Tresco Abbey
5065	Upton Castle		5093	Upton Castle
5066	Wardour Castle		5094	Tretower Castle
5067	St Fagan's Castle		5095	Barbury Castle
5068	Beverston Castle		5096	Bridgwater Castle
5069	Isambard Kingdom Brunel		5097	Sarum Castle
5070	Sir Daniel Gooch			

Fig. 76. 5048 Cranbrook Castle at Bristol Temple Meads, 1937. GREAT
WESTERN TRUST

One of the earliest of this batch was 5048 Cranbrook Castle, which was seen in 1937 at Bristol Temple Meads, waiting to take over a train complete with
horsebox (fig. 76). This is possibly a North to West
Express as Bristol was the usual engine change point
for such trains, an example of which is in the background with a Stanier 57ft (17.37m) LMS coach in a
train full of LMS coaches.

In 1936, as yet another accounting exercise, the
'Dukedog' 4-4-0 locomotives made an appearance,
combining the boiler of the Duke class with the running gear from the intermediate-diameter wheeled
Bulldog class 4-4-0 suitable for use on routes with
lighter traffic requirements, such as the Cambrian.

Both classes were originally first introduced in the
nineteenth century.

The revamped engines were produced in a quantity
of thirty, several of which were named after members of the peerage, specifically Earls. The problem was that the retirement of Stanley Baldwin as
Prime Minister and his elevation to the House of
Lords was reflected by the renaming of Castle 5063
to be Earl Baldwin. He had been a director of the
GWR and his family had long associations with the
company.

The noble lords objected to being associated with
nineteenth-century technology, while another of their
number was associated with the latest thing in steam
technology. Under pressure the GWR renamed the
Castles after their lordships, starting with 5043 and
ending with 5062. For a list of the name changes,
please *see* Appendix I.

It cut no ice that the Dukedog was descended from
the Duke, which was higher up in the aristocratic pyr-
amid. Paradoxically their lordships had no problem
with their ancient homes being associated with the
then modern steam age technology.

Changes were gradually made to bring earlier locomotives up to more recent standards. Here, for example, 4085 Berkeley Castle is seen at Exeter engine
sheds on 14 April 1936 (fig. 77), equipped with the
more modern whistle shield and front top lamp iron
on the smokebox door.

Fig. 77. 4085 Berkeley Castle at
Exeter sheds, 14 April 1936. GREAT
WESTERN TRUST

The 5013 class also had wider water spaces in the firebox. This, together with the overall firebox dimensions remaining the same, led to a small reduction in grate area. This meant exposing more water to the intensity of the firebox heat, although the reduced grate area didn't seem to have an effect on steam production, given the way the engine was fired.

The chimney was changed from 5044 onwards for a smaller pattern; the rest of the class caught up with this modification as they went through Swindon works and had boilers changed. The spring equalizing beams (*see* fig. 21) were discontinued from about 1930 as more flexible bogie springs were adopted.

The GWR even pre-empted the streamlining craze of British railways. Collett was said to have sent out for a tin of plasticine, with which he fashioned the rudiments of streamlining on a model of a Castle. The outcome was 5005 Manorbier Castle, produced in March 1935. Most of the modifications had been removed by the outbreak of World War II except the V-fronted cab. As they did not have a wind tunnel in which to test the changes, there were no claims as to performance benefits. The look of the engine was not improved and some of the streamlining caused operational difficulties. A King received similar treatment.

The appearance of 5005 Manorbier Castle about 1930, before the streamlining experiment, can be seen as it headed south to Padddington on Rowington

Troughs, also known as Lapworth Troughs (fig. 78). Note the mass of discarded sleepers at trackside; these did not last long, being soaked many times a day with water from the pickup process.

Some six years later Manorbier Castle was at Goring-on-Thames with a rake of uniform Collett coaches (fig. 79). The first streamlining fixings to go were the cylinder covers, following reports that the cylinders were overheating. The steps/handholds on the side of the smokebox are the sorts of devices to be found on the conning tower of a submarine. A tubular post signal has made an early appearance.

The onset of World War II brought a virtual cessation of Castle production as Swindon and the GWR came under government control. Much of Swindon's production was given over to the manufacture of munitions, armoured vehicles and aircraft components. A number of Stanier LMS 2-8-0 freight locos were built at Swindon and one of these was to provide the boiler for the new-build Hawksworth County Class 4-6-0 1014 County of Glamorgan, under construction at the GWS Didcot at the time of writing.

In 1935 5025 Chirk Castle was seen at Old Oak Common yard still in 1927 livery (fig. 80). One of the nameplates was on display in the café at the National Trust property for some years until its true value was realized.

Further west on the system, 5031 Totnes Castle was to outlast much of its surroundings at Plymouth North

Fig. 78. 5005 Manorbier Castle on Rowington Troughs, about 1930. GREAT WESTERN TRUST

Fig. 79. 5005 Manorbier Castle at Goring-on-Thames, about 1936. GREAT WESTERN TRUST

Fig. 80. 5025 Chirk Castle at Old Oak Common yard, 1935. GREAT WESTERN TRUST

Road, seen here on 3 September 1937 (fig. 81), as they disappeared under heavy air attacks during World War II. Totnes Castle carried on in service until 1963.

As a result of the exploits of the Royal Air Force in the Battle of Britain in autumn 1940, several Castles were renamed to commemorate the names of RAF aircraft, some of which had not taken part in the battle itself but were household names in the early part of the war.

In order to meet wartime blackout regulations, the Castles had their side windows plated over and

tarpaulins fitted. On the infrastructure front, ash shelters were built at several motive power depots lest the glow from dropped fires gave a beacon to incoming bombers; just such a structure survived at Banbury depot for some years.

When war broke out Collett was 69 years old, but he continued in office until Frederick Hawksworth took over in the spring of 1941.

The GWR express passenger engines had to survive the war on an inferior quality of coal. Hawksworth went some way to addressing this problem with

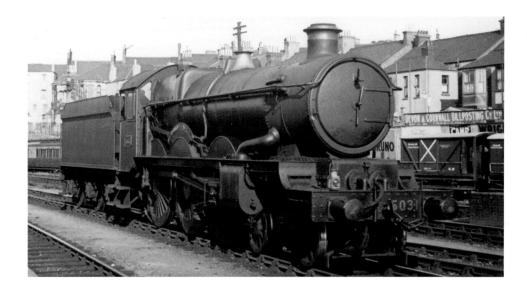

Fig. 81. 5031 Totnes Castle at Plymouth North Road, 3 September 1937. GREAT WESTERN TRUST

an improved superheater for his Modified Hall class locos.

The performance of engines on the road suffered as day to day maintenance and Swindon factory visits were curtailed. Combined with the poor quality coal, this led standards to drop. The initial wartime top speed of 60mph (98km/h), however, was later raised to 75mph (115km/h). Despite these difficulties, some prodigious feats of haulage were performed and the Castles had a proud war record of keeping the massive increase in trains running in very difficult circumstances.

One loco that saw plenty of change was 4016 The Somerset Light Infantry (Prince Albert's), photographed at Swindon Works Yard under the loading gauge in 1938 (fig. 82). This rebuilt Star, originally Knight of the Golden Fleece, had been renamed in January of that year. It bears the regimental crest on the nameplate splasher but retains the Churchward taper buffers.

Fig. 82. 4016 The Somerset Light Infantry (Prince Albert's), Swindon Works Yard, 1938. GREAT WESTERN TRUST

After the war the old era continued with the building of another ten new Castle engines in 1946:

5098	Clifford Castle
5099	Compton Castle
7000	Viscount Portal
7001	Denbigh Castle
7002	Devizes Castle
7003	Elmley Castle
7004	Eastnor Castle
7005	Lamphey Castle
7006	Lydford Castle
7007	Ogmore Castle

Number 7007 was the last express passenger engine built by the company and was renamed Great Western in February 1948, a matter of weeks after nationalization. The nameplate splasher carried the company's coat of arms.

Towards the end of the war, and even after, the coal supply situation became ever more desperate. Many of the miners had enlisted to fight in the armed forces and there was a crisis centred on who was going to dig the coal. Ernest Bevin, Minister of Labour and National Service, instituted a scheme from late 1943 by which young men between the ages of eighteen and twenty-five, known as 'Bevin Boys', were conscripted to work in the mines: the last conscripts worked until 1948.

The GWR had already prepared plans pre-war to electrify the GWR main line west of Taunton. Their solution to the coal crisis was to burn oil in their steam engines rather than coal. It was initially thought that Cornwall could be all oil-burning and then proceed eastwards, thus cutting out many long-haul coal trains needed just to bring loco coal to the depots.

Castles numbered 100A1, 5039, 5079, 5083 and 5091 were converted to burn oil, as were engines of the 28XX 2-8-0 heavy freight class and some Halls.

The Ministry of Fuel and Power promoted the GWR scheme as a solution to the nationwide coal crisis, until another government department at the Treasury pointed out that, as the nation was bankrupt after the war, it did not possess the foreign exchange to buy the oil. North Sea oil was, by this time, some forty years distant.

The Castles converted to oil burning were:

Number	Converted to oil burning	Reverted to coal burning
100A1	January 1947	September 1948
5039	December 1946	September 1948
5079	January 1947	October 1948
5083	December 1946	November 1948
5091	October 1946	November 1948

For a time life as the Western Region of British Railways continued much as it had under the GWR as the management were all company men until Hawksworth retired in 1949. Under British Railways in 1948 there was a series of locomotive exchanges in which Castles were not involved, but modifications were carried out to Castles as a result of the data gathered. An early BR experiment was a light green livery with BRITISH RAILWAYS applied to some Castle tenders. Blue liveries were similarly experimented with on Kings until the return to GWR mid-chrome green as the standard for express passenger and mixed traffic locomotives.

Another thirty engines were constructed under BR auspices, ending in 1950.

7008	Swansea Castle
7009	Athelney Castle
7010	Avondale Castle
7011	Banbury Castle
7012	Barry Castle
7013	Bristol Castle
7014	Caerhays Castle
7015	Carn Brea Castle
7016	Chester Castle
7017	G. J. Churchward
7018	Drysllwyn Castle
7019	Fowey Castle
7020	Gloucester Castle
7021	Haverfordwest Castle
7022	Hereford Castle
7023	Penrice Castle
7024	Powis Castle
7025	Sudeley Castle
7026	Tenby Castle
7027	Thornbury Castle
7028	Cadbury Castle
7029	Clun Castle
7030	Cranbrook Castle

7031	Cromwell's Castle
7032	Denbigh Castle
7033	Hartlebury Castle
7034	Ince Castle
7035	Ogmore Castle
7036	Taunton Castle
7037	Swindon

Fig. 83. The last Castle ever built was 7037 Swindon in 1950. The name and number plate are restored and kept at STEAM, Swindon, September 2017.

The last Castle ever built was 7037 Swindon in 1950 (fig. 83). The name, number plate and splasher have been restored and are kept at STEAM, Swindon. The splasher has the coat of arms of the Borough of Swindon. September 2017.

The General Strike of 1926, World War II and the locomotive exchanges of 1948 had emphasized the effect that sub-standard coal had on the performance of GWR engines. The lower calorific value of coal other than Welsh steam coal did not supply enough heat energy to make steam as efficiently. Standards of maintenance and driving were also not generally what they were pre-war, although there would be enough dyed in the wool GWR men left to turn in notable performances despite these deficiencies.

The GWR's policy of moderate superheat was called into question and larger three- and four-row superheaters were tried on many engines with considerable success.

Dynamometer car tests had shown that the back pressure from the exhaust was limiting the ability of the engine to run free and fast at the top end.

It was British Railways practice to introduce self-cleaning screens on all locomotives. A mesh grill was put in place to deflect larger pieces of exhaust burnt coal from being ejected up the chimney. This design was later modified. This had the effect of sharpening the blast and making the fire draw well, but it restricted the outflow of exhaust gases. As Churchward had gone to all the trouble of long-stroke piston valves to get the steam into the cylinders efficiently, if the process of getting it out were impeded, this limited the engine's performance at the top end and made them less free running. The front end was redesigned and double chimneys were fitted to many of the class.

These two modifications were originally carried out on the King class but were also to make significant differences to Castle class performance. This enabled timetables to be speeded up from 1954 and some higher top speeds were found to be possible.

The first main-line diesels were introduced in 1958, but the Western Region continued to fit Castles with double chimneys until 1961. Even though the postwar Castles had much more life in them, it was evident that the political climate and the unions wanted to be rid of steam quickly, rather than letting the taxpayers get their money's-worth, as had been the case in Germany.

Castle Class: Illustrated Details

In Chapter 2 much was made of the inner workings of the inside valve gear and generally beneath the engine. As the valve gear and some of the inner workings are the same for both Star and Castle class, this section concentrates more on the external visual details and major workings of the driver's controls. It is illustrated by a series of photographs of 4073 Caerphilly Castle, 4079 Pendennis Castle, 5043 Earl of Mount Edgcumbe, 5051 Drysllwyn Castle, 5080 Defiant and 7029 Clun Castle, all taken in 2017.

As will often happen, we will start with 5043 Earl of Mount Edgcumbe. The screw reverser visible on the right-hand – driver's – side of the cab has polished steel handles in the best GWR traditions (fig. 84). The brass graduated scale indicates the amount of gear in

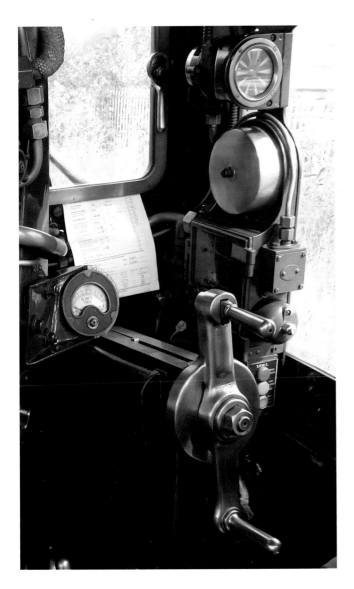

Fig. 84. 5043 Earl of Mount Edgcumbe: driver's controls, screw reverser, August 2017.

either direction that is selected by turning the gear handle. Full forwards is selected for setting off, and this would be wound back to 15–25 per cent for economical running at speed. The graduated scale may not be very accurate with an engine that was due for shopping as the ports around the valves would be subject to a build-up of carbon deposits. Many GWR drivers ignored the graduated scale and ran the engine by its sound and feel.

To the right of the reversing gear winding handle is the GWR-designed ATC apparatus, which would ring

the bell if all was well at a distant signal or sound the horn if it was ON or at caution. In addition the sunflower display above the bell would display black if the signal was in an OFF or go condition.

Below the ATC bell apparatus is the Train Protection and Warning System (TPWS) control panel, which is a development of ATC and is a compulsory fit on trains that use Network Rail.

The black speedometer is of the original GWR pattern and measures up to 100mph (160km/h).

There were two types of valve and cylinder lubricator on GWR engines: the sight feed and the mechanical lubricator. Sight feed or hydrostatic lubricators (fig. 85) require hands-on work by the driver to adjust

Fig. 85. 5051 Drysllwyn Castle: sight feed lubricator, October 2017.

each feed to each cylinder individually. Done properly the sight feed is as effective as the mechanical type, but does require concentrated effort from the driver.

The mechanical lubricator dispensed oil to the cylinders and valves by opening the engine's regulator: the wider the opening, the more oil delivered. The lubricator is the black box seen on the footplate (fig. 86) with the copper tubes connected to it. Locomotives of the earlier 4073 series had their mechanical lubricators on the side of the smokebox.

Dyed-in-the-wool GWR men, however, complained that engines with mechanical lubricators were sluggish. In BR days the mechanical lubricator of 7018 Dryslwyn Castle was adjusted to feed twice the rate of oil as normal, resulting in an engine that was said to be a flyer.

On this photograph of 5043 Earl of Mount Edgcumbe at speed on the Shakespeare Express (fig. 87), the mechanical lubricator can be seen located behind the outside steam pipe. The pipework in the vicinity can restrict access to the inside motion.

The mechanical lubricator cab gauge (fig. 88) was a necessary refinement for a displacement mechanical lubricator, which works by admitting steam with an open regulator into a vessel. As the steam condenses, the oil floats to the top and into delivery pipes to go to valves and cylinders. The more the regulator is opened the more steam and the more oil is consequently pushed out.

The purpose of the gauge is to remind the driver that if the regulator is completely closed no oil would be going to the cylinders. The driver is then advised to just 'crack' open the regulator to reintroduce the oil flow. The text on the gauge reads: 'When running

Fig. 86. 7029 Clun Castle: mechanical lubricator, October 2017.

Fig. 87. 5043 Earl of Mount Edgcumbe at speed: the mechanical lubricator is visible, August 2017.

Fig. 88. 5043 Earl of Mount Edgcumbe: mechanical lubricator cab gauge, August 2017.

with steam shut off / move regulator from full shut position / until pointer shows in white sector.'

5043 Earl of Mount Edgcumbe is equipped only with vacuum brakes, whereas other main-line engines currently use air brakes as well for running on Network Rail. The vacuum brake is a fail-safe system where the default position is brakes on: that is the position shown on the vacuum gauge in fig. 89. To release the brakes it is necessary to create a vacuum and sustain it. If there are any leaks or a pipe is broken the brakes will come on. The vacuum necessary to keep the brakes off on a GWR locomotive is 25 inches of mercury (0.85 bar); on other railways it is 21 inches of mercury (0.71 bar). Churchward understood that it was no use creating a powerful engine if the braking system wasn't up to stopping the heavy trains his engines were hauling. Recent innovations in the car industry with ceramic brake discs on high-performance cars have taken a leaf out of Churchward's tome of wisdom.

The ejector is a steam-driven device that creates the vacuum required to release the brakes.

To keep the brakes off while running, most GWR engines have a crosshead-driven vacuum pump, which assists in the process.

The gauge has two indicators: Train Pipe and Reservoir or Vacuum Cylinder. The brakes remain off while

Fig. 89. 5043 Earl of Mount Edgcumbe: vacuum brake gauge and driver's side boiler pressure gauge, August 2017.

the two vacuum values are the same, but the action of operating the brake valve admits air into the train pipe. This forces the piston in the brake cylinder to move and apply the brakes through the brake rigging. Although this instrument was British Railways issue, the higher vacuum that the GWR used means it was peculiar to the Western Region.

The large black handle with the circular pierced annular towards the bottom left of fig. 90 is the admitting valve for air to the vacuum system. When air is admitted the vacuum is partially destroyed and the brakes come on. There is a union with the lettering B900 on it and another black handle at right angles to the first and pointing vertically upwards. This is the valve to admit steam to the ejector to create a vacuum to release the brakes. The fitting directly below that with the bulbous housing, and yet another black handle, is the blower. The purpose of this is to use steam to create an artificial draught at the smokebox to better draw the fire. This is mostly used when the engine is stationary.

The underside of 4073 Caerphilly Castle (fig. 91) shows two bright rods heading south to north. These are the inside cylinder connecting rods and the black bar between them is part of the brake rigging. The cylinder in red at the top right, connecting to the right-hand internal crosshead, is the vacuum pump mentioned above.

The three pipes controlled by three black handles at the top of the cab backhead (fig. 92) are all to do with getting water into the boiler. The centre one is an exhaust injector, by which exhaust steam is used to

Fig. 90. 5043 Earl of Mount Edgcumbe: vacuum brake gauge and brake control handle, August 2017.

Fig. 91. 4073 Caerphilly Castle: crosshead-driven pump body on the right in red, September 2017.

Fig. 92. 5043 Earl of Mount Edgcumbe: regulator and injector controls and indications, August 2017.

force water into the boiler against its pressure. This only works when the loco is moving. Either side of the centre pipe are the left and right live steam injectors, which work when there is boiler pressure. The gauge glass on the centre left gives an approximate indication of how much water is in the boiler. A set of linkages close off the valves to the gauge for maintenance.

Just by the gauge glass there is a lamp bracket, as boiler contents was the one parameter that needed to be known at night. It is usually the fireman's job to maintain the water level in the boiler. Beneath the injector controls is the regulator, with its lever pointing to the driver's seat when closed, and the large cylindrical counterweight.

It is the fireman's job to maintain the boiler pressure and for this reason the boiler pressure gauge is fitted on the left-hand side of the cab. The fireman in this case is maintaining the boiler pressure at exactly the right level, just below blowing off when the safety valves operate. 5043 has a boiler pressure gauge on the driver's side as well, but it was not in operation on this occasion.

5051 Drysllwyn Castle has another bourdon tube-type pressure gauge, also on the fireman's side, but this time indicating the pressure required to provide

Fig. 93. 5043 Earl of Mount Edgcumbe: boiler pressure gauge, August 2017.

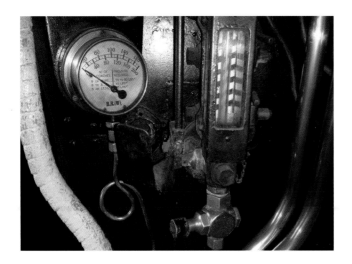

Fig. 94. 5051 Drysllwyn Castle: train heating gauge, November 2017.

ledge where the enamel tea can sits to keep hot. The fire would also be used to fry bacon and eggs on the fireman's shovel: loco crews have maintained that the food never tasted better.

A salient feature of the 5013 sub-class was the fire iron tunnel, here seen in use on the left.

Although the fireman was provided with a window and windscreen wiper (fig. 96), he would generally be posted to look out for signals en route as most signals would be on that side of the track.

steam heating in passenger coaches (fig. 94). The legend on the instrument face reads:

Number of coaches	Pressure required
9 or mores	70 to 80 lbs per square inch
6 to 9	60 lbs per square inch
5 or less	40 lbs per square inch

The four L-shaped levers in front of the firebox doors are dampers that control the flow of air to the fire (fig. 95). Above the firebox doors is the all-important

Fig. 95. 5043 Earl of Mount Edgcumbe: firehole doors, dampers and fire iron tunnel, August 2017.

Fig. 96. 5043 Earl of Mount Edgcumbe: fireman's view of the journey, August 2017.

Locomotives and cabs prior to the Churchward era were small and narrow. It was the practice of some engine crews to go for an excursion around the loco to check for hot axleboxes and other problems while it was on the road pulling a train. As the locos expanded to meet the available gauge width, the safety clearance between tunnels and bridges was further reduced and this kind of in-flight maintenance became even more hazardous (fig. 97).

Although 5043 Earl of Mount Edgcumbe is now in BR livery and the shed plate on the smokebox door reads 84E for Tyseley, old GWR habits die hard: the company's version, TYS, still appears inside the cab roof (fig. 98). Note the hooks on which to hang the weather sheet or tarpaulin. The condition of the cab roof is symptomatic of the care and attention given to the whole engine.

The L-handled large item with the vertical shaft in fig. 100 is the water scoop lowering handle. The driver can monitor the tender contents by the gauge sitting just above it, although these were known to be only

Fig. 98. 5043 Earl of Mount Edgcumbe: cab roof, August 2017.

Fig. 99. 5051 Drysllwyn Castle: flip-up driver's seat, Great Western Society Didcot shed, November 2017.

Fig. 97. 5043 Earl of Mount Edgcumbe: fireman's side warning plate, August 2017.

moderately accurate. The smaller handled item nearer the floor is the right side injector water feed controller; there is a similar lever on the left-hand side for the left injector, together with the tender handbrake standard. The tender shown here is a Collett 4,000 gallon (18,184ltr) type (fig. 100); the Hawksworth equivalent is seen behind, coupled to the Hawksworth Modified Hall 6998 Burton Agnes Hall.

Coal space on the Collett 4,000 gallon tender was limited to 6 tons (6.1 tonnes). The inclination of the

Fig. 100. 5051 Drysllwyn Castle: tender controls, November 2017.

coal space is evident here (fig. 101). Note how battered the tool box lids become when there is so much coal around.

5051 Drysllwyn Castle is out of service awaiting overhaul, but is still kept in fine cosmetic condition by the Great Western Society at Didcot Motive Power Depot (fig. 102). The standard superheater blister can be seen on the outside of the smokebox/boiler, just above the handrail and ejector pipe pairing. The locomotive retains the single chimney it was built with. The stablemate is 56XX Collett 0-6-2 tank engine no. 6697.

A different superheater design is seen here on 7029 Clun Castle, posed on the turntable at Tyseley on the day of its presentation to the public after overhaul (fig. 103). The four-row superheater was a BR development. This, together with improved draughting of the double blast-pipe and chimney, was one of reasons why Clun Castle distinguished itself in the last years of BR Western Region service.

The four-row superheater and double chimney were also retrofitted to 5043 Earl of Mount Edgcumbe, here seen at speed through Wilmcote station (fig. 104). The mechanical lubricator is positioned behind the steam pipe. The mass of copper pipes to the various surfaces to be lubricated show up well, as does the

Fig. 101. 5051 Drysllwyn Castle: tender coal space, November 2017.

Fig. 102. 5051 Drysllwyn Castle: superheater blister, November 2017.

Fig. 103. 7029 Clun Castle on the turntable at Tyseley, October 2017.

lagged steam input via the regulator that powers the lubricator. In addition the engine has several drip-feed dashpots: two of these are visible as the small brass objects, one cylindrical device in front of the right-hand outside valve chest and one rectangular piece above the inside cylinder valve chest. Also on the valve chest covering is a diamond chequer plate to assist the crews' safety while clambering on the engine. The brass fitting on the outside of the smokebox door is a bayonet steam lance connection, to which a flexible hose and lance is connected to clean the smokebox and front of the engine. The only gases escaping are those from the chimney. The engine is a credit to Tyseley Locomotive Works.

Another locomotive undergoing restoration at Didcot is 4079 Pendennis Castle (fig. 105). The inside cylinder valve chest cover is more like that of a Star on this early Castle example. The grey primer paint on many of the components indicate that the restoration is nearing completion. The OZ home depot is an antipodean reference to the loco's former home in Australia.

Fig. 104. 5043 Earl of Mount Edgcumbe at speed through Wilmcote station, August 2017.

Fig. 105. 4079 Pendennis Castle at Didcot, November 2017.

Fig. 106. 7029 Clun Castle nameplate and outside motion detail, October 2017.

The boiler of 7029 Clun Castle is equipped with a blowdown valve (fig. 106). The red plate reads:

WARNING
BLOW DOWN VALVE

THIS VALVE <u>MUST NOT</u> BE OPENED
UNTIL IT HAS BEEN ASCERTAINED
THAT NO ONE IS UNDER THE ENGINE.
TO OPEN TURN CLOCKWISE.

The purpose of this device is to remove forcibly by steam pressure the accumulation of dissolved deposits in the boiler water or steam after boiler treatment.

The collection of these deposits particularly affects the efficiency of the superheater and any other heat exchanger-type surfaces. Perhaps this could be likened to a rather macho type of kettle de-scaler. The valve opens in the opposite sense to most valves. Blow down valves are more common in the United States. A standard nameplate style is fitted.

5080 Defiant illustrates the way the nameplate was displayed with a non-Castle type name (fig. 107), although peers such as Earl of Mount Edgcumbe were not similarly treated. The addition of the Castle Class sobriquet seems to have been a post-World War II feature.

After a locomotive has been restored it is commonplace for the observation to be made that not much

Fig. 107. 5080 Defiant boiler and nameplate, October 2017.

Fig. 109. Collett 4,000 gallon (18,191 l) tender in need of restoration at Didcot, Great Western Society, August 2017.

of the original remains. It is easy to see why when the restorers are faced with a challenge like this Collett 4,000 gallon (18,191ltr) tender at Didcot (fig. 109). The brake standard is on the right and the water scoop pickup handle on the left.

Fig. 108. 5080 Defiant loco and tender coupling and buffing gear, October 2017.

CHAPTER FIVE

CASTLE CLASS LOCOMOTIVES: ALLOCATION AND WORK

As with their illustrious forebears, the Stars, Castles were initially restricted to the West of England main line and consequently the longest distance and heaviest express passenger trains. This extreme top link assignment, however, did not last as long as that enjoyed by the Stars, for within four years the King class was to take over the most long-distance and heaviest trains on the railway. In Cornwall, however, where Kings were prohibited from crossing the Royal Albert Bridge, Castles still held sway as the top motive power west of the Tamar.

An early example was 4009 Shooting Star, rebuilt as a Castle in 1925 and renamed No. 100 A1 Lloyds in January 1936. It is seen here at Swindon station on 13 August 1939 (fig. 110). The driver is attending to the inside cylinder valve rods. Note the cranked angle on the water crane, which was necessary after the introduction of the larger Collett tenders.

Castles distinguished themselves in every other area of passenger haulage, serving on named expresses such as the Cheltenham Spa Express, Bristolian, Torbay Express, Merchant Venturer, Cornishman, Devonian, Cathedrals Express, the Ocean Mails Special Atlantic liner expresses, Pembroke Coast Express, Cambrian Coast Express and Capitals United Express. Some of these were British Railways innovations.

The example of these services shows the Plymouth to Paddington up Ocean Mails special, reporting number 002, at Dawlish with a presumably empty bullion van in about 1939 (fig. 111). It is headed by 5039 Rhuddlan Castle, one of the stars of the Cheltenham Flyer. Access to the nation's gold wealth was restricted by having doors on only one side, which made marshalling and allocating arrival platforms an additional administrative task.

Fig. 110. 100 A1 Lloyds, the rebuilt and renamed 4009 Shooting Star, at Swindon station, 13 August 1939. GREAT WESTERN TRUST

Fig. 111. 5039 Rhuddlan Castle on the Plymouth to Paddington Ocean Mails special at Dawlish with a presumably empty bullion van, about 1939. GREAT WESTERN TRUST

The first forty engines were allocated between Paddington (Old Oak Common), Newton Abbot and Laira:

Paddington (OOC)
4073, 4074, 4075, 4076, 4077, 4078, 4079, 4080, 4081, 4082, 4083, 4089, 4090, 4091, 4092, 4093, 4094, 4097, 4099, 5000, 5001, 5002, 5005, 5006, 5010

Newton Abbot (NA)
5003, 5011, 5012

Laira (LA)
4084, 4085, 4086, 4087, 4088, 4095, 4096, 5004, 5007, 5008, 5009

Castles became more widely dispersed after the late 1920s, following the introduction of the King class and coincident with more engines being built. The situation in later years was:

1932
Paddington 10, Bristol Bath Road 2, Exeter 1, Newton Abbot 8, Laira 6, Wolverhampton Stafford Road 2, Cardiff Canton 6, Chester 2.

No appearance at either Worcester or Hereford, although Stars and Saints were prominent.

1936
Paddington
111, 4037, 4073, 4075, 4084, 4090, 4099, 5000, 5004, 5005, 5006, 5008, 5014, 5018, 5022, 5027, 5029, 5037, 5038, 5039, 5040, 5043, 5044, 5045, 5054, 5055, 5056

Bristol Bath Road
4016, 4081, 4082, 4096, 5042, 5048

Exeter
4074, 4076, 4085, 4087, 5009, 5025

Newton Abbot
4077, 4093, 4098, 5003, 5019, 5021, 5024, 5026, 5034, 5057

Plymouth Laira
4032, 4088, 4092, 4094, 4097, 5011, 5013, 5015, 5017, 5028, 5041

Penzance
5016

Cardiff Canton
4079, 4083, 4091, 5001, 5002, 5010, 5012, 5023, 5030, 5046, 5052

Swansea Landore
4078, 4080, 4089, 4095, 5020, 5047, 5051

Wolverhampton Stafford Road
5007, 5031, 5033, 5035, 5036

Shrewsbury
4000, 5032, 5053

Worcester
4086, 5049, 5050

Swindon Stock
100A1

1938
Paddington 32, Bristol Bath Road 7, Exeter 7, Newton Abbot 9, Laira 11, Penzance 2, Wolverhampton Stafford Road 8, Shrewsbury 3, Gloucester 1, Worcester 4, Cardiff Canton 12, Landore 8.

1947
Paddington 33, Reading 1, Bristol Bath Road 16, Exeter 3, Newton Abbot 14, Laira 13, Penzance 1, Taunton 2, Wolverhampton Stafford Road 10, Shrewsbury 8, Gloucester 3, Worcester 6, Hereford 1, Cardiff Canton 14, Landore 14.

1950
Paddington 33, Reading 2, Oxford 3, Bristol Bath Road 16, Swindon 7, Exeter 2, Newton Abbot 15, Laira 16, Penzance 1, Wolverhampton Stafford Road 9, Shrewsbury 7, Chester 3, Gloucester 3, Worcester 6, Hereford 1, Cardiff Canton 20, Landore 16, Carmarthen 1.

1954

The complete allocation of the class for the year is given as:

Paddington
4037, 4082, 4097, 5004, 5014, 5029, 5034, 5035, 5038, 5040, 5044, 5055, 5056, 5060, 5065, 5066, 5081, 5082, 5087, 5093, 5095, 7001, 7004, 7010, 7024, 7025, 7027, 7030, 7032, 7033, 7036

Reading
4085, 5036

Oxford
5012, 5026, 7008

Bristol Bath Road
4073, 4075, 4084, 4091, 4094, 4096, 5000, 5019, 5025, 5037, 5048, 5064, 5067, 5069, 5074, 5076, 5085, 5094, 5096, 7011, 7014, 7019, 7034

Swindon
5009, 5062, 5068, 5083, 5084, 7015, 7037

Exeter
5003, 5021

Newton Abbot
4077, 4080, 4088, 4098, 4099, 5011, 5024, 5028, 5041, 5047, 5059, 5071, 5078, 5079, 7000, 7029

Plymouth Laira
4086, 4089, 5027, 5058, 5098, 7031

Penzance
4087, 5023

Cardiff Canton
5001, 5005, 5006, 5007, 5020, 5030, 5046, 5049, 5052, 5054, 5077, 5080, 5089, 5099, 7016, 7017, 7020, 7022, 7023

Swansea Landore
4074, 4078, 4081, 4093, 4095, 5002, 5013, 5016, 5051, 5072, 7002, 7003, 7009, 7012, 7018, 7021, 7028

Carmarthen
5039, 5043

Wolverhampton Stafford Road
4000, 4079, 4083, 4090, 4092, 5008, 5010, 5015, 5022, 5027, 5031, 5032, 5045, 5053, 5070, 5088, 7026

Shrewsbury
5050, 5073, 5091, 5097

Chester
4076, 5033, 5061, 5075

Worcester
5063, 5086, 5090, 5092, 7005, 7007, 7013

Gloucester
5017, 5018, 5042, 7006, 7035

The following table gives details from engine record cards of trains worked by Castles in the 1930s, providing a snapshot of a few of the engines in daily service at odd days between the wars. There are a few vacuum freights and only one ordinary freight train. Together with postal services, these made up the only diversion from passenger trains in ordinary service.

Fig. 112. 5029 Nunney Castle in 1934 livery near Westbury, about 1936. The fireman is seen looking out for signals. This early optically aligned engine was to survive into preservation. GREAT WESTERN TRUST

Fig. 113. 5025 Chirk Castle, another noted Cheltenham Flyer performer, in its as-built 1927 livery with a light engine lamp at Plymouth North Road, 1934. The position of the engine on the middle through road suggests that it is perhaps waiting to take over the down Cornish Riviera Express from the King that would have brought the train from Paddington. GREAT WESTERN TRUST

Fig. 114. 5016 Montgomery Castle at Plymouth North Road on A lamps with a Cornwall-bound passenger train, 28 August 1937. GREAT WESTERN TRUST

Castle Class Workings, 1930s

DD/MM/YY	Loco	From	To	Descriptor	Details
		Old Oak Common			
9/8/30	4085	12/20 Newquay	Paddington	Passenger	9 coaches from Ply
5/10/30	5000	10.30 Paddington	Newport	Excursion	12 coaches
1/8/31	4076	9/25 Paddington	Neyland	Passenger	12 coaches & Mail
15/6/32	5001	12/15 Paddington	Oxford	Passenger	
3/9/32	4089	8.10 Taunton	Paddington	Passenger	
11/8/33	4071	7/55 Paddington	Newport	Excursion	2nd Part
20/1/34	4078	9/0 Penzance	Paddington	Passenger	
9/7/34	4071	7/15 Paddington	Bristol	Passenger	
14/9/34	5022	8/30 Paddington	Weymouth	Passenger	
26/3/35	5029	2/30 Cheltenham	Paddington	Passenger	
16/6/35	5029	6/35 Weymouth	Paddington	Excursion	
14/3/36	5006	7/20 Plymouth	Paddington	Passenger	
16/5/36	4099	10/15 Paddington	Plymouth	Freight	Vacuum fitted
12/9/36	4073	5.10 Fishguard	Paddington	Passenger	2nd Part 15 coaches
13/1/37	111	8.40 Paddington	Snow Hill B'ham	Passenger	
17/9/38	5037	3/55 Paddington	Carmarthen	Passenger	13 coaches
22/7/39	5008	12/15 Minehead	Paddington	Passenger	2nd Part 10 coaches
		Bristol Bath Road			
15/7/33	4016	5/15 Bristol	Paddington	Passenger	
28/5/34	4081	7/45 Bristol	Paddington	Passenger	
31/12/35	4096	2/35 Shrewsbury	Penzance	Mail	
7/1/36	4081	9/50 Paddington	Penzance	Passenger	
27/7/36	5042	7/10 Taunton	Bristol	Passenger	
12/9/36	4096	11.0 Minehead	Paddington	Passenger	9 coaches
4/1/37	5042	5/15 Bristol	Paddington	Passenger	
4/1/37	5042	9/50 Paddington	Penzance	Passenger	
10/3/38	5025	9/50 Paddington	Penzance	Passenger	
		Taunton			
11/8/34	4081	1/30 Paddington	Penzance	Passenger	15 coaches
		Exeter			
6/12/34	4074	1/30 Paddington	Penzance	Passenger	
22/8/36	5009	3/30 Paddington	Penzance	Passenger	2nd Part 12 coaches
13/1v1/36	4074	6.35 Hackney (NA)	Exeter	Freight	
18/5/38	4099	11.32 Oxford	Wolverhampton	Passenger	to Worcester
18/5/38	4099	2/45 WOS Shrub Hill	Malvern Wells	Passenger	
		Newton Abbot			
7/6/30	4075	10.40 Wolverhampton	Penzance	Passenger	12 coaches
7/6/30	5009	10.30 Paddington	Penzance	Passenger	13 coaches from Ply
31/3/31	5004	11.15 Paddington	Bristol	Passenger	
25/7/31	4080	7.7 Kingswear	Crewe	Passenger	
19/11/31	4084	7/35 Kingswear	Exeter	Passenger	
19/11/31	4084	5/5 Penzance	Manchester	Passenger	from Exeter to Bristol
19/11/31	4084	10/10 Paddington	Penzance	Postal	from Bristol
5/5/32	4074	7/35 Kingswear	Exeter	Passenger	
5/5/32	4074	5/5 Penzance	Manchester	Passenger	from Exeter to Bristol
5/5/32	4074	9/50 Paddington	Penzance	Passenger	from Bristol
27/8/32	4080	10.35 Manchester	Paignton	Passenger	

(continued)

DD/MM/YY	Loco	From	To	Descriptor	Details
7/7/34	5016	12/0nn Paddington	Kingswear	Passenger	
9/3/1935	4090	11.25 Cardiff General	Paignton	Passenger	
12/12/35	5016	10.32 Crewe	Plymouth	Passenger	
20/12/35	5017	11/40 Ply Millbay	Paddington	Passenger	Ocean Mails Special
12/9/36	5019	10.40 Paddington	Newquay	Passenger	7 coaches
5/1/38	5028	11.30 Exeter	Kingswear	Passenger	
5/1/38	5028	7/25 Kingswear	Newton Abbot	Passenger	
19/8/39	5072	9.10 Liverpool	Penzance	Passenger	11 coaches to Plym
24/8/1939	5060	7.45 Penzance	Crewe	Passenger	6 coaches to Plym
		Laira			
18/1/30	5008	11.00 Paddington	Paignton	Passenger	Luxury Pullman
19/9/30	4086	11.50 Paddington	Penzance	Passenger	14 coaches from Pad
1/12/30	5002	1/25 Penzance	Paddington	Passenger	
14/7/33	5010	9/0 Penzance	Paddington	Passenger	
4/8/34	5021	10.40 Wolverhampton	Penzance	Passenger	
29/12/35	5000	9/0 Penzance	Paddington	Passenger	1st Part
12/7/36	5041	9/0 Penzance	Paddington	Passenger	
		Truro			
31/7/37	4087	11.10 Penzance	Paddington	Passenger	9 coaches to Plym
20/8/38	4032	8.19 Truro	Penzance	Passenger	4 coaches
20/8/38	4032	10.00 Penzance	Paddington	Passenger	11 coaches 3rd Part
		Penzance			
13/8/38	4087	9.5 Wolverhampton	Penzance	Passenger	14 coaches from Ply
		Cardiff			
19/7/30	4077	11.25 Milford Haven	Paddington	Passenger	10 coaches
27/4/32	4092	8.00 Pembroke Dock	Paddington	Passenger	
15/6/32	4083	12.24 Reading	Cardiff	Freight	Vacuum fitted
17/1/33	5017	6.45 Cardiff	Paddington	Passenger	
24/1/33	5017	5/55 Paddington	Fishguard Harbour	Passenger	
25/6/34	5003	4/35 Swansea	Hereford	Passenger	
25/6/34	5003	8/17 Crewe	Cardiff	Passenger	
12/9/35	5012	9.30 Paddington	Cheltenham	Passenger	
29/2/36	4083	8.15 Cardiff	Paddington	Passenger	
23/9/36	5052	10.55 Cardiff	Bourneville	Passenger	Excursion
24/3/37	5012	11.25 Milford Haven	Paddington	Passenger	
21/4/37	5052	9/10 Swansea	Cardiff	Passenger	
2/6/38	4083	11/10 Cardiff	Paddington	Freight	Vacuum fitted
		Landore Swansea			
14/8/33	4037	1/0 Neyland	Paddington	Passenger	
22/7/36	4089	9/25 Paddington	Swansea	Passenger	
30/5/36	4050	12/35 Swansea	Paddington	Passenger	6 coaches
28/8/37	4095	3/55 Paddington	Carmarthen	Passenger	15 coaches
3/9/38	4095	5/30 Paddington	Swansea	Passenger	9 coaches
22/7/39	4078	3/55 Paddington	Carmarthen	Passenger	
22/7/39	5051	5/30 Paddington	Swansea	Passenger	
22/7/39	5048	5/55 Paddington	Swansea	Passenger	
		Wolverhampton Stafford Road			
7/8/32	4016	9.32 Paddington	Wolverhampton	Passenger	Excursion
24/10/33	4096	10/45 Penzance	Wolverhampton	Passenger	
31/10/33	4096	10/45 Penzance	Wolverhampton	Passenger	

DD/MM/YY	Loco	From	To	Descriptor	Details
22/8/36	5035	9.35 Pwllheli	Paddington	Passenger	14 coaches
31/7/37	5033	10.45 Penzance	Wolverhampton	Passenger	13 coaches from Ply
30/7/38	5035	10.20 Paddington	Aberystwyth	Passenger	11 coaches
21/8/39	4090	7/10 Penzance	Plymouth	Passenger	4 coaches
Worcester					
12/9/36	4086	6.50 Wolverhampton	Paddington	Passenger	8 coaches
27/8/37	5049	4/55 Paddington	Wolverhampton	Passenger	12 coaches
17/9/38	5050	8.23 Wolverhampton	Paddington	Passenger	10 coaches + 1
29/7/39	5017	12/55 Hereford	Paddington	Passenger	8 coaches
Gloucester					
30/7/38	5092	8.00 Cheltenham	Paddington	Passenger	10 coaches
3/9/38	5092	5/0 Paddington	Cheltenham	Passenger	7 coaches
10/7/38	4086	11.40 Cheltenham	Paddington	Passenger	10 coaches

Notes: Workings by Depot, 4/15 indicates 4.15 pm or 16:15 hrs, nn = noon. From/to Bristol, Br indicates the engine worked from that point onwards or to that point. 2nd Part means the train was run in multiple parts because of traffic demand. Red places, other than GWR including joint lines. The + designation in one of the workings means that extra non-passenger vehicles have been added to the train. These might be the following types: 6-wheel milk tanker empty, SYPHONS C, D, F, G, H, J for milk churns or parcels, FRUIT vans, passenger brake vans, horse boxes and other vehicles for parcels-type traffic authorized to run at passenger train speeds.

Fig. 115. 5014 Goodrich Castle on B lamps piloting a Star at Exeter St. Davids, 1935. Until BR days it was commonplace for the more powerful locomotive to head the train. GREAT WESTERN TRUST

Castles were ousted from the Cornish Riviera Express by Kings in the late 1920s but they continued to distinguish themselves on the Cheltenham Spa Express, popularly later known as the Cheltenham Flyer, and the train introduced for the centenary of the GWR in 1935, The Bristolian. Castles were also regular performers on the Torbay Express from Kingswear to Paddington and thus used the single track from Paignton to Kingswear.

The Cheltenham Spa Express

This service, which was present in all but name before World War I, would have seemed an unlikely vehicle for a world speed record. The up train set off from Cheltenham behind a 45XX 2-6-2 tank engine, which could deal with the short Golden Valley route to Gloucester. There an Old Oak Common Star or Saint, initially, would take the usually lightly loaded seven coaches from Gloucester down the main line parallel with the former Midland line from Birmingham to Bristol. The train turns left, as it were, at Standish Junction for the next Golden Valley past Stonehouse, Stroud and Brimscombe along a twisty and hilly route through Sapperton Tunnel to Kemble. After the stop at Kemble, then the junction for both Cirencester and Tetbury, the train initially ran straight through Swindon. It was only then that a fast run could be achieved. The sinuous Thames Valley through Goring-on-Thames, where water would be picked up, and Pangbourne provided the last theoretical obstacles to a speedy run to Paddington.

In July 1923 the train, now named the Cheltenham Spa Express, was headed by 2915 Saint Bartholomew. The engine demonstrated that a Churchward engine could maintain the set schedule of 75 minutes for the 77.3 miles (124km) from Swindon to Paddington at an average speed of 61.8mph (99km/h). This was enough to wrest the speed title of the rails from the North Eastern Railway, which had set a record average speed of 61.5mph on the race track that is the 44 mile (71km) section from Darlington to York. This was no flash in the downhill pan. The engine showed it could keep time even when subject to a delay of up to five minutes. The 2-cylinder engine had demonstrated that there was plenty in reserve.

Cecil J. Allen, an LNER employee and no friend of the GWR, was later to comment:

> Under 70 minutes net for a journey of 77.3 miles, and a slow finish to avoid too early an arrival! If the Great Western Railway is setting out seriously to capture the blue riband of start-to-stop railway speed, as I remarked previously, in such circumstances as these it would seem idle for any other aspirant to compete!

Sir Felix Pole's objective was first to wrest the title and then put it beyond others' reach. The Castles were to provide the tools to get the job done.

An early harbinger of what was to come with Castle power was 5003 Lulworth Castle's haulage of the train in the winter of 1929. With nine coaches the engine achieved an average speed of 84.5mph (136km/h) for the 20.5 miles from Steventon to Reading on minimally advantageous gradients of between 1 in 754 and 1 in 1760. This is remarkable when it is realized that the maximum speed recorded was only 86.5mph (139km/h).

These early encouraging results only spurred on the GWR to higher average speeds. In 1931 a modest cut

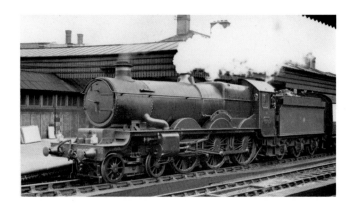

Fig. 116. 5052 Eastnor Castle at Newport, 31 May 1936. One year later the engine was to be elevated to the peerage as Earl Radnor. The lower top lamp iron and speedometer are modern features. The coach is a bow-ended Collett corridor coach. GREAT WESTERN TRUST

Fig. 117. 5057 Earl Waldegrave on platform 4 at Shrewsbury, about 1938. This engine had formerly been Penrice Castle and this name eventually ended up on number 7023. The train was going to cross Crewe Junction and head for Chester. GREAT WESTERN TRUST

Fig. 118. 5080 Ogmore Castle near Haddenham, between Princes Risborough and Bicester on the Paddington to Snow Hill route, 27 May 1939. It would appear that some coaches have been slipped. The engine would later become Defiant, in which guise it has been preserved and is now resident at Tyseley. Haddenham was one of the speedy parts of the route and speeds above 90mph (145km/h) were quite common. GREAT WESTERN TRUST

of three minutes was followed by attempts over three days by different crews with 5000 Launceston Castle. The fairly tight schedule of 67 minutes was easily broken with times of 59 minutes 20 seconds, 58½ minutes and an authenticated world record of 58 minutes and 20 seconds. This was from an engine manufactured before the introduction of the Zeiss optical alignment system (see Chapter 4). What might have been possible with laser-like production methods?

Fig. 119. A hazy view of 5000 Launceston Castle, about 1930, heading east from Penzance, the only way possible. The sea wall is the boundary marker here, as opposed to the more usual fencing. GREAT WESTERN TRUST

The Cheltenham Flyer					
Locomotive: 5000 Launceston Castle					
Load: 6 Coaches 184 tons (187 tonnes) tare, 195 tons					
(198 tonnes) full					
16 September 1931					
(GREEN Actual time denotes in front of schedule)					
Distance miles (km)	Place on journey	Schedule time mins	Actual time mins.s	Speeds mph	(km/h)
0 (0)	Swindon Junction	0	0.00	–	
2.3 (4)	Milepost 75		–	–	
5.7 (9)	Shrivenham		6.15	80	(129)
10.8 (17)	Uffington		9.55	85	(137)
13.4 (22)	Challow		11.45	85	(137)
16.9 (27)	Wantage Road		14.10	87	(140)
20.8 (34)	Steventon		16.50	90	(145)
24.2 (39)	DIDCOT		19.05	88	(142)
28.8 (46)	Cholsey and Moulsford		22.15	87	(140)
32.6 (52)	Goring-on-Thames		24.55	82	(132)
35.8 (58)	Pangbourne		27.10	85	(137)
38.7 (62)	Tilehurst		29.15	84	(135)
41.3 (66)	READING		31.05	85	(137)
46.3 (75)	Twyford		34.35	86	(138)
53.1 (85)	Maidenhead		39.15	88	(142)
58.8 (95)	SLOUGH		43.15	85	(137)
64.1 (103)	West Drayton		46.55	85	(137)
68.2 (110)	Southall		49.55	84	(135)
71.6 (115)	Ealing Broadway		52.20	84.5	(136)
76.0 (122)	Westbourne Park		–	–	
77.3 (124)	PADDINGTON	67	58.20		

The booked time worked out at an average speed of 69.2mph (111km/h), a world record, but Launceston Castle's fastest time was an average of 79.5mph (128km/h), a truly astonishing value when the average car of the time could get up to about 50mph (80km/h).

At any rate the drivers were instructed to avoid trying to run even faster, so we have the unusual scenario of a railway whose trains were too fast for itself. It was probably a blessing, safety-wise, that ATC had been installed along the Thames Valley by this time.

The world record had been held by the Reading Railroad in the eastern United States, where the 55½ miles (89km) from Camden Philadelphia, Pennsylvania, to Atlantic City, New Jersey, were covered

The Cheltenham Flyer Locomotive: 5006 Tregenna Castle Load: 6 Coaches 186 tons (189 tonnes) tare, 195 tons (198 tonnes) full 6 June 1932 (GREEN Actual time denotes in front of schedule)					
Distance miles (km)	Place on journey	Schedule time mins	Actual time mins.s	Speeds mph	(km/h)
0 (0)	Swindon Junction	0	0.00	–	
2.3 (4)	Milepost 75		3.28½	64	(103)
5.7 (9)	Shrivenham		6.15	81	(130)
10.8 (17)	Uffington		9.51	85.5	(138)
13.4 (22)	Challow		11.42	87	(140)
16.9 (27)	Wantage Road		14.05	89	(143)
20.8 (34)	Steventon		16.40	90	(145)
24.2 (39)	DIDCOT		18.55	91	(146)
28.8 (46)	Cholsey and Moulsford		21.59	91	(146)
32.6 (52)	Goring-on- Thames		24.25	92	(148)
35.8 (58)	Pangbourne		26.33	90	(145)
38.7 (62)	Tilehurst		28.28	92	(148)
41.3 (66)	READING		30.12	91	(146)
46.3 (75)	Twyford		33.31	89	(143)
53.1 (85)	Maidenhead		38.08	87	(140)
58.8 (95)	SLOUGH		42.10	87	(140)
64.1 (103)	West Drayton		45.51	84	(135)
68.2 (110)	Southall		48.51	81.5	(131)
71.6 (115)	Ealing Broadway		51.17	84.5	(136)
76.0 (122)	Westbourne Park		54.40	–	
77.3 (124)	PADDINGTON	67	56.47		

twisty with gradients around the 1 in 1350 to 1 in 1500 down, except at Goring-on-Thames, which is level and consequently is the water trough pick-up point.

By Reading 5006 was nearly a minute ahead of 5000. Reading was taken at 91mph (146km/h), which must have rattled the points at all the junctions, yards and sidings, as well as exceeding the speed limit there, although this was then a commonplace occurrence.

At Slough Tregenna Castle was more than a minute up. Both engines were doing 84.5mph (136km/h) at Ealing Broadway with about 5 miles (8km) to go

Fig. 120. 4096 Highclere Castle on B lamps at Kensal Green, near Paddington, with a pristine Collett coach in the background and newly installed colour light signals on view, about 1933. There is a mixture of Collett and Churchward coaches in the train with what looks like a SIPHON at the rear. GREAT WESTERN TRUST

in 42 minutes 33 seconds, which produced an average speed of 78.3mph (126km/h). Both the NER and the Reading records were over shorter distances than the GWR's 77.3 miles (124km).

Nevertheless the GWR sought to put the record beyond the reach of most competitors with a staged series of record runs. The engine carefully selected was 5006 Tregenna Castle, another early engine, but clearly a flyer.

Tregenna Castle was only four seconds up on Launceston Castle over the nearly 11 miles to Uffington, but at this point whereas 5000's speeds were in the eighties, 5006 was in the nineties. This part of the journey down the Thames Valley is quite

Fig. 121. 4086 Builth Castle at Slough with a motley collection of GWR coaches in the old company's livery, 17 May 1948. The numerous 5ft (1.5m) signal arms, with their tapered wooden posts, represent the old school in signalling. GREAT WESTERN TRUST

before Paddington. Tregenna Castle shaved more than 1½ minutes off an already fast time that itself had been a world record.

The final run in the trilogy is the exploit of an optically aligned 5039 Rhuddlan Castle some five years later in 1937. Rhuddlan Castle was twenty seconds slower to Shrivenham than either 5000 or Tregenna Castle. This is understandable as it was hauling an all-up load some 20 per cent higher than either of its classmates. By Didcot, however, after continuous running at 90mph (145km/h), 5039 was almost as fast as 5006 and faster than 5000. When the engine reached Slough it had pulled away and remained ahead until Ealing Broadway, where the loco was eased. This caused a loss of five minutes rather than Tregenna Castle's thrilling run into the

capital at about 85mph (137km/h). If it had not been for that final slowing Rhuddlan Castle showed every sign of beating the record – and with a heavier loading.

All the engines involved were based at Old Oak Common, where arguably the best of the top link drivers were based. Old Oak also had a repair shop that would assist in keeping the hand-picked engines in top form for these record runs.

Exactly as Sir Felix Pole had planned, the world's spotlight was on the GWR. The company had been able to call on the dedication and maximum effort from the staff involved and rely on the best steam coal from south Wales. To this heady recipe was added Churchward's brilliance and Collett's practical adaptability. No wonder they were world beaters.

All this was achieved with a specially prepared engine in the shape of 5006 Tregenna Castle. It might have been comforting for the opposition to point out that the GWR could only do it with a lightly loaded train and hand-picked engines in balmy summer weather, but the following runs go some way to debunking that argument.

They cover the winter of 1937 and are runs of engines in ordinary daily service and with loads of up to 13 coaches or 435 tons (442 tonnes) gross, more than twice the usual tariff.

Lydford Castle with an extra coach on top of 5006 Tregenna Castle's load was within a minute and a half up to and including Reading. It only started to fall

The Cheltenham Flyer Locomotive: 5039 Rhuddlan Castle Load: 7 Coaches 223 tons (189 tonnes) tare, 235 tons (198 tonnes) full 30 June 1937 (GREEN Actual time denotes in front of schedule)					
Distance miles (km)	Place on journey	Schedule time mins	Actual time mins.s	Speeds mph	(km/h)
0 (0)	Swindon Junction	0	0.00	–	
2.3 (4)	Milepost 75		3.43	59	(95)
5.7 (9)	Shrivenham		6.35	80.5	(130)
10.8 (17)	Uffington		10.10	90	(145)
13.4 (22)	Challow		11.57	90	(145)
16.9 (27)	Wantage Road		14.12	94	(151)
20.8 (34)	Steventon		16.45	95	(153)
24.2 (39)	DIDCOT		18.57	90.5	(146)
28.8 (46)	Cholsey and Moulsford		21.58	91	(146)
32.6 (52)	Goring-on- Thames		24.25	88	(142)
35.8 (58)	Pangbourne		26.40	86.5	(139)
38.7 (62)	Tilehurst		28.40	90	(145)
41.3 (66)	READING		30.27	86.5	(139)
46.3 (75)	Twyford		33.50	90	(145)
53.1 (85)	Maidenhead		38.17	93	(150)
58.8 (95)	SLOUGH		42.08	90.5	(146)
64.1 (103)	West Drayton		45.47	84	(135)
68.2 (110)	Southall		48.46	82	(132)
71.6 (115)	Ealing Broadway		51.40	eased	
76.0 (122)	Westbourne Park		57.40	–	
77.3 (124)	PADDINGTON	67	61.07		

Fig. 122. 5040 Stokesay Castle, a production engine constructed using the Zeiss system, rattling the points at Reading heading the Cheltenham Flyer, 7 August 1939. The loco on the left looks like a Hall and is signalled to MAIN on the 'cash register' type signal. GREAT WESTERN TRUST

The Cheltenham Flyer Locomotive: 5055 Lydford Castle Load: 7 Coaches 218 tons (221 tonnes) tare, 230 tons (233 tonnes) full 1 January 1937 (GREEN Actual time denotes in front of schedule)			
Distance miles (km)	Place on journey	Schedule time mins	Actual time mins.s
0 (0)	Swindon Junction	0	0.00
2.3 (4)	Milepost 75		—
5.7 (9)	Shrivenham		6.43
10.8 (17)	Uffington		10.22
13.4 (22)	Challow		—
16.9 (27)	Wantage Road		14.25
20.8 (34)	Steventon		—
24.2 (39)	DIDCOT	21	19.13
28.8 (46)	Cholsey and Moulsford		—
32.6 (52)	Goring-on-Thames		25.02
35.8 (58)	Pangbourne		27.32
38.7 (62)	Tilehurst		—
41.3 (66)	READING	34	31.47
46.3 (75)	Twyford		35.38
53.1 (85)	Maidenhead		40.33
58.8 (95)	SLOUGH	47½	44.39
64.1 (103)	West Drayton		48.26
68.2 (110)	Southall	54½	51.33
71.6 (115)	Ealing Broadway		54.10
76.0 (122)	Westbourne Park	61	59.00
77.3 (124)	PADDINGTON	65	61.49

behind further after Ealing Broadway, when the engine was being eased down on its approach to Paddington. Nevertheless the engine was more than three minutes inside the scheduled time. The maximum speed of 93.5mph (150km/h) at Wantage Road was followed by 90mph (145km/h) at Didcot, although the engine slowed to 76.5mph (123km/h) at Goring-on-Thames over the troughs. Until this point the engine had been battling side winds as it headed south, but after the turn eastwards, and assisted by the prevailing wind, it picked up time and was almost three minutes early at Slough.

5025 Chirk Castle was labouring under the same sort of weather conditions as its classmate Lydford, but with two more coaches from Tregenna Castle had hauled, resulting in a train 38 per cent heavier.

This run was characterized by high winds and wintery showers, and time was just kept to Didcot.

The Cheltenham Flyer Locomotive: 5025 Chirk Castle Load: 8 Coaches 248 tons (252 tonnes) tare, 270 tons (274 tonnes) full Winter 1937 (GREEN Actual time denotes in front of schedule)			
Distance miles (km)	Place on journey	Schedule time mins	Actual time mins.s
0 (0)	Swindon Junction	0	0.00
2.3 (4)	Milepost 75		—
5.7 (9)	Shrivenham		7.02
10.8 (17)	Uffington		11.01
13.4 (22)	Challow		—
16.9 (27)	Wantage Road		15.31
20.8 (34)	Steventon		—
24.2 (39)	DIDCOT	21	20.44
28.8 (46)	Cholsey and Moulsford		—
32.6 (52)	Goring-on-Thames		26.48
35.8 (58)	Pangbourne		29.11
38.7 (62)	Tilehurst		—
41.3 (66)	READING	34	33.17
46.3 (75)	Twyford		37.00
53.1 (85)	Maidenhead		41.50
58.8 (95)	SLOUGH	47½	45.50
64.1 (103)	West Drayton		49.41
68.2 (110)	Southall	54½	52.43
71.6 (115)	Ealing Broadway		55.13
76.0 (122)	Westbourne Park	61	59.19
77.3 (124)	PADDINGTON	65	62.15

Fig. 123. 5021 Whittington Castle is only a few miles from its namesake at Shrewsbury platform 4, seen here with a heavy Chester-bound train, about 1938. The Castle would come off at Chester and the train might then proceed to Birkenhead, usually hauled by a GWR 51XX 2-6-2 tank engine. The pilot engine inside the Castle appears to be a Hall. GREAT WESTERN TRUST

Fig. 124. 4090 Dorchester Castle is seen here in early condition, but it is just possible to discern the words British Railways on the tender. It was heading a stopping passenger service at St. Austell about 1950. The vehicle behind the engine appears to be a FRUIT D. *GREAT WESTERN TRUST*

The Cheltenham Flyer			
Locomotive: 5018 St. Mawes Castle			
Load: 10 Coaches 317 tons (322 tonnes) tare, 340 tons (345 tonnes) full			
Winter 1937			
(RED Actual time denotes behind schedule, GREEN in front or on time)			
Distance miles (km)	Place on journey	Schedule time mins	Actual time mins.s
0 (0)	Swindon Junction	0	0.00
2.3 (4)	Milepost 75		–
5.7 (9)	Shrivenham		7.16
10.8 (17)	Uffington		11.19
13.4 (22)	Challow		–
16.9 (27)	Wantage Road		15.58
20.8 (34)	Steventon		–
24.2 (39)	DIDCOT	21	21.22
28.8 (46)	Cholsey and Moulsford		–
32.6 (52)	Goring-on-Thames		27.36
35.8 (58)	Pangbourne		29.59
38.7 (62)	Tilehurst		–
41.3 (66)	READING	34	34.08
46.3 (75)	Twyford		37.56
53.1 (85)	Maidenhead		43.04
58.8 (95)	SLOUGH	47½	47.22
64.1 (103)	West Drayton		51.24
68.2 (110)	Southall	54½	54.39
71.6 (115)	Ealing Broadway		57.12
76.0 (122)	Westbourne Park	61	60.41
77.3 (124)	PADDINGTON	65	63.04

Despite a slowing for Goring-on-Thames troughs, this did not impede Chirk Castle to any degree as the engine hammered along at an average speed of 82.6mph (133km/h) over the 59.1 miles (95km) from the Wiltshire/Berkshire border (as it then was pre-1974) at Uffington to the outskirts of London at Hanwell and Elthorne. The presence of a GATSO camera at Reading might have been revealing had it then been invented.

Fig. 125. 5042 Winchester Castle storming Sapperton Bank in Gloucestershire with a Fruit D, Milk Tank, inside frame SIPHON Gs, BR General Utility Vans (GUV), Southern Railway Utility Vans and other parcels and coaches, 30 May 1955. *GREAT WESTERN TRUST*

Fig. 126. 5022 Wigmore Castle, from Wolverhampton Stafford Road shed, crosses the River Dee on its approach to Chester, about 1954. The tracks here were quadruple along the North Wales coast and the GWR double track from Wrexham joined these tracks before crossing the River Dee by the racecourse. Hereabouts the railway crosses over a canal and a road crosses over both. *GREAT WESTERN TRUST*

The engine showed the ability to sustain high speeds over a long distance and yet there was no outstanding top speed; the maximum was 86.5mph (139km/h) at Maidenhead. The aim was an early arrival with a regular service train, not a newspaper headline dash.

On the next winter run 5018 St. Mawes Castle left Gloucester with a load 74 per cent greater than the record run of Tregenna Castle. The first appearances of red on the log of the runs shows what a valiant fight the crew and the engine put up to arrive at Paddington nearly two minutes early as the train was slightly behind time with 70 per cent of the journey completed. Once again there was no fireworks maximum, just the sustaining of more than 80mph (130km/h)

for most of the journey. (The maximum speed was 82mph/132km/h at Wantage Road, Reading and Ealing Broadway.) The schedule called for an average speed of 71.6mph (115km/h).

The maximum speed of 5023 Brecon Castle was 79mph (127km/h) at Didcot, but it should be remembered that this was achieved hauling thirteen coaches, which amounted to a load 123 per cent greater than that of Tregenna Castle. A net time for the run was not given, but using the average of times for Maidenhead to Slough and Ealing to Westbourne Park for the

Fig. 127. 5022 Wigmore Castle was seen at Old Oak Common on 5 June 1948, shortly after Nationalization. The British Railways lettering is in the Egyptian Serif style of the old company. Corporate branding had not yet occurred to BR. GREAT WESTERN TRUST

Fig. 128. Class D and class E engines, 5067 St Fagans Castle and 3864 Collett 2-8-0, toy with a train of milk tanks at Aller Junction, Devon, 17 September 1955. The Castle may just be working to its next passenger turn; this was done to cut down on light engine moves and hence track occupancy. The two six-wheel SIPHON C wagons at the rear would be for churn traffic, as opposed to bulk liquid in the tankers. GREAT WESTERN TRUST

Distance miles (km)		Place on journey	Schedule time mins	Actual time mins.s
0	(0)	Swindon Junction	0	0.00
2.3	(4)	Milepost 75		–
5.7	(9)	Shrivenham		8.00
10.8	(17)	Uffington		12.17
13.4	(22)	Challow		–
16.9	(27)	Wantage Road		17.07
20.8	(34)	Steventon		–
24.2	(39)	DIDCOT	21	26.15
28.8	(46)	Cholsey and Moulsford		–
32.6	(52)	Goring-on-Thames		31.44
35.8	(58)	Pangbourne		34.01
38.7	(62)	Tilehurst		–
41.3	(66)	READING	34	36.06
46.3	(75)	Twyford		40.03
53.1	(85)	Maidenhead		45.20
		Adverse signal check		
58.8	(95)	SLOUGH	47½	52.20
64.1	(103)	West Drayton		57.19
68.2	(110)	Southall	54½	60.58
71.6	(115)	Ealing Broadway		63.48
		Adverse signal check		
76.0	(122)	Westbourne Park	61	68.35
77.3	(124)	PADDINGTON	65	71.41

The Cheltenham Flyer
Locomotive: 5023 Brecon Castle
Load: 13 Coaches 401 tons (407 tonnes) tare, 435 tons (442 tonnes) full
Winter 1937
(RED Actual time denotes behind schedule)

other runs it can be estimated that the signal delays accounted for six minutes overall. When this is taken into account the train would be less than a minute late with a load more than twice that normally contemplated when the schedule was introduced. The two minutes difference between 5018 and 5023 at Maidenhead would indicate that Brecon Castle was on schedule for a right time arrival.

The Bristolian

The GWR sought to celebrate the centenary of incorporation of the company in 1835 in many ways. One of these was the introduction of a fast train between the two cities whose heraldic crests are constituents of the company's coat of arms, London and Bristol, and between which had been the original route of the GWR.

The down train from Paddington to Bristol Temple Meads used Brunel's original route via Bath, a distance of 118.3 miles (190km), but up trains left Bristol via Filton and used the South Wales direct line as far as Wootton Bassett Junction, a distance of 117.6 miles (189km). The slightly shorter up route had more adverse gradients, particularly the climb out of Filton, than the down. The schedule was 105 minutes for both up and down trains.

Initially locomotives of the King class were used, but the seven Collett coaches were adequately hauled

Fig. 130. 5098 Clifford Castle with double chimney and four-row superheater inside an unidentified locomotive at Exeter St. David's, 17 June 1960. 5098 is still carrying its headlamps and it is reasonable to assume that the other engine has just backed on to assist. Clifford Castle was another flyer used for tests and special trains. GREAT WESTERN TRUST

by mostly Bristol Bath Road Castles. The service was suspended at the outbreak of World War II.

The service was finally resumed in 1954 using Castles, although King class locomotives were again used for the Friday trains, which were usually strengthened by two coaches. The updating of the Castles, which took place about this time, coincided with the zenith of the train's performance in the mid- to late 1950s. Double-chimney Castles with four-row superheaters

Fig. 129. 5071 Spitfire pauses at Oxford on the Cathedrals Express to Worcester and Hereford, 18 July 1959. Only the first four or five coaches would go on to Hereford. The engine carries an 85A Worcester shed plate. GREAT WESTERN TRUST

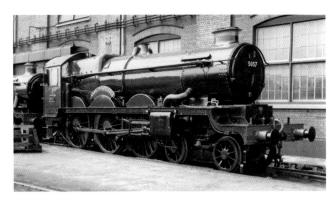

Fig. 131. 5057 Earl Waldegrave, seen awaiting a tender at Swindon works, also has the double chimney and four-row superheater at Swindon works, 6 May 1962. Compare this with Figure 117. This is probably its last heavy general overhaul. The loco is fitted with windscreen wipers, mechanical lubricator and speedometer. It carries a shed plate for 81A, Old Oak Common. GREAT WESTERN TRUST

Fig. 132. 5008 Raglan Castle at its own Worcester Loco Sheds, 85A, under the shadow of Rainbow Hill, 3 June 1962. There were two distinct depots at Worcester, for passenger and freight. Although the steam engine sheds and subsequent diesel depot closed, this area is still (2018) controlled by Worcester Tunnel Junction signal box. GREAT WESTERN TRUST

Fig. 133. 5042 Winchester Castle on express passenger duties at Gloucester, 12 September 1955. The large disc or 'Banjo' signal above 5042's tender was to control split movements onto the long platform at Gloucester by means of a crossover halfway along. In 2018 Worcester Shrub Hill retains this arrangement and a Banjo signal. GREAT WESTERN TRUST

Fig. 134. 5047 Earl of Dartmouth at Knowle and Dorridge station with an up express, 12 October 1958. The first coach is a Hawksworth bow-ended type and others are Collett productions. The Knowle part of the name was later dropped and the station is now simply Dorridge. GREAT WESTERN TRUST

were – and are – real speed machines. In recent times 5043 and 7029, which are similarly equipped, have confirmed the mid-1950s promise.

In the above table a reworked Castle, 4090 Dorchester Castle with double chimney and four-row superheater, headed the down train, which was subjected to the prevailing headwinds. The gradients are minimally adverse as far as Swindon. After Wootton Bas-

sett Junction the line falls at a gradient of 1 in 100 down Dauntsey bank, where the maximum speed of 95mph (153km/h) was achieved, and then rises at 1 in 660 to Corsham, where another 1 in 100 down grade takes the train through Box Tunnel. After Box station the line gently falls through Bath and on to Bristol Temple Meads station. In this latter section the greatest fall is 1 in 850 and the shallowest 1 in 1320, with some level running. On this run the net time was 98¼

	The Bristolian Locomotive: 4090 Dorchester Castle – (double chimney) Load 7 Coaches 246 tons (240 tonnes) tare, 265 tons (254 tonnes) full 1958, Driver Harris, Old Oak Common (GREEN Actual time denotes in front of schedule)					
Distance miles (km)	Place on Journey	Schedule time mins	Actual time mins.s	Speed mph	(km/h)
0.0 (0.0)	PADDINGTON	0	0.0		
5.7 (9.2)	Ealing		8.32	62.5	(100)
9.1 (14.6)	Southall		11.32	72	(116)
13.2 (21.2)	West Drayton		14.53	77	(124)
18.5 (29.8)	SLOUGH		18.55	79/74	(127/119)
24.2 (38.9)	Maidenhead		23.23	78.5	(126)
31.0 (49.9)	Twyford		28.26	82	(132)
	Permanent Way Slack				
36.0 (57.9)	READING		33.33		
41.5 (66.8)	Pangbourne		38.47	75	(121)
48.5 (78.1)	Cholsey and Moulsford		44.11	77.5	(125)
53.1 (85.5)	DIDCOT		47.44	78	(126)
60.4 (97.2)	Wantage Road		53.20	77	(124)
66.5 (107)	Uffington		58.03	78	(126)
71.5 (115)	Shrivenham		61.49	79.5	(128)
77.3 (124)	SWINDON JUNCTION		66.14	78	(126)
82.9 (133)	Wootton Bassett		70.26	81.5	(131)
87.7 (141)	Dauntsey		73.47	95	(153)
91.0 (146)	Milepost 91		75.52	91	(146)
94.0 (151)	CHIPPENHAM		78.02	78	(126)
98.3 (158)	Corsham		81.23	75.5	(122)
101.9 (164)	Box		84.09	80/72	(129/116)
106.9 (172)	BATH		88.34		
113.8 (183)	Keynsham		95.01	72	(116)
118.4 (191)	BRISTOL TEMPLE MEADS	105	100.47		

Fig. 135. *4079 Pendennis Castle, with a proud history of achievements behind it, could look forward to more after a 1964 overhaul at Swindon Works, but mostly in private ownership. The ovoids in the tender will not assist the process. The temptation to convert to double chimney and four-row superheater has been resisted.* GREAT WESTERN TRUST

Fig. 136. *4093 Dunster Castle with a 87E Landore shed plate heads the Pembroke Coast Express from Paddington, 30 April 1960. The engine has a Hawksworth tender and white painted buffer heads, and is towing a BR Mark 1 coach. A tank locomotive of either the 51XX or 45XX class would have hauled the train the last leg to Pembroke Dock.* GREAT WESTERN TRUST

Fig. 137. 5056 Earl of Powis speeds through Swindon with the Royal train carrying the reigning monarch, King George VI, 22 May 1946. 5056 was another flyer and one of the last Old Oak Castles to survive. STEAM, MUSEUM OF THE GREAT WESTERN RAILWAY

Fig. 138. 7016 Chester Castle is seen at Swindon in early non-standard BR livery, but still bearing the GWR code CDF on the footplate for Cardiff Canton, late 1940s. It was still the GWR at this point, although with a different name on the tender. STEAM, MUSEUM OF THE GREAT WESTERN RAILWAY

minutes, ahead of schedule, and the average speed was 71.4mph (115km/h).

The fastest-recorded Castle-hauled Bristolian service was by 7018 Drysllwyn Castle in April 1958, taking a total of 93 minutes 50 seconds with a top speed of 102mph (164km/h). There were also other instances of Castles 'doing the ton' on this service.

Castle Class Workings, 1940s

The following table is taken from engine record cards again after hostilities ceased in Europe (the earliest recorded working is June 1945). Much of what was happening on the railways in wartime was subject to the Official Secrets Act (1939).

Whereas the table above covering the 1930s presented a snapshot of all Castle workings, here, later on in their careers, Castles are shown working untypical or unusual types of train rather than the Paddington passenger services to and from major destinations that the engines were still doing. Some of the workings are pilot or standby locomotives that don't involve a train or a destination.

Notes: Workings by Depot, 4/15 indicates 4.15pm or 16:15hrs, nn = noon. From/to Bristol, Br indicates the engine worked from that point onwards or to that point. 2nd Part means the train was run in multiple parts because of traffic demand. Red places, other than GWR including joint lines. The + designation means that extra non-passenger vehicles have been added to the train. These were of the types: six-wheel milk tanker empty, SYPHONS C, D, F, G, H, J for milk churns or parcels, FRUIT vans, passenger brake vans, horseboxes and other vehicles for parcels-type traffic authorized to run at passenger train speeds.

DD/MM/YY	Loco	From	To	Descriptor	Details
		Old Oak Common			
2/2/46	5036	6/40 Penzance	Paddington	Postal	From Exeter
29/9/46	5014	10.50 Swansea	Sheffield	Assist	
11/1/47	5023	3/50 Whitland	Kensington	Milk	5/50 Felin Fran
20/4/47	5022	10.30 Paddington	Taunton	Passenger	Relief
22/8/47	5029	2.30 Paddington	Bristol	Newspaper	
31/10/47	4076	12/30 Carmarthen	Cheltenham	Passenger	1/50 Swdn-Glos
13/12/47	5038	3/0 St Austell	Tavistock Junction	Freight	
24/5/48	4037	2/15 Kensington	Penzance	Milk Empties	
17/7/48	5065	8/25 Swindon	Banbury	ECS	Empty coach stock
2/10/48	5056	Banbury		Pilot	Passenger
		Oxford			
13/11/48	7008	6/45 Paddington	Great Malvern	Passenger	
23/11/48	7008	9.20 Birkenhead	Bournemouth	Passenger	10 coaches
		Bristol Bath Road			
25/2/46	5082	9.10 Liverpool	Plymouth	Passenger	
18/11/46	4093	10.15 Bradford	Kingswear	Passenger	from Bristol 4/5
31/12/46	4096	2/35 Shrewsbury	Penzance	Mail	
23/7/47	5096	10.30 Cardiff	Portsmouth	Passenger	
21/8/47	5025	2/25 Neyland	Pontypool Road	Passenger	5/30 Swdn – Cardiff
13/2/48	4089	4/30 Exeter	Bristol	Passenger	+ Milk
20/8/48	5019	10/10 Paddington	Penzance	Postal	from Bristol to NA
25/8/48	5042	5.10 Bristol	Weston-super- Mare	Freight	
6/1/49	5025	1/0 Plymouth	Liverpool	Passenger	4/35 Bristol to Salop
		Swindon			
8/3/48	5091	8.48 Fishguard Harbr	Paddington	Parcels	
25/11/48	5091	12/45 Old Oak Comm	Neyland	Empties	Fish and Milk
22/12/48	5083	5.30 Marston Sidings	Bristol	Fish	
		Newton Abbot			
21/2/46	5028	10/10 Paddington	Penzance	Postal	
2/6/46	5047	7.30 Newton Abbot	KIngswear	Lt Engine	
22/11/47	5011	10.35 Hackney Yard	Kingswear	Freight	
22/11/47	5011	2/45 Kingswear	Hackney Yard	Freight	
29/4/48	5062	5.45 Laira	Hackney Yard	Freight	
8/10/48	5058	6/40 Penzance	Paddington	Postal	Truro—Newton Abbot
		Laira			
4/5/46	5095	12/0nn Penzance	Crewe	Passenger	
24/4/47	4088	10/10 Paddington	Penzance	Postal	
7/5/48	5050	9/32 Old Oak Comm	Penzance	Freight	
9/7/48	5050	4.0-12/0nn Ranelagh		Pilot	
22/9/48	5050	10/15 Paddington	Plymouth	Parcels	
		Penzance			
13/11/48	5098	9/55 Bristol	Penzance	Freight	13 Vac + 14 + Brake V
27/11/48	5098	6/20 Penzance	Kensington	Milk	
		Cardiff Canton			
4/6/45	4094	6/35 Penzance	Paddington	Postal	

(*continued*)

DD/MM/YY	Loco	From	To	Descriptor	Details
17/10/46	5007	1.0 Paddington	Swansea	Pilot	West End
11/4/47	5010	11/55 Manchester	Cardiff	Passenger	from Hereford
11/4/47	5010	12.25 Cardiff	Crewe	Passenger	to Hereford
1/5/49	5049	8/30 Bournemouth	Cardiff	Excursion	
		Landore Swansea			
4/4/46	5013	10/10 Paddington	Penzance	Assist	NA to Plymouth
4/4/46	5013	7.45 Penzance	Manchester	Passenger	
12/8/46	5016	9/50 Victoria Basin	Cardiff	Freight	from Gloucester
24/12/47	7003	10/0 Carmarthen	Tyseley Carr Sid	ECS	Empty Coach Stock
6/4/49	5093	11/55 Yeovil	Neyland	Parcels	
		Wolverhampton Stafford Road			
18/1/46	5053	5/35 Birkenhead	Paddington	Passenger	
5/4/46	5015	9.45 Paddington	Hereford	Passenger	
9/12/46	5018	11/5 Paddington	Shrewsbury	Passenger	
14/1/47	5018	11.00 Milford Haven	Paddington	Passenger	
11/11/48	4076	5/25 Leamington Spa	Oxford	Passenger	5 coaches
		Shrewsbury Coleham			
8/7/46	5021	12/0nn Penzance	Crewe	Passenger	
11/6/48	5073	8.45 Plymouth	Crewe	Passenger	5/0 Chester-Wolves
16/7/48	5086	10/38 Bristol	Shrewsbury	Passenger	
21/12/48	5064	8.45 Plymouth	Crewe	Passenger	
24/5/49	5073	10.35 Crewe	Cardiff	Passenger	11.28 Salop-Cardiff
		Worcester			
30/3/46	4092	1/45 Paddington	Stourbridge Junction	Passenger	1/2 from WOS
27/4/46	5092	7.33 Malvern Wells	Paddington	Passenger	
18/11/49	7005	6/45 Paddington	Great Malvern	Passenger	
		Hereford, Barton			
6/7/48	4079	2/0 Penzance	Crewe	Perishable	

The same locomotives are seen doing the more menial tasks, such as 5091 from Swindon and 5011 from Newton Abbot: the latter would appear to be a pickup goods, the lowest of the low freight turns. These would not appear to be filling in turns, as we had with the Stars on freights in Cornwall, but a shed allocating low-power work to engines that were badly in need of overhaul after the war, as indeed many of them were.

Paradoxically Worcester was able to keep its engines on passenger work, albeit some minor turns. Express milk delivery and the subsequent running of the empties occupied Castles on the Penzance and Whitland

jobs, but Dorrington in Shropshire was not a Castle turn and the GWR took the train only as far as Banbury.

Castle Class Workings, 1950s and 1960s

In this section, instead of expressing the engines' usage as a table, the opportunity has been taken to illustrate the period by a photographic record. The photographs are from the author's collection, except where indicated.

Fig. 139. 5047 Earl of Dartmouth leaves Teignmouth station with one pristine Collett coach and another less so, July 1947. This was one of the quintessential GWR photographic locations as photos can be taken from the footpath that runs along the trackside. AUTHOR'S COLLECTION

Fig. 140. 5068 Beverston Castle at Bathampton, heading a mixture of Collett and Hawksworth coaches all in GWR livery, 29 December 1951. The Bristolian service was not resumed until 1954. STEAM, MUSEUM OF THE GREAT WESTERN RAILWAY

Fig. 141. 7037 Swindon at Bath Spa station, 1950s. The engine is appropriately allocated to 82C Swindon and appears to be on a running in turn on B lamps. STEAM, MUSEUM OF THE GREAT WESTERN RAILWAY

Fig. 142. 7018 Drysllwyn Castle at Kingkerswell with the Torbay Express and Churchward dynamometer car, 26 July 1956. Drysllwyn Castle was another flyer on which the oil supply could be doubled by a setting in the mechanical lubricator. This is the post-war engine with that name, condemned in 1963. Confusingly, Earl Bathurst, the name 5051 was given in 1937, has largely been dropped for the earlier Drysllwyn Castle at the Didcot depot of the GWS. STEAM, MUSEUM OF THE GREAT WESTERN RAILWAY

Fig. 143. 5070 Sir Daniel Gooch at Paddington's platform 1, the premier departure platform, 1948. Some of the buildings behind in Westbourne Terrace, which were GWR offices, are now Grade 1 listed. The loco name and number plates are part of the NRM collection. The same name has also been given to a class 47 diesel loco. Sir Daniel Gooch Place, the forecourt to Swindon station, has a similar name plate. AUTHOR'S COLLECTION

Fig. 144. 5004 Llanstephan Castle arrives at Paddington with an express from Fishguard Harbour comprising Hawksworth, Collett and BR coaches, 14 August 1954. AUTHOR'S COLLECTION

Fig. 145. 5034 Corfe Castle is pictured at Exeter St. David's with an express for Paignton, 7 August 1954. Corfe Castle was a destination on the LSWR Swanage branch of the Southern Railway, which is now the Swanage Railway. Passengers before World War I had been known to mistake the loco name plate for the train's destination. AUTHOR'S COLLECTION

Fig. 146. 5042 Winchester Castle arrives at Paddington from Cheltenham Spa, passing the massive goods station and the Paddington Arrivals signal box, 14 August 1954. AUTHOR'S COLLECTION

Fig. 147. 5038 Morlais Castle reverses away from Paddington towards Ranelagh Bridge after arriving with an express from Weston-super-Mare, about 1954. At this time the carriage shunting was shared between 57XX and the newer 94XX pannier tanks; earlier 45XX tanks had been used. AUTHOR'S COLLECTION

Fig. 148. 5014 Goodrich Castle arrives from Swindon at Weston-super-Mare, 28 August 1954. Weston-super-Mare was the most popular destination for the Swindon Trip, when the whole town decamped for a day out courtesy of the GWR. A 57XX Pannier tank is carriage shunting in the background. AUTHOR'S COLLECTION

Fig. 149. 5034 Corfe Castle provides a steamer connection from Fishguard Harbour on its arrival at Paddington, 7 May 1955. This was only a few months after the working for Paignton seen in fig. 145. AUTHOR'S COLLECTION

Fig. 150. 7022 Hereford Castle pilots a Hall on a Plymouth-bound express from Liskeard, 1955. The train is about to go over the top of the Looe branch, which has a separate platform to the left of the train. AUTHOR'S COLLECTION

Fig. 151. 5044 Earl of Dunraven at Paddington, about 1955. The first coach looks like Collett sunshine stock of 1936 with the deep windows and a lower waistline than its neighbour. In the background there appears to be a 61XX Prairie tank. AUTHOR'S COLLECTION

Fig. 152. 5019 Treago Castle at Bristol Bath Road shed, identified by the BR code 82A, with a light engine tail lamp, about 1955. There appears to be another 5013 class Castle behind. The signal box is of the 1930s update to colour light signalling at Bristol Temple Meads. There is a 20 ton loco coal wagon between the loco and signal box. AUTHOR'S COLLECTION

Fig. 153. 5022 Wigmore Castle at Stafford Road, about 1955, with a reporting number ex-Kingswear, and what looks like red name and number plate backgrounds, which were a trademark of Stafford Road Works. AUTHOR'S COLLECTION

Fig. 154. 5080 Defiant drifts past Paddington Arrival signal box with a train from Paignton with a Hawksworth brake coach, leading, and Collett coaches, about 1955. AUTHOR'S COLLECTION

Fig. 155. 5035 Coity Castle idles past Paddington Goods depot with an express from Cardiff, about 1956. A 1930s enamel sign for Virol adorns the goods depot. AUTHOR'S COLLECTION

Fig. 156. 5027 Farleigh Castle has come off a stopping passenger to Reading shed yard by the over-girder turntable, about 1956. 5982, in the background, was one of Reading's Halls. AUTHOR'S COLLECTION.

British Railways Castle Swansong

Diesel traction had been a fact of life on the Western Region since 1958. Although some updates to Castles continued long after the introduction of their successors, by the early 1960s the end of Castle working on BR was in sight.

There were to be a number of runs to celebrate the Castle's long and glorious career and they were to go out with a cataclysmic bang rather than an ignominious whimper. Their actions were to inspire others to preserve some of the remaining engines and leave a legacy that steam enthusiasts can enjoy to this day.

Fig. 157. 5030 Shirburn Castle, with a Cardiff Canton shed plate, at Bristol Temple Meads on a B lamps stopper, likely a running in turn from Swindon, about 1954. 4575 class 2-6-2T is in the background. AUTHOR'S COLLECTION

Fig. 158. 5090 Neath Abbey in repose at Shrewsbury's Coleham depot, about 1955. Like much else at Shrewsbury, the depot was shared with the LNWR, later LMS. AUTHOR'S COLLECTION

High Speed Test Run
Wolverhampton to Paddington
Locomotive: 7030 Cranbrook Castle
Load: 5 Coaches 176 tons (179 tonnes) tare, 180 tons (183 tonnes) full
15 May 1962
(RED Actual time denotes behind schedule, GREEN in front or on time)

Distance miles (km)		Place on journey (including junctions)	Schedule time mins	Actual time mins.s	Speeds mph	(km/h)
0		WOLVERHAMPTON LOW LEVEL	0	0.00	—	
5.2	(8)	Wednesbury		3.43	—	
10.0	(9)	Handsworth	15	13.45	69	(111)
12.6	(20)	SNOW HILL, BIRMINGHAM	20	17.08	38*	(61)
13.4	(22)	*Tyseley*	24	20.24	70	(113)
19.6	(32)	Solihull		24.02	80	(129)
		Permanent way slack				
23.0	(37)	Knowle and Dorridge	29½	27.23	—	
25.5	(41)	Lapworth		31.54	86	(134)
29.7	(48)	Hatton	34½	35.21	65*	(105)
39.9	(64)	Warwick		38.38	84	(135)
35.9	(58)	LEAMINGTON SPA	40	41.10	—	
		Station Stop				
6.1	(10)	Southam Road		7.15	68/78	(109/126)
11.2	(18)	Fenny Compton		11.21	76	(122)
16.2	(26)	Cropredy		15.17	86	(138)
19.8	(32)	BANBURY	17	17.58	78*	(126)
24.9	(40)	Aynho Junction	21	22.14	80/65*	(129/105)
30.1	(48)	Ardley	25	26.32	76	(122)
33.9	(55)	BICESTER	27½	29.07	98	(158)
36.9	(59)	Blackthorn		30.55	103	(166)
39.9	(64)	Brill		32.53	85	(137)
43.2	(70)	Ashendon Junction	34	35.42	61*	(98)
47.2	(76)	Haddenham		39.04	80	(129)
52.6	(85)	PRINCES RISBOROUGH	41½	43.31	62*	(100)
55.8	(90)	Saunderton		46.25	68	(109)
58.5	(94)	West Wycombe		48.48	81/48*	(130/77)
60.8	(98)	HIGH WYCOMBE	50½	51.59	—	
		Station Stop				
4.8	(8)	Beaconsfield		5.15	68	(109)
9.1	(15)	Gerrards Cross		8.21	91	(146)
11.7	(19)	Denham	10½	10.01	103	(166)
16.2	(26)	Northolt Junction	13½	13.11	—	
19.7	(32)	Greenford	15	14.40	—	
23.2	(37)	Old Oak West Junction	18½	18.25	40*	(64)
		Permanent way slack			15	(24)
25.2	(41)	Westbourne Park	20½	21.55	—	
26.5	(43)	PADDINGTON	26	25.15	—	

* Speed restriction

This was intended to be a high-speed test run. The most powerful diesels of the day on the Western Region, however, could just about manage 100mph (160km/h), while many were limited to less than that. As a result one of the fast-disappearing steam engines was chosen. All the Kings were to be withdrawn in 1962, so a Castle it was.

This run in 1962 was with a lighter load than Tregenna Castle's exploits on the Cheltenham Flyer, but it was on a more up and down route with speed restrictions that were adhered to and two station stops at Leamington Spa and High Wycombe. Although the train was

behind time for most of the route, it showeds a very spirited run with two maxima of 103mph (166km/h). What passengers on the platform at Bicester made of the train at almost 100mph (160km/h) can only be imagined. This run was all the more remarkable as the engine had been in store at Old Oak Common prior to the run.

The day of 9 May 1964 was to go down in the annals as a Castle day par excellence. 4079 Pendennis Castle made a start from Paddington and showed all the signs of repeating its earlier good work in 1925 until it melted the firebars and grate. The engine had to be

Fig. 159. 4099 Kilgerran Castle heads the Capitals United Express at Rumney, east of Cardiff, 31 July 1959. The engine carries an 87E Landore, Swansea shed plate. AUTHOR'S COLLECTION

Fig. 161. 5013 Abergavenny Castle in magnificent condition and a credit to Landore depot staff, is seen at Swansea waiting to depart with the Pembroke Coast Express for Paddington, about 1959. The first coach looks like a Centenary coach, which is way off its usual routes. AUTHOR'S COLLECTION

Fig. 160. 5023 Brecon Castle, with the 82C Swindon shed plate, on ECS Empty Coaching Stock working waits for the 'off' at Newton Abbot, 1959. In the 1930s this engine was one of the stars of the Cheltenham Flyer and its work is examined in detail earlier in this chapter. AUTHOR'S COLLECTION

Fig. 162. 4095 Harlech Castle, with a Laira shed plate, hauling some ex-LNER Gresley teak coaches, about 1959. LNER coaches would often come onto the GWR at either Banbury or Oxford from the Great Central routes. AUTHOR'S COLLECTION

taken off at Westbury, where a Modified Hall 6999 Capel Dewi Hall substituted and acquitted itself well, followed by 7025 Sudeley Castle to Plymouth.

The run from Plymouth to Bristol by 7029 Clun Castle demonstrated a performance that was to save her from the breaker's yard. After Cowley Bridge Junction, near Exeter, it was as if 7029 had been shot from a gun and the acceleration in the passenger's seats was palpable. Speeds in the nineties reeled off with frightening rapidity but speed limits and slacks were strictly adhered to, denying Clun Castle a three-figure maximum speed down Wellington Bank or the opportunity to eclipse City of Truro's record. Nevertheless

the engine achieved a record run of 128 minutes net for the 127.4 miles from Plymouth to Bristol. O.S. Nock, the most seasoned observer of engine performance, was almost beside himself.

That memorable day was rounded off by a thrilling run from Bristol Bath Road by Castle 5054 Earl of Ducie from Bristol Temple Meads to Paddington. The run was overseen by a locomotive inspector, Jack Hancock, and possibly that meant there was no liberal interpretation of speed limits to achieve a three-figure maximum. The running was a fine epilogue to a stirring day, with an overall average speed of 74.13mph

Fig. 165. 5091 Cleeve Abbey on ECS/Parcels at Mitre Bridge, Scrubs Lane, near Paddington, about 1961. An Eastern Region 'Blue Spot' fish van has found its way onto the GWR and behind the Castle. New colour light signalling by BR is being installed. AUTHOR'S COLLECTION

Fig. 163. 4078 Pembroke Castle, with a 81D Reading shed plate, on shed there, about 1958. Reading was an indicator of past glories in the sense that the loco would be sent there to work out its days on secondary work. AUTHOR'S COLLECTION

Fig. 164. 5024 Carew Castle on a B lamps stopper at Aller Junction, about 1960. An LMS 57ft Stanier coach is leading, followed by Collett coaches. AUTHOR'S COLLECTION

Fig. 166. 7007 Great Western, the last GWR built Castle, with a 85A Worcester shed plate, gets a refill at Shrewsbury's Coleham depot after working a B lamps stopper, about 1961. AUTHOR'S COLLECTION

(119km/h) and a sustained high-speed dash between Swindon and Paddington at an average of 80.59mph (130km/h). The journey was completed in 95 minutes and 18 seconds for the 117¾ mile (189km) distance – a proper Bristolian job.

Other special Castle trains were run from the now London Midland Region shed of Tyseley, coded 2A, and this continued for some months with privately purchased engines after the end of Western Region steam in December 1965.

The Castle Story Continues

The generally accepted belief in the later 1960s was that Castles had reached the end of the line in terms of active service, and with BR that was certainly the case. It was thought there would be 4073 Caerphilly Castle in the Science Museum in Kensington and that would be it.

Privately preserved Castles were to continue the story after BR had originally banned steam from its metals, with the exception of the Vale of Rheidol, which it still owned, and the LNER's Flying Scotsman, which the wily Alan Pegler had contractually obliged BR to run on their tracks when he purchased the engine.

This summary of the remaining eight preserved Castles does not include their numerous workings on heritage preserved railways within Britain. Much of their later work both on and off Network Rail metals is available to view commercially on video or free to view at the point of delivery on YouTube.

4073 Caerphilly Castle
Science Museum, Kensington, June 1961; the National Railway Museum, York; then STEAM Museum of the Great Western Railway, Swindon (fig. 167).

4079 Pendennis Castle
Hauled the last Birkenhead to Paddington express as far as Birmingham on 4 March 1967. The engine was sold to Hamersley Iron in Australia in 1977. It was repatriated in 2000 to the Great Western Society at Didcot, where the locomotive is being overhauled to main-line running condition in 2018 (fig. 168).

Fig. 167. 4073 Caerphilly Castle with the tender coupling correctly stowed under the left hand buffer at STEAM, Museum of the Great Western Railway, Swindon, September 2017. AUTHOR'S COLLECTION

Fig. 168. 4079 Pendennis Castle nears completion at the Great Western Society's works at Didcot, November 2017. AUTHOR'S COLLECTION

5029 Nunney Castle
Bought from Woodham's scrapyard in 1976, it was moved to the GWS Didcot, where it was first steamed in 1980. Owned by Jeremy Hosking, the locomotive left Didcot in the mid-1990s to work on the main line on heritage excursions. After a period out of service it returned to the main line in 2008, but is currently out of service at Williton West Somerset Railway. It is expected to be back in service during 2018.

5043 Earl of Mount Edgcumbe
Bought by the then Birmingham Railway Museum to provide spare parts for 7029 Clun Castle in 1973. After a thorough overhaul the loco first steamed in

Fig. 169. 5043 Earl of Mount Edgcumbe glides effortlessly and silently towards Wilmcote Station from Stratford-upon-Avon with the Shakespeare Express, August 2017. AUTHOR'S COLLECTION

2008. It has distinguished itself on main-line running with its regular Shakespeare Express and other Vintage Trains runs (fig. 169). In 2014 the engine astonished the steam world by beating Clun Castle's fifty-year-old record set on 9 May 1964. This was from an engine that is limited on the main line to 75mph (121km/h)!

5051 Drysllwyn Castle or Earl Bathurst

Both names are used. Arrived at GWS Didcot in 1970 and was restored to main-line running order in 1980, appearing at the Rocket 150 celebrations in May that year. The engine was subsequently a star performer during the GWR 150 celebrations in 1985 and hauled many trains that summer, both as a singleton and double-headed. The engine also hauled the

GWS vintage train of restored GWR coaches. The locomotive's boiler certificate expired in 1990 and it returned to the tracks in 1998. Following a second expiry in 2008, the engine now awaits resources for a further overhaul (fig. 170).

5080 Defiant

This loco left the Barry scrapyard in 1974 bound for Tyseley and intended as a donor engine for 7029. It was restored to running condition in 1988. When its boiler certificate expired it was moved to the Buckinghamshire Railway Society at Quainton Road, near Aylesbury, where it was a static exhibit until 2017. The engine was then returned to Tyseley with a view to a further restoration to running condition (fig. 171).

Fig. 170. 5051 Dryslwyn Castle awaits its turn for overhaul at the GWS depot at Didcot, October 2017. 5900 Hinderton Hall also waits. AUTHOR'S COLLECTION

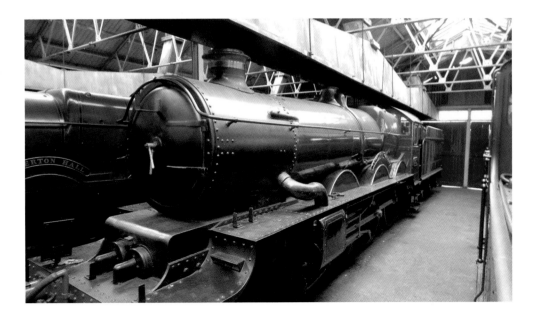

Fig. 171. 5080 Defiant also awaits overhaul at Tyseley in the company of 4965 Rood Ashton Hall (left) and 5043 Earl of Mount Edgcumbe (right), October 2017. AUTHOR'S COLLECTION

Fig. 172. 7029 Clun Castle is in immaculate condition and a credit to Tyseley Locomotive Works after its re-dedication ceremony, October 2017. 5080 Defiant, without its smokebox number plate, and 5043, with its own in place, look on. AUTHOR'S COLLECTION

7027 Thornbury Castle

Another acquisition from Woodham's Barry scrapyard by the Birmingham Railway Museum in 1972. The loco was subsequently acquired by Pete Waterman, the music producer, television personality, railway entrepreneur and noted railway modeller. The loco was sold in 2016 to the owner of Crosville motor services, who also owns 4936 Kinlet Hall. Parts of the loco reside in a bus depot in Weston-super-Mare, while others are away under restoration. The aim is to run the loco in after overhaul on the West Somerset Railway and then offer it out for main-line running.

7029 Clun Castle

This loco never suffered the ignominy and uncertainty of a Barry stay as it was bought straight from British

Railways and formed the nucleus of the Tyseley fleet. The engine distinguished itself over Shap and on the Settle and Carlisle line in 1967, arriving at Hellifield almost seventeen minutes early on a journey scheduled for seventy minutes. Later on 7029 was to share the plaudits with 5051 during the Great Western 150 celebrations in 1985. After another overhaul the loco was re-dedicated in October 2017 at a ceremony at Tyseley (fig. 172), where she was joined by 5043, 5080 and other Great Western engines.

Castles were always the doyen of GWR locomotives and they have retained that status in the public eye. They have now been working longer in preservation than they were in railway service, although not at the same level of intensity, and have an assured long-term future.

CHAPTER SIX

KING CLASS LOCOMOTIVES

A Speedy Genesis

The story of the Castles in Chapter 4 alluded to the introduction of the Southern Railway's Lord Nelson class, which was to exceed the theoretical tractive effort figure of the Castles, a value the GWR and Sir Felix Pole had made much of in their publicity at the introduction of the Castles in 1923. The Castle figure was 31,625lb (141kN) and Lord Nelson 33,500lb (149kN).

Castles distinguished themselves on the LNER and LMSR, and yet the nine days of the General Strike in 1926 stopped the flow of Welsh steam coal and forced the importation of foreign coal, mostly of inferior steaming quality.

Castles began to lose time on the heaviest West of England expresses. The answer to the coal problem, as was found later, would have been to increase the superheater effectiveness. Coupled with the Lord Nelson issue, however, it was decided to design a new engine that would take care of both the Southern Railway and the perceived lack of power on the heaviest of trains.

The overriding influence of the Civil Engineers Department was brought into this mix, since they imposed the maximum axle loading that the bridges carrying track could withstand. Before any substantial increase in weight from larger locomotives could be contemplated, some bridge strengthening and negotiation had to take place. Collett had already had to compromise with the Castle's boiler when that class had to have a specially constructed boiler to keep within the then axle loading limits of 20 tons (20.3 tonnes).

Fig. 173. 6000 King George V surrounded by fellow GWR locomotives and exhibits at STEAM, Museum of the Great Western Railway, Swindon, September 2017. AUTHOR'S COLLECTION.

J. C. Lloyd, the Chief Civil Engineer, was sent for and it transpired that only four bridges needed to be strengthened on the proposed routes to accommodate the 22 ton (22.4 tonnes) axle load. This meant that originally Kings would be restricted to routes from Paddington to Plymouth and Wolverhampton, although this was later relaxed to include Cardiff and Shrewsbury.

Sir Felix Pole then issued two directives in the winter of 1926. The first was to the Civil Engineering department, requiring them to have all bridges on the routes required capable of carrying an axle load of 22 tons (22.4 tonnes). He then required the Chief

Mechanical Engineer to have a new class of locomotive ready for traffic for the summer of 1927, and with a maximum axle load of 22 tons (22.4 tonnes) and with the highest possible tractive effort figure.

At the time Pole had not acquired the finance to pay for either scheme, but he saw that as a minor obstacle, believing that he could easily persuade the Board to stump up the cash. He was held in the highest regard by the Board, while his mastery over the publicity surrounding the locomotive exchanges and the coup of getting the King to drive one of the GWR's engines was seen as a masterstroke for the company's prestige.

The pressure was well and truly on for the Chief Mechanical Engineer's department, faced with challenges from the Southern's Lord Nelson, the much anticipated LMS Royal Scot and the rejuvenated LNER A3 Pacifics, the changes to which were largely brought about thanks to observation of Pendennis Castle at the exchange.

Sir Felix Pole was expecting a Super Castle. The selection of 'Cathedral' class as the prototype's working title was common knowledge in Swindon and the surrounding district.

The tractive effort formula used was this:

$$\text{Tractive Effort} = \frac{\begin{array}{c}\text{Boiler Pressure} \times \text{No. of} \\ \text{Cylinders} \times \text{Piston Dia.} \times \text{Stroke} \\ \times\ 85\%\end{array}}{\text{Driving Wheel Diameter}}$$

The high tractive effort required meant that everything on the top line needed to increase, while the driving wheel diameter reduction could be decreased to increase the final figure. The notional value of 85 per cent took account of mainly heat losses from the boiler and firebox. A theoretically perfectly insulated boiler and firebox would have a 100 per cent value.

In the end the cylinders were increased to 16¼in (41cm) and the stroke to 28in (71cm), compared with a Castle at 16in (41cm) by 26in (66cm).

Boiler pressure was raised from 225psi (15.51 bar) on the Castle to 250psi (17.23 bar) on the Super Castle or Cathedral.

A reduction of driving wheel diameter from 6ft 8½in (2.04m) on the Castle to 6ft 6in (1.98m)

was enough to swing the tractive effort value to be 40,300lb (179.26kN).

This was way in excess of any other British passenger steam locomotive at the time and was to remain so. Paradoxically the 40,300lb (179.26kN) figure was downgraded at subsequent overhauls by the use of 16in (41cm) cylinders.

F. W. Hawksworth then translated this data into terms for a workable engine within a few months. By December 1926 Castle class 5001 Llandovery Castle was trialled with 6ft 6in (1.98m) driving wheels and the engine ran like this until 1928 in order to establish if there were any in-service issues with the smaller diameter driving wheel. It would have been surprising if there had been, as the new dimension was only at the lower limit of tyre wear on the larger wheels. Nevertheless, the data had to be acquired.

A King in the United States

The Baltimore and Ohio Railroad on the eastern seaboard of the United States was to celebrate its centenary in 1927 and there was to be a cavalcade of the latest in motive power. It was only natural that the birthplace of the railways should be asked to send a representative to help them celebrate. The B&O president commissioned the noted author and enthusiast Edward Hungerford to visit the Stockton and Darlington Railway celebrations in 1925, where he met Sir Felix Pole. Hungerford proposed that a British engine visit Baltimore in 1927 for the celebrations, which would be known as the 'Fair of the Iron Horse'. Sir Felix Pole could see the publicity opportunity for the GWR and readily agreed, provided it was a GWR engine. It was originally thought a Castle would suffice, as they had at Wembley, but the Super Castle was well enough developed for it to go.

Pole realized that a GWR engine at the B&O celebrations was representing not just the GWR but Great Britain, as no other British railway would be present. His publicity antennae were fully extended when he also realized that a class name change from Cathedral was necessary and desirable. King George V was consulted and readily agreed that the prototype locomotive be named after him; the other Kings would also be similarly honoured with names from Royal ancestry.

The first locomotive was to cost £7,546, a hefty increase from the first Castle, but there were additional tooling costs as well as the non-standard driving wheels and bogie.

This was another of Pole's publicity coups bordering on genius. The cost of shipping the first engine, 6000 King George V, to the USA and its associated support costs paled into insignificance against the priceless publicity and promotion the GWR was to receive. The King class would follow on from the other GWR publications and the advertising copy almost wrote itself: the King of Locomotives, power, Majesty and so on.

In one fell swoop Pole had demolished the rest of the 'Big Four' opposition. The Southern's Lord Nelson, which had been out for only a few months, was comprehensively trounced in the tractive effort stakes, as was Royal Scot from the LMS, which was to suffer from indifferent steaming qualities until Stanier re-boilered the class with a GWR-type taper boiler and Belpaire firebox years later. The LNER managed a bit better with the A3 boiler pressure increased to 220psi (15.2 bar), but that still gave a tractive effort of only 36,465lb (162.2kN). Even the LNER A4 introduced in 1935 could not compete in tractive effort terms, while the LMS Duchess approached the King's figure but did not eclipse it.

When the designers and draughtsmen finalized the design it turned out that the axle loading was now 22½ tons (22.86 tonnes). The civil engineers were once again consulted and this time they acquiesced to the request that the engines be permitted to run over the bridges on the line from Paddington to Plymouth and from Wolverhampton to Paddington via Bicester, instead of via Oxford.

Although tractive effort was a largely theoretical value, this was what mattered in the minds of the public as then they had no other data to go on. Years later both A4s and Duchesses would be seen to be the more powerful engines after dynamometer car tests, but then they were much larger engines at 102 and 108 tons (104 and 110 tonnes) respectively, compared with a King at only 89 tons (90.4 tonnes), all excluding tenders and their loads.

Before King George V went to Maryland it was exhibited at a series of events on the GWR system described as the most powerful locomotive in the land. It attracted large crowds. a small entrance fee was charged and the proceeds were put towards the 'Helping Hand' fund, which typically supported widows and children of GWR employees who had died in service. The engine was turned out as the last example to use the 1922 livery of the garter crest; all successive engines that year would have the 1927 livery of the twin heraldic shields on lined-out locomotives.

Just before despatch to the USA, King George V was fitted with a Westinghouse pump on the right-hand side of the smokebox to brake US coaching stock. Westinghouse pumps and braking systems were common on the GE section of the LNER, but not used on the GWR.

In the few months between Pole's edict and the finished engine being shipped to the USA, all stops were pulled out at Swindon to ensure the locomotive would acquit itself with distinction across the Atlantic.

The engine upheld the proud tradition of the Stars and Castles on the Cornish Riviera Express on 20 July 1927, but by 3 August the boiler was off the frames and the engine was loaded onto the SS *City of Chicago* at Roath Dock, Cardiff, for the almost three-week journey to the United States.

Whatever Pole's expectations were as to the engine's reception, they were to be exceeded by the hyperbole generated by the *New York Tribune* even before the engine landed. This article was printed while 6000 King George V was still on the high seas.

A DISTINGUISHED ENVOY

This Great Western Railway of England will send as an exhibit to the Baltimore and Ohio centenary this fall the first of its new 'King' class locomotives. Breathes there a man with no soul so dead that he doesn't thrill a little at such news? Especially when he learns that this engine, now under construction, will be capable of a speed of eighty miles an hour, the most powerful locomotive ever built for an English railway.

Somewhere in the breast of every normal homo sapiens there stretches a chord that vibrates only to the sight of a fine locomotive. Even now, with aeroplanes and motors to bid against it in its own field of romantic interest, the steam locomotive retains its fascination. There are probably a number of reasons for this. We can think of at least two — its unusually demonstrative nature and its extraordinary beauty.

Man has devised no other machine that expresses its feelings so frankly and so unmistakably. A locomotive sighs, it pants, it coughs, it barks; it emits empassioned (sic) shrieks and mournful toots; it puts forth staccato protests at hauling a heavy load or climbing a steep grade; it purrs ecstatically as it romps along the rails at a mile a minute; it can hiss and throb and snort and tinkle. And in addition to all these auditory forms of expression it has its visual signs, its plumes of steam spelling surplus energy, its belchings of black smoke denoting determination, its sparks at night registering passion.

This new English locomotive that is coming over, the first of its race to pay us a visit since the Chicago World's Fair in 1893, will bear the name King George V and be one of twenty, each bearing the name of an English monarch.

Despite several inaccuracies in the text and the omission that a good deal of the GWR was in Wales, the article created widespread interest that was only surpassed when the engine took to the rails across the pond.

The quality of the finish and the sewing machine-like progress of the engine impressed all as much as the clear exhaust, indicating complete coal combustion. The engine, although small by US standards, impressed all who saw her and some railways even modified their own engines to resemble the Swindon product.

As Britain had been pioneers in commercial rail travel, King George V was given the honour of leading the procession of the exhibits.

Driver Young of Old Oak Common, who had distinguished himself in the Castle locomotive exchanges of 1925 and 1926, was the natural choice as driver.

Meanwhile, the remaining five of the first batch of six engines were hard at work on the West of England main line. There had been reports of instability at high speed and the engines rolling alarmingly as though they were 2-cylinder engines with out of balance valve gear and driving wheels, or even resembled the River class tank engines on the London, Brighton and South Coast Railway years earlier. This culminated in the derailment of a bogie of 6003 King George IV at Midgham on the Berks and Hants line on 10 August 1927. This might be regarded as a misfortune, but even here the GWR was lucky in that the derailment took place on a piece of plain track and the engine was brought safely to a halt with only minimal damage

and no casualties. This event took place from a speed of 60mph (97km/h). Had the engine been running over points or a crossing it would almost certainly have been fully derailed with injury and/or death and serious damage.

The fault was quickly traced to a deficiency in the bogie springing and Stanier was contacted in the US to make a simple adjustment to enable King George V to run safely on the B&O main line.

King George V's ability to run up to 75mph (121km/h) with the test train on the main line was to cause consternation among the passengers, many of whom were unused to such speeds in the USA. There was a report of requests to slow down from some of the contingent, but this turned out to be a kind of warning that coming up ahead there was a curve upon which there was a 30mph (49km/h) speed limit. Driver Young had to learn the road as he drove along it, although he had a pilot-man with him.

King George V was presented with a bell, which in the US is a mandatory warning device for road crossings and such; the engine carried it for its entire working life and beyond.

Upon completion of the visit the locomotive was also presented with two pairs of commemorative gold medallions, which adorn the cab side to this day.

Back in Britain the 247-minute timing of the Cornish Riviera Express from Paddington to Plymouth was cut to the even 240 minutes. In addition the GWR advertised a trip from Paddington to Swindon to visit Swindon Works – the birthplace of the Kings and hauled by a King. This was for an all-in price of 5 shillings (25p). The inaugural run with 700 passengers was sold out and a further excursion a week later had to have two complete trains to accommodate the eager passengers. As the GWR would have put it, the passengers were 'boys of all ages'.

It is worth noting that the Cheltenham Flyer of the period was allowed 75 minutes for the Swindon to Paddington leg of the journey, which 6001 King Edward VII completed in 68½ minutes.

King Class: Design Details

Hawksworth was Chief Draughtsman at the time of the Kings' design and it fell to him to produce the design that would fit the specification outlined by Sir Felix Pole.

The boiler had to be considerably enlarged and lengthened by an amount that was to make the coupled wheel spacing 1ft 6in (45.7cm) longer than the Castle, thereby making it impossible to swap coupling rods between the different classes of engines in the way we have reported with Stars and Castles. The rest of the valve gear layout, however, remained the same as those predecessors but with larger piston valves. The enlarged boiler was given the designation Standard No 12.

The reduced driving wheel diameter put more space pressure on an area of the bogie that was already tight for space. The bogie wheel diameter was similarly reduced by 2in (5cm) to 3ft (0.91m), the same amount by which the driving wheels had been reduced.

The Churchward bogie had its weaknesses with riveted joint failures. It was decided that a plate frame bogie, in the case of the Kings, would solve this problem. The inside cylinders were in the way and this led to a front bogie wheel with an outside frame and the trailing wheel with an inside frame, a completely novel arrangement for the GWR and one of the Kings' most distinctive external features. Inside and outside bearing bogie axleboxes had been seen before, but not a mixture on the same bogie. Between the bogie wheels was a cross shaft upon which was mounted the lateral side-play springs of the bogie mounting, in further shades of de Glehn. The cross-shaft ends protruded beyond the bogie plate frame sides, another distinctive Kings feature.

Fig. 174. 6000 bogie with outside framed front wheel with coil springs (added after the Midgham derailment) and inside frame rear. The lateral springing cross shaft appears prominently. *STEAM, Swindon, September 2017. AUTHOR'S COLLECTION.*

The equalizing bar present on the Stars wouldn't fit on a bogie that had outside and inside axleboxes and was consequently abandoned. The bogie wheels had originally been fitted with short laminated springs, but under test after the Midgham derailment it was found that the vertical play of the front axle was very limited, which meant that if there were a small change in track level the wheels would not be touching the rail: a clear case for instability and an explanation of the rolling movement reported earlier. Substantial coil springs were fitted to the leading axle with increased vertical travel.

The longer wheelbase of the coupled wheels led to the fitting of slides to allow the rear driving wheels to move laterally. To accommodate this movement the rear coupling-rod bush was made spherical. This was similar to a device called a Cartazzi slide, which was used in rear pony trucks on GWR 2-6-2 tank engines and LNER Pacific and V2 pony trucks.

Kings in Production

King George V was the prototype in July 1927, but a further five locomotives quickly followed a month later:

6001	King Edward VII
6002	King William IV
6003	King George IV
6004	King George III
6005	King George II
6006	King George I

The naming of the class worked backwards from the current reigning monarch, although some changes were made to this system in later years.

The similarly named members of the Star class were renamed 'Monarch' as opposed to King. This affected numbers 4021–4030 (for details *see* Appendix I). Even though the legendary, if mythical, King Arthur did not a feature in the new class, the ancient Duke 4-4-0 3257 King Arthur had its name removed.

The class was brought up to twenty in 1928 by the addition of another fourteen class members:

6007	King William III
6008	King James II
6009	King Charles II
6010	King Charles I
6011	King James I
6012	King Edward VI
6013	King Henry VIII
6014	King Henry VII
6015	King Richard III
6016	King Edward V
6017	King Edward IV
6018	King Henry VI
6019	King Henry V

The Cartazzi slides that had been introduced earlier to afford some lateral play to the rear driving axle were removed.

The last ten Kings weren't built until 1930, by when the Depression was firmly under way.

6020	King Henry IV
6021	King Richard II
6022	King Edward III
6023	King Edward II
6024	King Edward I
6025	King Henry III
6026	King John
6027	King Richard I
6028	King Henry II
6029	King Stephen

This build rounded off the class to numbers compatible with the other railways' crack express locomotives: SR Merchant Navy, LMS Duchesses and LNER A4.

These last engines varied slightly externally from their forebears in the nature of the inside cylinder valve covers (figs. 175 and 176).

6029 was renamed in May 1936 upon the accession of Edward VIII, although the name was not changed again after the abdication, despite the fact that he had not been crowned or anointed.

After the abdication of Edward VIII, 6028 was renamed King George VI, the latest reigning male monarch, in January 1937 while the engines were in revenue service.

Fig. 175. 6016 King Edward V with original inside cylinder valve covers and with 1934 'shirt button' livery at Swindon works, about 1936. GREAT WESTERN TRUST

Fig. 176. A steamy 6023 King Edward II with later inside cylinder valve covers, as built on engines 6020–29, Didcot, August 2017. AUTHOR'S COLLECTION

Kings in Detail: Modifications

Although the Kings were a small class of locomotives, there were detail differences between class members throughout their lives. Some details, such as upper lamp bracket positions and the smokebox door step, evolved much as the Stars and Castles had done in the 1930s and later. In early BR days a light blue livery was experimented with, as well as a darker blue. The former livery appears in some images of 6023 in preservation.

Streamlining

As with the Castles, the streamlining experiment was extended to a King, 6014 King Henry VII. The engine later lost all the streamlining fittings except the V fronted cab. The engine also had a cab roof ventilator. This feature proliferated through the rest of the class, but not until 1954.

Mechanical Lubricators and Steampipes

Initially the engines were fitted with sight feed lubricators.

The earlier mechanical lubricator position was behind the steam pipe on the right-hand side (fig. 177). The later position was in front of the steam pipe on the same side (fig. 178). The move was reputedly due to inside motion access issues. The steampipes are a later modification to prevent cracking due to flexing.

Fig. 178. 6000 at the STEAM Museum with the later position lubricator fitted on the first locomotive, November 2017. The wooden bell plinth is visible and this modification also affected the centre lamp iron. The loco carries an 82C Swindon shed plate, to which it was never allocated, but is rather a homage to its current home. AUTHOR'S COLLECTION

Slotted Bogie Cross-Member

Some class members were fitted with a slotted bogie cross-member (fig. 179), which was said to increase cooling to the bogie bearing surfaces.

Small Cab Side Window

Only one of the class, 6001 King Edward VII, was fitted with this seemingly extraordinary feature (fig. 181).

Coned or Parallel Locomotive Buffer Shanks

Some class members were built with Churchward-type coned buffer shanks and others with the parallel Collett-type buffer shanks.

Fig. 177. 6023 at Didcot with the earlier pattern lubricator position on a later locomotive, August 2017. AUTHOR'S COLLECTION

Fig. 179. 6021 King Richard II on an express passenger train at Knowle and Dorridge station, heading for Paddington from Snow Hill, 31 March 1962. The loco has a slotted front bogie cross member. There was a fatal crash at the station in 1963 involving a shunting goods train and a diesel hydraulic of the Western class. GREAT WESTERN TRUST

Fig. 180. 6029 King Edward VIII with 83D Laira shed plate at Dawlish with solid bogie stretcher, 22 June 1954. The Collett coaches are still in GWR livery. GREAT WESTERN TRUST

Fig. 181. 6001 King Edward VII, featuring an Old Oak Common shed plate and a small window on the cab side, draws an express at Norton Fitzwarren heading for Taunton and Bristol, about 1954. It was around here that a King came to grief during World War II. STEAM, MUSEUM OF THE GREAT WESTERN RAILWAY

Fig. 182. 6017 King Edward IV, with an 83D Laira shed plate with the appended SC for a Self-Cleaning smokebox, on what looks like a running in turn from Swindon works at Bristol, June 1957. The engine has a double blast pipe and chimney and a four-row superheater, but it retains the older coned engine buffers. GREAT WESTERN TRUST

Fig. 183. 6024 King Edward I, displaying an Old Oak Common shed plate, at Wolverhampton Stafford Road, by which time Kings would run to Shrewsbury with the Cambrian Coast Express, September 1960. Visible are a double blast pipe and chimney, four-row superheater and parallel buffer shanks. GREAT WESTERN TRUST

Double Blast Pipes and Chimneys and Four-Row Superheaters

BR introduced these features after experiments following the 1948 Locomotive Exchanges. Eventually all class members were so treated (fig. 183), transforming them into even more free-running engines with greater economy on substandard coal.

Forward Frame Lifting Eyes

A minor modification was to cut out a circular piece from the forward frames, just by the inside cylinder spindle covers, and bush it for use by a lifting crane (*see* figs 176 and 182).

Bogie Strengtheners

Even with the specially designed bogie there were problems with cracking. This was solved by bolting and welding strengthener pieces onto the bogie side frames (fig. 184).

6000 Bell Plinth

A minor modification that only affected King George V was the addition of a wooden plinth underneath the bell mounted on the front bufferbeam. This also affected the position of the centre bufferbeam lamp bracket.

Fig. 184. The strengthening pieces on the bogie of 6023 are those in front of the rear bogie wheel and those behind the front bogie wheel, secured with eight bolts and faintly U-shaped. August 2017. AUTHOR'S COLLECTION

		Summary of King Class Modifications
Year	Loco numbers	Detail
1947	6022	Four row superheater, mechanical lubricator
1948	6009 to 6025	Dark blue livery, red cream and grey lining
		Square edged step to inside cylinder valve spindle casing and chequer plate
1949	Class members	Programme of four-row superheater fit to rest of class
1950	Class members	Light blue livery, black and white livery
1952	6001 to 6017	Precursor to double chimney with sleeve and modified jumper top – improved draughting. Self-cleaning smokebox. Reversion to GWR mid-chrome green
1953	6001	After improved draughting, ran 796 ton (809 tonnes) 25-coach train from Reading to Stoke Gifford, near Bristol
1954	Class members	Sliding cab-roof ventilators fitted to rest of class
1955	6000, 6003, 6020	Large-diameter single chimney fitted
	6015	First double chimney and double blast-pipe, rolled out to other class members, fourteen in all
1956	Class members	Class withdrawn for bogie strengthening plates fit
	6004	First standard cast iron chimney, designed by North Eastern Region of BR
1958	Class members	Basket-type spark arresters
1959	Class members	New pattern buffers, partial fit

CHAPTER SEVEN

KING CLASS LOCOMOTIVES: ALLOCATION AND WORK

As with all top-link express engines, the majority were put to work on the heaviest West of England trains, with some going to Wolverhampton Stafford Road for Birmingham services. Later, with the advent of diesels in the west, some went to Cardiff. Bristol Bath Road had Kings for the restored post-war Bristolian, but they didn't last there.

The allocations for the first sheds of their existence were as follows:

1927
Paddington: 6000, 6001, 6003, 6005
Laira: 6002, 6004

1928
Paddington: 6007, 6009, 6011, 6013, 6015, 6017
Laira: 6006, 6008, 6010, 6016, 6018
Newton Abbot: 6012, 6014
Stafford Road: 6019

1930
Paddington: 6021, 6025, 6026, 6027, 6028, 6029
Laira: 6020, 6022, 6024
Newton Abbot: 6023

Fig. 185. 6028 King Henry II is pictured with a down express in Sonning cutting, near Reading, about 1931. The engine is in its as built condition with the later smoothed-over inside cylinder valve spindle covers but has the top lamp iron on the smokebox top, complete with a small step on the smokebox door to access it. The engine is in 1927 livery and heading for Reading. GREAT WESTERN TRUST

At the end of the GWR's existence their allocations were as follows:

31 December 1947
Paddington: 6001, 6003, 6007, 6009, 6013, 6014, 6015, 6021, 6025
Laira: 6000, 6002, 6004, 6010, 6012, 6016, 6017, 6019, 6020, 6022, 6026, 6029
Newton Abbot: 6018, 6023, 6024, 6027, 6028
Stafford Road: 6005, 6006, 6008, 6011

1950 Summary
Paddington 10; Bristol Bath Road 3; Laira 10; Stafford Road 7

At the end of their existence on BR the home sheds were as follows:

1962
Paddington: 6000, 6005, 6009, 6010, 6011, 6018, 6019, 6021, 6025, 6026, 6028, 6029
Stafford Road: 6001, 6002, 6006, 6007, 6008, 6012, 6013, 6014, 6015, 6016, 6017, 6020, 6022, 6027
Cardiff Canton: 6003, 6004, 6023, 6024

The King class soon settled down to regular hard work after their teething problems over weights and springing had been addressed. They became the steadiest of locomotives at speed and a byword for hauling power on the GWR.

An experienced GWR crewman from Didcot shed recounted: 'To ride on a King was as near to riding on a turbine one could get on a steam engine, the power was almost unbelievable, you opened the regulator and it responded immediately.' It's only fair to say he was not used to crack express engines generally.

He also revived the tale of a piece of string fitted to the bell on King George V and would kid newcomers that to fire a King properly you had to ring the bell at the front of the engine. In other words, throw the coal down to the far end of the firebox, and while doing this, pull the string as a demonstration. Of course the rooky fireman would never be able to ring the bell by normal firing.

One feature of the Kings that was inherited from its illustrious predecessors was the sure-footedness of the engine enhanced by the higher overall weight. Traction and, to some extent, acceleration were enhanced and Kings became a cliché for power unlimited. Train crews have said Castles to be happiest when running in the speeds of the eighties, but Kings were said to be good in the nineties; later tests, however, proved that both classes could exceed 100mph (160km/h).

The early work of King class locomotives is examined in the following tables. The same down journey or part of it has been examined so that direct comparisons can be made. The down journey was always more demanding by nature of the prevailing winds and slightly adverse gradients out of Paddington as far as Reading.

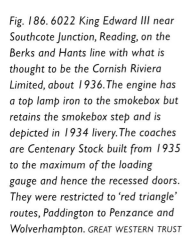

Fig. 186. 6022 King Edward III near Southcote Junction, Reading, on the Berks and Hants line with what is thought to be the Cornish Riviera Limited, about 1936. The engine has a top lamp iron to the smokebox but retains the smokebox step and is depicted in 1934 livery. The coaches are Centenary Stock built from 1935 to the maximum of the loading gauge and hence the recessed doors. They were restricted to 'red triangle' routes, Paddington to Penzance and Wolverhampton. GREAT WESTERN TRUST

Fig. 187. 6003 King George IV, equipped with earlier valve spindle covers but lowered top lamp bracket and step, arrives with an Express at Kingswear, 1938. The single track from Paignton is now the Paignton and Dartmouth Steam Railway and the train's final destination was Dartmouth, which could only be accessed on the GWR ferry The Mew across the River Dart. STEAM, MUSEUM OF THE GREAT WESTERN RAILWAY

The Down Cornish Riviera Express
Date: July 1927
Locomotive: 6011 King James I
Load to Westbury 14 Coaches 492 tons (500 tonnes) tare, 525 tons (533 tonnes) full
Load to Taunton 12 Coaches 421 tons (428 tonnes) tare, 450 tons (457 tonnes) full
Load to Exeter 10 Coaches 357 tons (363 tonnes) tare, 380 tons (386 tonnes) full
Load to Plymouth 7 Coaches 253 tons (257 tonnes) tare, 270 tons (274 tonnes) full
(RED Actual time denotes behind schedule, GREEN in front)

Distance miles (km)		Place on journey		Schedule mins	Actual time mins.s	Speeds mph	(km/h)
0.0	(00.0)	PADDINGTON		0	0.0		
1.3	(2.09)	Westbourne Park			3.05		
5.7	(9.17)	Ealing			9.10		
9.1	(14.6)	SOUTHALL		11	12.45	59	(95)
13.2	(21.2)	West Drayton			16.55	65	(105)
18.5	(29.8)	SLOUGH		20	21.35	70.5	(113)
24.2	(38.9)	Maidenhead		25½	26.40	66	(106)
36.0	(57.9)	READING	Slack	37	37.30	40	(64)
44.8	(72.1)	Aldermaston			46.55	65	(105)
53.1	(85.4)	NEWBURY		55½	54.55	61	(98)
58.5	(91.1)	Kintbury			60.10	62.5	(100)
61.5	(98.9)	Hungerford			63.15	61.5	(99)
66.4	(107)	Bedwyn		68½	68.15	58.5	(94)
68.6	(110)	Grafton Curve Junction	P Way Slack		70.50	20	(32)
70.1	(113)	Savernake	Slack		73.55	42.5	(68)
75.3	(121)	Pewsey			79.05	71.5	(115)
81.1	(131)	Patney			83.50	80.5	(130)
86.9	(140)	Lavington Slack	Permanent Way		88.35	20	(32)
95.6	(154)	WESTBURY	Slack	96	98.35	35	(56)
98.5	(159)	Milepost 112¾			102.05	54	(87)

Distance miles (km)	Place on journey		Schedule mins	Actual time mins.s	Speeds mph	(km/h)
101.3 (163)	FROME	Slack		105.30	35	(56)
106.6 (172)	Witham			112.00	53.5	(86)
108.5 (175)	Milepost 122¾			114.15	50.5	(81)
111.9 (180)	Bruton			117.15	83.5	(134)
115.3 (186)	CASTLE CARY	Slack	118	120.00	50	(80)
120.2 (193)	Keinton Mandeville			124.55	67	(108)
125.7 (202)	Somerton			129.45	75	(121)
131.0 (211)	Curry Rivell Junction			134.05	79	(127)
137.9 (222)	Cogload Junction	P Way Slack	140	140.55	10	(16)
142.9 (230)	TAUNTON		144½	147.45	58.5	(94)
144.9 (230)	Norton Fitzwarren			149.45	62.5	(100)
147.5 (237)	Milepost 167¾			152.10	64	(103)
150.0 (241)	Wellington			154.40	58.5	(94)
152.8 (246)	Milepost 173			157.55	42.5	(68)
153.8 (248)	Whiteball Signal Box			159.25	44	(68)
158.8 (256)	Tiverton Junction			164.05	76.5	(123)
161.1 (259)	Cullompton			165.55	80.5	(130)
170.2 (274)	Stoke Canon			173.05	76.5	(123)
173.7 (280)	EXETER ST. DAVIDS		174½	175.55	70	(113)
178.4 (287)	Exminster			179.40	82	(132)
		Permanent Way Slack			10	(16)
188.7 (304)	Teignmouth	Slack		195.25	65	(105)
193.9 (312)	NEWTON ABBOT	Slack	198½	201.25	25	(40)
195.7 (315)	Milepost 216			204.13	50.5	(81)
197.7 (318)	Dainton Signal Box		204½	207.50	60	(97)
202.5 (326)	Totnes		210½	213.35	53	(85)
204.7 (329)	Milepost 225			216.49	31.5	(51)
205.3 (330)	Tigley Signal Box			217.50	29	(47)
207.1 (333)	Rattery Signal Box			221.15	36	(58)
209.4 (337)	Brent		219½	224.10	54	(87)
211.6 (341)	Wrangaton	Permanent Way Slack		226.40	25	(40)
219.0 (352)	Hemerdon Signal Box		231	235.55	68	(109)
221.7 (357)	Plympton			238.30	50	(80)
225.4 (363)	Mutley	Adverse signals				
225.7 (363)	PLYMOUTH NORTH ROAD		240	245.35		

Where the original log taken indicated two speeds the higher of the two has been used, although the overall performance time is the same.

The run was distinctive in that, even with a total of thirteen different impediments put in the way of the train, it managed to arrive at Plymouth North Road only five minutes late. If the net time of 228 minutes is used, discounting all the enforced delays, the train was actually twelve minutes early on the already improved schedule of 240 minutes, as opposed to the previous value of 247 minutes.

This unlikely event was in fact confirmation of the new engine's ability to handle the heaviest long-distance trains and be ahead of the schedule despite difficulties faced by the locos in service. Of course it needed superb handling by the crews to get the best out of the locomotives and the GWR had the right people on the footplate. In a modern-day context Network Rail would have been culpable for the delays and fined.

The next King run considered was two years later. Although the starting load was a bit less, no coaches

Fig. 188. 6019 King Henry V sets out from Paddington with a down express passing Kensal Green, August 1931. Unusually the fireman is looking out of the window instead of hanging over the side by the cab window.
GREAT WESTERN TRUST

The Down Cornish Riviera Express
Date: July 1929
Locomotive: 6000 King George V
Load to Westbury 14 Coaches 479 tons (500 tonnes) tare, 510 tons (533 tonnes) full
Load to Taunton 11 Coaches 378 tons (428 tonnes) tare, 405 tons (457 tonnes) full
Load to Exeter 11 Coaches 378 tons (363 tonnes) tare, 405 tons (386 tonnes) full
(RED Actual time denotes behind schedule, GREEN in front)

Distance miles	(km)	Place on journey		Schedule time mins	Actual time mins.s	Speeds mph	(km/h)
0.0	(00.0)	PADDINGTON		0	0.0		
1.3	(2.09)	Westbourne Park			2.55		
5.7	(9.17)	Ealing			9.10		
9.1	(14.6)	SOUTHALL		11	12.00	60	(97)
13.2	(21.2)	West Drayton					
18.5	(29.8)	SLOUGH		20	20.20	73	(117)
24.2	(38.9)	Maidenhead		25	25.00	72	(116)
31.0	(49.9)	Twyford		30½	30.50	69	(111)
36.0	(57.9)	READING	Slack	36	35.15		
37.8	(60.8)	Southcote Junction			37.20	56	(90)
44.8	(72.1)	Aldermaston					
53.1	(85.4)	NEWBURY		54	51.35	62	(99)
58.5	(91.1)	Kintbury					
61.5	(98.9)	Hungerford					
66.4	(107)	Bedwyn		67	64.05	64	(103)
70.1	(113)	Savernake			68.00	52	(84)
75.3	(121)	Pewsey			72.55	75	(121)
78.8	(127)	Woodborough	P Way Slack		76.10	15	(115)
81.1	(131)	Patney			83.50	55	(89)

Distance miles (km)	Place on journey		Schedule time mins	Actual time mins.s	Speeds mph	(km/h)
86.9 (140)	Lavington					
91.4 (147)	Edington			89.00	82	(32)
95.6 (154)	WESTBURY	Slack	94	92.40		
98.5 (159)	Milepost 112¾			102.05	54	(87)
101.3 (163)	FROME			105.30	35	(56)
106.6 (172)	Witham					
108.5 (175)	Milepost 122¾			108.45	82	(132)
111.9 (180)	Bruton					
115.3 (186)	CASTLE CARY	Slack	116	114.35	60	(97)
120.2 (193)	Keinton Mandeville					
125.7 (202)	Somerton			124.00	72	(116)
129.9 (209)	Langport	Adverse Signals				
137.9 (222)	Cogload Junction	Adverse Signals	137	134.45	55	(89)
142.9 (230)	TAUNTON		142	139.55	57	(92)
144.9 (230)	Norton Fitzwarren					
147.5 (237)	Milepost 167¾					
150.0 (241)	Wellington			147.25	54	(87)
152.8 (246)	Milepost 173					
153.8 (248)	Whiteball Signal Box			153.20	26	(42)
158.8 (256)	Tiverton Junction			158.25	72	(116)
161.1 (259)	Cullompton					
170.2 (274)	Stoke Canon			167.30	81	(123)
173.7 (280)	EXETER ST. DAVIDS (pass)	Slack	171½	170.20	60	(113)

were slipped at Taunton so the load through to Exeter was eleven coaches, a coach more than two years previously. There was only one fewer delay than with 6011 and yet 6000 was able to bring the train to pass Exeter St. David's a full minute before time, with a net time of 166 minutes. This was with a schedule that was three minutes tighter to Exeter than the run two years before.

The long 1 in 1320 climb past Twyford caused a blip into the red, but this was to be the last debit in the journey. The arduous climb to Savernake was breasted at 52mph (84km/h); as this was pre-1933, the Westbury cut-off had not been put in place so there was a slack there at the station, which reduced the credit to nearer 1½ minutes from almost 3 minutes. Similarly the Frome cut-off was only constructed in 1933 during the works to alleviate unemployment during the Great Depression: King George V must have rattled Hannaford's train shed at Frome only slightly at a modest 35mph (56km/h) rather than twice that after the cut-off had been built.

Fig. 189. 6002 King William IV heads away from Paddington to an unknown destination in 1929. The two staff members in the four foot seem oblivious of trains on both sides or of the possibility of one coming along the track they are walking along. STEAM, MUSEUM OF THE GREAT WESTERN RAILWAY

The summit at Whiteball imposed a quite marked speed reduction, but the downhill section from there through Exeter produced a maximum of 81mph (123km/h) at Stoke Canon, just before Cowley Bridge Junction, Exeter.

The train continued past Exeter, still with the eleven coaches that made it about 18 tons (18.3 tonnes) more than the maximum unassisted load usually permitted. Despite a succession of slacks as far as Newton Abbot, King George V met with no further delays and brought the train in to Plymouth North Road in precisely 237 minutes, a full three minutes before time.

The next run described, with 6020 King Henry IV heading the Cornish Riviera Express in 1930, was again on the Berks and Hants line, but this time the recorder, a Major Myers, was only travelling as far as Taunton so the journey ends there. It is nonetheless a remarkable piece of running with 505 tons

Fig. 190. 6018 King Henry VI in repose at Bristol Bath Road in 1934 'shirt button' livery, 1937. Although generally clean, the footplate needs to be swept down to remove ash from opening the smokebox door. GREAT WESTERN TRUST

The Down Cornish Riviera Express
Date: 1930
Locomotive: 6020 King Henry IV
Load to Westbury 505 tonnes (513 tonnes) full
Load to Taunton 430 tons (437 tonnes) full
(RED Actual time denotes behind schedule, GREEN in front)

Distance miles	(km)	Place on journey		Schedule time mins	Actual time mins.s	Speeds mph	(km/h)
0.0	(00.0)	PADDINGTON		0	0.0		
1.3	(2.09)	Westbourne Park			2.37		
5.7	(9.17)	Ealing			8.13		
9.1	(14.6)	SOUTHALL		11	11.36	63	(101)
13.2	(21.2)	West Drayton					
18.5	(29.8)	SLOUGH		20	19.42	76.5	(123)
24.2	(38.9)	Maidenhead		25	24.28	71.6	(115)
31.0	(49.9)	Twyford			30.03	74	(119)
36.0	(57.9)	READING	Slack	36	34.15	45	(72)
37.8	(60.8)	Southcote Junction					
44.8	(72.1)	Aldermaston			43.25	68	(109)
53.1	(85.4)	NEWBURY		54	50.58	62.5	(100)
58.5	(91.1)	Kintbury			55.58	67	(108)
61.5	(98.9)	Hungerford			58.54	61	(98)
66.4	(107)	Bedwyn		67	63.31	65	(105)
70.1	(113)	Savernake			67.19	53	(85)
75.3	(121)	Pewsey			72.03	77.5	(125)
78.8	(127)	Woodborough					
81.1	(131)	Patney			76.42	70.5	(113)
86.9	(140)	Lavington			81.13	79	(127)

Distance miles (km)	Place on journey		Schedule time mins	Actual time mins.s	Speeds mph	(km/h)
91.4 (147)	Edington					
95.6 (154)	WESTBURY		94	89.24		
98.5 (159)	Milepost 112¾			102.05	51	(82)
101.3 (163)	FROME	P Way Slack				
106.6 (172)	Witham					
108.5 (175)	Milepost 122¾			108.26	51	(82)
111.9 (180)	Bruton			111.38	82	(132)
115.3 (186)	CASTLE CARY	Slack	116	114.29	60	(97)
120.2 (193)	Keinton Mandeville			118.57		
125.7 (202)	Somerton			123.54	65	(105)
129.9 (209)	Langport			127.39	77.5	(125)
137.9 (222)	Cogload Junction		137	134.41	70.5	(113)
142.9 (230)	TAUNTON		142	140.57		

(513 tonnes) from Paddington and without the benefit of the Westbury and Frome cut-offs.

This gave a net time of 138 minutes. The Taunton arrival time is that of the slip coach, whereas on other such runs it was the passing time.

The start out of Paddington seemingly always produced some deficit as far as Southall when lifting a prodigious load with a newish fire; but by Slough the train was ahead of time and remained so comfortably throughout the journey to the slip at Taunton. The delays were kept to a minimum and not one could be attributed to the signallers, who would be under strict instructions to ensure a clear road for the train.

Next attention swings to the Birmingham line via Bicester. The accelerated speeds brought to the Paddington to Bristol trains were not thought necessary or achievable with the runs to Snow Hill. Here the GWR was in competition with the LMS out of Euston and a lightly loaded seven-coach express was not seen to be useful or rewarding commercially. Consequently the Birmingham trains were much more

Fig. 191. 6023 King Edward II *drifts down Hemerdon Bank, near Plymouth, with a stopping train, 28 August 1937. No two vehicles are alike, including an inside and outside frame SIPHON G, a MONSTER and a clerestory coach.*
GREAT WESTERN TRUST

Paddington to Leamington Spa
Locomotive: 6017 King Edward IV
415 tons (422 tonnes) tare, 445 tons (452 tonnes) full to Bicester
380 tons (386 tonnes) tare, 407 tons (414 tonnes) full to Banbury
314 tons (319 tonnes) tare, 335 tons (340 tonnes) full to Leamington Spa
(RED Actual time denotes behind schedule)

Distance miles (km)	Place on journey		Schedule mins	Actual time mins.s	Speeds mph	(km/h)
0.0 (00.0)	PADDINGTON		0	0.0		
1.3 (2.09)	Westbourne Park	Adverse Signal		3.6		
3.3 (5.31)	OOC West	P Way Slack		7.31		
7.8 (12.5)	Greenford	P Way Slack	13	16.02		
10.3 (16.6)	Northolt Junction		15.5	20.40		
14.1 (22.7)	Milepost 3¾	P Way Slack				
14.8 (23.8)	Denham			27.57	56	(97)
17.4 (28.0)	Gerrard's Cross			30.55	52	(97)
21.7 (34.9)	Beaconsfield			35.36	51.5	(83)
26.5 (42.6)	HIGH WYCOMBE		32	40.64		
28.8 (46.3)	West Wycombe					
31.5 (50.7)	Saunderton			45.56	47	(76)
33.0 (53.1)	Milepost 22¾					
34.7 (55.8)	PRINCES RISBOROUGH		42	49.10		
40.1 (64.5)	Haddenham			53.00	91.5	(147)
44.1 (71.0)	Ashendon Junction			55.57		
50.4 (81.1)	Blackthorn			61.34	80	(117)
51.6 (83.0)	Milepost 7½ (from Ashendon Jn)					
53.4 (85.9)	BICESTER		58½	63.59		
57.1 (91.9)	Milepost 13					
57.2 (92.0)	Ardley			67.32	63.5	(83)
62.4 (100)	Aynho Junction		67	72.00		
67.5 (109)	BANBURY		72	76.44		
71.1 (114)	Cropredy				69	(117)
76.3 (123)	Fenny Compton			80.52		
81.2 (131)	Southam Road			85.15		
81.2 (131)	Fosse Road				91	(146)
87.3 (140)	LEAMINGTON SPA		90½	92.59		

heavily loaded, with something of a switchback route compared to the Bristol run.

The first run, which finished at Leamington Spa, was another example of a train delayed by external forces but valiantly trying to make up for lost time.

By the end of the London suburbs at Denham the train was about seven minutes behind time with the most challenging parts of the run to come. At Saunderton summit the engine managed 47mph (76km/h), which was creditable enough but not enough to stop the deficit rising to more than seven minutes at Princes Risborough. The top speed of 91.5mph (132km/h)

was achieved at Haddenham shortly afterwards; this was almost equalled at Fosse Road on the run into Snow Hill.

The eventual deficit was cut by two-thirds, giving a net time of 83 minutes. This was a very creditable performance in a comparatively short journey.

Another run over the same route is worthy of inclusion as it shows a King hauling a heavier load at high speed.

The Stafford Road crew left Paddington as if shot from a gun. As a result they encountered traffic and signals before they had even left London. It is a fair

Fig. 192. 6009 King Charles II passes Kensal Green Gasworks on its way out of London with an express, about 1933. The engine is in almost original condition in 1927 livery. STEAM, MUSEUM OF THE GREAT WESTERN RAILWAY

Paddington to Leamington Spa
Locomotive: 6008 King James II
476 tons (484 tonnes) tare, 505 tons (513 tonnes) full to Bicester
445 tons (452 tonnes) tare, 470 tons (476 tonnes) full to Banbury
374 tons (380 tonnes) tare, 400 tons (406 tonnes) full to Leamington Spa
(GREEN Actual time denotes in front of schedule)

Distance miles (km)		Place on journey		Schedule mins	Actual time mins.s	Speeds mph	(km/h)
0.0	(00.0)	PADDINGTON		0	0.0		
1.3	(2.09)	Westbourne Park	Adverse Signal				
3.3	(5.31)	OOC West	Adverse Signal		6.43		
7.8	(12.5)	Greenford		13	12.01		
10.3	(16.6)	Northolt Junction		15.5	14.36		
14.1	(22.7)	Milepost 3					
14.8	(23.8)	Denham			19.04	65	(105)
17.4	(28.0)	Gerrard's Cross			21.46	57.5	(93)
21.7	(34.9)	Beaconsfield			26.22	56.5	(91)
26.5	(42.6)	HIGH WYCOMBE		32	30.44		
28.8	(46.3)	West Wycombe					
31.5	(50.7)	Saunderton			37.04	52	(84)
33.0	(53.1)	Milepost 22¾					
34.7	(55.8)	PRINCES RISBOROUGH		42	40.28		
40.1	(64.5)	Haddenham			44.30	90	(145)
44.1	(71.0)	Ashendon Junction			47.35		
50.4	(81.1)	Blackthorn			53.30	76	(122)
51.6	(83.0)	Milepost 7½ (from Ashendon Jn)					
53.4	(85.9)	BICESTER		58½	55.58		
57.1	(91.9)	Milepost 13					
57.2	(92.0)	Ardley			59.37	62	(98)
62.4	(100)	Aynho Junction		67	64.19		
67.5	(109)	BANBURY	Permanent Way Slack	72	69.12		
71.1	(114)	Cropredy			73.31	52	(84)
76.3	(123)	Fenny Compton			79.01		
81.2	(131)	Southam Road			83.02		
81.2	(131)	Fosse Road	Adverse Signal		84.59	80	(129)
87.3	(140)	LEAMINGTON SPA		90½	89.23		

Fig. 193. 6014 King Henry VII with part of its streamlining removed at Horfield, near Bristol, about 1937. The train would appear to be the Bristolian with Sunshine coaches with the low waistline. The buffet car with the higher waistline looks like the 'Quick Lunch Bar Car' of 1936 that is now at Swindon. Tubular post signals are making an early appearance. STEAM, MUSEUM OF THE GREAT WESTERN RAILWAY

summation to say they were Stafford Road men going home. Even at Greenford the train was almost a minute in credit and by Bicester it was 2½ minutes. A remarkable part of the story is that the train achieved its maximum speed at Haddenham before any coaches were slipped and loaded to 505 tons (513 tonnes). The net time for the run was 86¾ minutes.

The last run to the Midlands also concerns 6008 King James II, through to Snow Hill this time.

The net times were Paddington to Leamington Spa 87¾ minutes, and Leamington Spa to Birmingham Snow Hill 24½ minutes.

A fair load and a speedy run were had as far as just outside Banbury, where the train was brought to a stand outside the station. This meant that there would not be the requisite momentum to slip the Banbury coaches and an unscheduled stop had to be made to detach the slip coaches in the platform. A run that produced timings in which the train was about 1½ minutes in credit saw the balance tip the other way with a 5 minute deficit. Nevertheless the vigorous start from Banbury may well have showered the coach roofs with cinders after depositing 85 tons (86 tonnes) of coaches at the platform. A fine run to Leamington Spa ensued. With the timing slate wiped clean, 6008 brought its train into Snow Hill just inside the scheduled time. Once again a train that was the victim of circumstances beyond its control was brought back to reasonably prompt running by the performance of

the engine and crew. As before there was fine running with the heavier load.

The Shrivenham Collision

In January 1936 the up Penzance sleeper was in collision with five goods vehicles that had become detached from an up mineral train hauled by 2802 from Aberdare to Old Oak Common, due to a broken draw hook. The

Fig. 194. 6028 King Henry II seen at about the time of the Abdication Crisis in 1936. Within a few months it would carry the name King George VI. The location is thought to be between Taunton and Bristol. There is a horsebox between the engine and coaches. GREAT WESTERN TRUST

Paddington to Birmingham Snow Hill
Date: 1930
Locomotive: 6008 King James II
14 coaches 457 tons (464 tonnes) tare, 490 tons (498 tonnes) full to Banbury
12 coaches 405 tons (411 tonnes) tare, 435 tons (442 tonnes) full to Leamington Spa
10 coaches 370 tons (376 tonnes) tare, 400 tons (406 tonnes) full to Snow Hill
(RED Actual Time denotes behind schedule, GREEN in front)

Distance miles (km)		Place on journey		Schedule time mins	Actual time mins.s	Speeds mph	(km/h)
0.0	(00.0)	PADDINGTON		0	0.0		
1.3	(2.09)	Westbourne Park					
3.3	(5.31)	OOC West	Slack	7	7.33	40	(64)
7.8	(12.5)	Greenford			13.03	58	(93)
10.3	(16.6)	Northolt Junction		15.5	15.37	58	(93)
14.8	(23.8)	Denham			20.05	63	(101)
17.4	(28.0)	Gerrard's Cross			22.45	54.5	(88)
21.7	(34.9)	Beaconsfield			27.27	59	(95)
24.2	(38.9)	Tylers Green				69	(111)
26.5	(42.6)	HIGH WYCOMBE	Slack	32	31.50	42	(68)
28.8	(46.3)	West Wycombe			34.45		
31.5	(50.7)	Saunderton			37.58	50.5	(81)
32.2	(53.1)	Milepost 22			38.46	50	(80)
34.7	(55.8)	PRINCES RISBOROUGH		41	41.18	70	(113)
40.1	(64.5)	Haddenham			45.27	83.5	(134)
44.1	(71.0)	Ashendon Junction		49	48.36	52	(84)
47.1	(76.3)	Brill			52.02	69	(111)
50.4	(81.1)	Blackthorn			54.30	75	(121)
53.4	(85.9)	BICESTER		58	56.55	67.5	(109)
57.2	(92.0)	Ardley			60.32	68	(109)
62.4	(100)	Aynho Junction	Slack	67	65.20	60	(97)
64.0	(103)	Kings Sutton			66.55		
67.0	(108)	Milepost 85¾	Adverse Signal Stop		70.27		
67.5	(109)	BANBURY	Unscheduled Station Stop	72	77.00		
71.1	(114)	Cropredy			6.20	51	(82)
76.3	(123)	Fenny Compton			11.35	73.5	(118)
81.2	(131)	Southam Road			15.40	81	(130)
86.3	(139)	Milepost 105	Mileage via Didcot		19.35		
87.3	(140)	LEAMINGTON SPA	Station Stop	91	21.28		
2.0	(3.22)	Warwick			3.20	54.5	(84)
6.2	(9.97)	Hatton			8.12	46	(74)
10.2	(16.4)	Lapworth			12.24	64	(103)
12.9	(20.8)	Knowle and Dorridge			14.51	63	(101)
16.3	(26.2)	Solihull			17.57	68	(109)
21.7	(34.9)	Tyseley			20.58	75	(121)
22.2	(35.7)	Bordesley			22.40		
23.3	(37.5)	BIRMINGHAM SNOW HILL		26	24.35		

Fig. 195. 6018 King Henry VI with dynamometer car passes Ferme Park carriage sidings at Hornsey, in north London, during the Locomotive Exchanges in May 1948. The LNER N2/4 with the condensing apparatus in the background was allocated to King's Cross in 1948. STEAM, MUSEUM OF THE GREAT WESTERN RAILWAY

complete train was 1,100ft long (335m) and weighed 1,100 tons (1,117 tonnes). The collision took place at Shrivenham, some way northeast of Swindon in the Vale of the White Horse.

The 24 ton (24.4 tonne) six-wheeled 'TOAD' brake van took the brunt of the impact. The passenger train engine, 6007 King William III, was forced over onto its right side and the driver was killed, although the fireman escaped serious injury. In the ensuing pile-up one passenger in the sleeper was killed and ten seriously injured.

It was fortunate that, although some of the wooden-bodied coaches had originally been gas lit, they had all been converted to electric lighting, so there was no fire. The signaller, freight train guard and the broken hook were all adjudged to be contributory factors.

The locomotive was so badly damaged that it had to be written off, although some parts were used in its replacement that emerged from the Swindon works in March 1936.

World War II

Kings followed the pattern set by the other two classes covered so far: grindingly relentless hard work with minimal or missed maintenance. Most were worn out at the end of the war. Kings, in common with Castles, had their cab side windows plated over and tarpaulins fitted over the cab and tender fall-plate in order to comply with blackout regulations.

No one incident exemplified the pressure under which the railway and its staff were working than that on 4 November 1940 at Norton Fitzwarren, near Taunton, which involved members of the King class locomotives.

The engine driver was an Old Oak Common man from Paddington. His house had been bombed the previous night but he had still reported for duty as usual. The train he was driving had been delayed by routing through Bristol for operational reasons and was running sixty-eight minutes late.

6028 King George VI, heading an express passenger train of thirteen coaches, was driven from Taunton on the quadruple tracks heading west. These tracks eventually come down to two at Norton Fitzwarren, the junction for the GWR's branch lines to Barnstaple and Minehead.

In the utter darkness of the blackout the driver did not notice that his train had been routed onto the down slow line, which was usually the province of freight and other slower moving traffic. The signal for the down fast was already lowered for an over-taking newspaper King-hauled train of only five vehicles. 6028's driver mistook that signal for his own. Lieutenant Colonel Sir Alan Mount's report does not mention the other King by name or number as locomotive movements were not generally made public in wartime.

On the train's approach to the end of the tracks and the point where it would rejoin the down fast, the ATC siren sounded to warn the driver that he had passed a distant signal at caution, the unmistakeable conclusion being that the next home signal was at danger as the points were set for the overtaking newspaper train on the down fast line. The driver subconsciously reset the warning.

The driver only realized his mistake when the newspaper train overtook his own. A full emergency brake application was not much use at this point and the train ran off the trap points at the end of what had become a loop at 40mph (64km/h). The loco slewed round across the down fast and tipped over on its left

Fig. 196. 6017 King Edward IV with the up Cornish Riviera Express near Burbage in the Vale of Pewsey, Wiltshire, 22 July 1949. The GWR had a wharf and goods shed serving the Kennett and Avon Canal nearby. STEAM, MUSEUM OF THE GREAT WESTERN RAILWAY

side. The fireman and twenty-six of the 900 passengers were killed and seventy-two were injured.

Even in disaster the GWR was fortunate in that, had the newspaper train been a little slower, the derailed engine would have collided with that train causing a far more serious incident. The newspaper train's guard was alerted by the crashing sound of ballast being thrown against his van from 6028's derailment and the sound of a broken window caused by a sheared rivet expelled from the bogie of 6028.

6028 was retrieved and repaired. The incident was not given much publicity as it was thought a bad omen for such a catastrophe to befall an engine named after the reigning monarch.

The driver accepted full responsibility for his actions. After forty years of exemplary service, he was a broken man and died within the year.

This horrific crash only served to emphasize what a safe railway the Great Western was. Its very nature and consequences were so out of keeping with the way the railway was run.

The 1948 Locomotive Exchanges

The GWR ceased to exist on 31 December 1947. The new order of British Railways sought to adopt best practice from the 'big four', whatever that might be. A series of exchanges took place in which locomotives from the big four ran trains on what had been their competitors' lines. Kings were chosen from the GWR engines to represent express passenger types. Owing to gauging issues, the route chosen was King's Cross to Leeds Central or the Great Northern route. The engine chosen was 6018 King Henry VI.

British Railways was more concerned about fuel economy than performance. Although dynamometer cars were used to provide measured data, the exchanges were used to confirm more or less what the board had already agreed: the LMS was to form the basis of the new standard classes of steam locomotive. The exchanges were more about politics than investigation.

Fig. 197. 6009 King Charles II in early blue livery at Leamington Spa, headed for Paddington, 11 July 1948. The coach is in post-war GWR livery. STEAM, MUSEUM OF THE GREAT WESTERN RAILWAY

The Kings were found to use more coal with substandard product than with the Welsh steam coal they had been designed for. The remedy was seen to be a higher degree of superheat than the moderate level propagated by Churchward and his successors. Finally the GWR was seen to have slipped behind the rest somewhat, although the 28XX Churchward freight locomotives were found to be superior to the rest and Hawksworth's Modified Halls gave a good account of themselves.

British Railways and the Kings

The section on modifications in Chapter 6 details the changes made after nationalization that brought the

Kings to their mechanical zenith, prior to their early demise. The Western Region of British Railways was keen to demonstrate that they were ahead of the modernization game. All thoughts of a proper evaluation of the cost and benefits of retaining modernized steam engines to amortize their working lives and so give good value to the taxpayer went out of the window. The Germans retained steam until 1976, working those trains in areas of the Rhine with access to a good deal of heavy mineral traffic. They could fairly be said to have had their money's-worth, although admittedly their engines were mostly built after World War II.

The decision to remove steam from the Western Region of BR was largely political and supported by the unions, who wanted better conditions for their

Fig. 198. An unidentified King rushes through Savernake Low Level station on the Berks and Hants line with a Penzance express bound for the capital, 6 April 1958. Savernake is in the Burbage area and the low level station was the junction for Marlborough. STEAM, MUSEUM OF THE GREAT WESTERN RAILWAY

workers. Many of the diesel hydraulics that replaced steam, however, were unreliable and unsatisfactory and lasted only a few years in service. A step change in performance was not apparent until the introduction of the HST in the mid-1970s.

As a result the Kings, which were now thirty to thirty-five years old, lasted only until 1962. Whereas Castles were relegated to freight and other menial tasks, the Kings were not degraded in this way. It must be admitted, though, that the later built Castles were less than fifteen years old before they too were scrapped. The Kings were the oldest top-link express passenger engines in BR service and were showing signs of ageing with cracked frames, a common weakness in all the 4-cylinder 4-6-0s.

There were to be more fireworks on the road, however, before their demise. Experiments with enhanced exhaust arrangements and four-row superheaters in in the early 1950s would lead to an examination of the maximum steam-raising capabilities of the re-draughted and superheated engine. On the test plant at Swindon it was found that the boiler's steaming capacity at its maximum had been raised by up to 30 per cent, a phenomenal increase in capability.

A series of dynamometer car test runs were carried out in July 1953 to determine whether what had been achieved on the plant at Swindon could be repeated under conditions of heavy load. The two runs of particular note concerned 6001 King Edward VII and its extraordinary load of twenty-five coaches, weighing in at 798 tons full (811 tonnes). The journey was from Reading to Stoke Gifford Yard, near Bristol, and return.

The 73 miles (117km) of the test were achieved in just over 80 minutes and just under 77 minutes, respectively. Top speeds of 72 and 78mph (116 and 126km/h) were the highlights, underpinned by continuous rates of steaming that had never been seen before with the King class. A value of about 2,000 indicated horse power (1491.4kW) was achieved.

One outstanding result of the tests was to illustrate that the disparity in performance with soft steam coal and 'Northern' hard coal was down to low levels. The disappointment with Kings in the 1948 loco exchanges using coal of a lower calorific value had been overcome.

The result was to accelerate the post-war schedules to match the capacity of the engines for high power outputs.

Far less in the public eye were the Newbury Race specials, which were often hauled by Kings and used Super Saloon coaches, the last word in pre-war luxury. One run recounted by D. S. M. Barrie recorded a higher power output than on the twenty-five coach test train. This was to overcome two very bad checks at Slough and still bring the train in two minutes early.

The accelerated schedules came into force in June 1954. Kings on the restored Bristolian were able to bring trains in before time consistently. In addition

Fig. 199. 6029 King Edward VIII, with an 83D Laira shed plate, hustles through Dawlish with a Paddington-bound express from Plymouth, mostly GWR liveried coaches, 22 June 1954. The tall signal box behind the engine has gone but Dawlish station has mostly survived. GREAT WESTERN TRUST

Fig. 200. 6015 King Richard III waits at Newton Abbot with an express from the Torbay line, 12 July 1953. The handsome headquarters building on the right, built in 1927, survives in 2018. AUTHOR'S COLLECTION

Fig. 201. 6013 King Henry VIII powers through Newbury with a Paddington to Penzance express, 25 April 1952. Newbury was then the junction for the Didcot, Newbury and Southampton line and the Lambourn branch. Both branches were used extensively during World War II but little afterwards. STEAM, MUSEUM OF THE GREAT WESTERN RAILWAY

parts of the track had been brought up to a standard where the running instruction was to the effect that crews could work their engines up to speeds that were 'as high as necessary' to regain lost time. This was a gauntlet thrown down to the more enterprising crews to see what could be achieved on favourable stretches of track.

A recorded highlight was a run by the down Bristolian of only seven coaches, headed by 6018 King Henry VI. The junction at Wootton Bassett was taken at 85mph (137km/h) down the 1 in 660 there. This was followed by a maximum of 102.5mph (165km/h) down Dauntsey bank, which is a down grade of 1 in 100. The slightly less than 17 miles (27km) from

Fig. 202. Kings Unlimited! 6025 King Henry III and 6015 King Richard III storm what is believed to be Rattery Bank near Totnes, Devon, with the down Cornish Riviera Express, 4 August 1950. GREAT WESTERN TRUST

Fig. 203. 6024 King Edward I at Chippenham on a running in turn from Swindon works, 28 November 1957. There appears to be a small FRUIT van followed by a Hawksworth coach and then some Collett coaches. STEAM, MUSEUM OF THE GREAT WESTERN RAILWAY

Swindon to Chippenham was covered in 11½ minutes, instead of the scheduled 12 minutes. The engine was eased coming into Chippenham, which it passed at 80mph (129km/h) on the 1 in 660 up gradient.

There were to be many reported instances of similar speeds with both Castles and Kings in the heady days of the mid- to late 1950s.

Kings in Preservation

Initially, and for some years, it was thought that only King George V, as part of the national collection, would survive, and for years this was the sole running survivor.

Fig. 204. 6012 King Edward VI pulls into Banbury General station about the time of the rebuilding, 4 April 1958. At this time the London and North Western Railway's Merton Street station was in operation, so a distinction had to be made. GREAT WESTERN TRUST

Fig. 205. 6000 King George V heads north through Abergavenny on its way to Shrewsbury and Chester on the Welsh Marches Pullman, 16 September 1972. The signal box and signalling at Abergavenny station remain much the same in 2018, as well as its disused goods shed and largely original station. GREAT WESTERN TRUST

6000 King George V

The loco was restored to running condition in 1968 by HP Bulmer and Co., the Hereford cider makers. The work was done at an engineering firm in Newport. To begin with the engine ran short demonstration trips with a rake of Pullman coaches at Bulmer's Railway Centre in Hereford.

In October 1971 the engine was the first main-line engine to break the BR steam ban that had been in place since 1969. It first ran a Bulmer promotion tour and then regular excursions from June 1972. Initially BR insisted that the engine only work along the Welsh Marches from Hereford to Chester and kept the engine away from the classic GWR routes. BR did not wish to sully its image with out-of-date technology running on its main lines, which had been the *raison d'être* for the steam ban in the first place. In 1985, however, the loco was a star of the GWR 150 celebrations in events organized by BR across the old company's tracks.

The engine was returned to the National Railway Museum in 1987 and no further overhaul to running condition was undertaken, since 6024 was nearing the end of its restoration. In 2015 it began a detachment, reportedly for five years, to STEAM, the Museum of the Great Western Railway.

The engine was thought to be out of gauge for many other lines and the situation has worsened with higher ballast piles for 125 running reducing bridge clearances and, more recently, the electrification of the GWR main line.

6023 King Edward II

The engine had languished for many years in Dai Woodham's scrapyard at Barry in South Wales. This was an unwanted engine: on arrival at Barry it had derailed and some way out of this difficulty was to flame-cut the rear driving wheels. It was sold in 1984 for £12,000.

Harvey's of Bristol Cream fame bought it for static display for £22,000 at Bristol Temple Meads station during the GWR 150 celebrations in 1985. A picture on the flickr website depicts 6023 and 6000 together in 1985 at the Fish Dock at Temple Meads station.

After purchase and massive restoration by the GWS at Didcot, in 2011 the engine steamed again

Fig. 206. 6023 King Edward II with Laira shed plate and cut-down boiler mountings on the running line at the Great Western Society, Didcot Railway Centre, August 2017. The visitor rides are included in the entrance ticket price.
AUTHOR'S COLLECTION

for the first time since 1962. It has carried the experimental BR blue livery, most recently in 2017 (fig. 206). The engine is at Didcot Railway Centre in 2018. The engine's boiler mountings have been cut down to try to meet Network Rail's gauging requirements and work continues to make it main-line ready.

6024 King Edward I

The King Preservation Society bought the engine from Dai Woodham's for £4,000 in 1974. A lengthy restoration period at the Buckinghamshire Railway Centre at Quainton Road, near Aylesbury, culminated in

a recommissioning ceremony presided over by HRH The Duke of Gloucester in 1989. After a spell at Tyseley the engine finally took to revenue rails in 1990. In March 1995 the loco was withdrawn from traffic for overhaul and taken to the former MoD site at Kineton in Warwickshire.

After overhaul the loco was entrusted with solo running over the line to Plymouth (fig. 207). It set the steam haulage record for the Plymouth to Exeter section of 58 minutes and 6 seconds in 2002.

The King Preservation Society carried out a second overhaul at Tyseley works and the engine was fitted with modern main-line signalling and data collection equipment.

Fig. 207. 6024 King Edward I with Old Oak Common shed plate on shed at Didcot (81E), Great Western Society, 2001. AUTHOR'S COLLECTION

In 2011 the locomotive was sold to the Royal Scot Locomotive and General Trust, which is chaired by the noted businessman and steam enthusiast Jeremy Hosking. A further overhaul was started in 2012 at the West Somerset Railway at Minehead, with work sub-contracted to Ian Riley at Bury and the South Devon Railway.

In 2017 new cylinders were cast and fitted. Thes are of slightly smaller size to enable greater route availability on main-line running.

To close, here are a few images of Kings during their later years in service.

Fig. 208. 6021 King Richard II at Weston-super-Mare, 11 May 1960. At this time the resort's excursion station, called Locking Road, was still open. GREAT WESTERN TRUST

Fig. 209. 6006 King George I at Shrewsbury, facing Chester, December 1956. Shrewsbury was joint GWR and LNWR and they shared the signalling installation. The King is about to pass Crewe Junction LNWR signal box after it has been given the 'off' with GWR signals. STEAM, MUSEUM OF THE GREAT WESTERN RAILWAY

Fig. 210. 6006 King George I has the 'off' at Banbury to head for Paddington, about 1958. Note that both cab roof ventilators are open. The crack King-hauled expresses would normally slip coaches for Banbury; the last such operation took place at Banbury in 1960. STEAM, MUSEUM OF THE GREAT WESTERN RAILWAY

Fig. 211. 6019 King Henry V hurries south near Lapworth towards Leamington Spa, 26 April 1959. The coaches are a mixed bag of Collett, Hawksworth and BR. GREAT WESTERN TRUST

Fig. 212. 6027 King Richard I, with a 84A Stafford Road shed plate, races south through Hatton Junction towards Paddington, 9 July 1960. STEAM, MUSEUM OF THE GREAT WESTERN RAILWAY

Fig. 213. Unidentified flying King on the sea wall near Teignmouth with the Cornish Riviera Limited, 1958. The rounded inside cylinder valve rod covers tell us it's one of the last batch of ten. STEAM, MUSEUM OF THE GREAT WESTERN RAILWAY

LOCOMOTIVE DETAILS
AND TIMELINES

Star Class Technical Summary

The initial technical data for the Star Class Locomotive no. 40 as an Atlantic 4-4-2 is as follows. Many changes were carried out over the life of the succeeding engines, particularly over boiler variations.

Cylinders (4)	Diameter 14¼in (35.6cm), Stroke 26in (69cm)
Boiler	
Barrel	14ft 10in (4.52m)
Diameter outside	4ft 10¾in (1.5m) and 5ft 6in (1.68m)
Pitch	8ft 6in (2.51m)
Firebox	
Length from outside	9ft (2.74m)
Tubes	250, diameter 2in (5cm)
Heating Surface	
Tubes	1,988.65sq ft (185m²)
Firebox	154.26sq ft (14.33m²)
Total	2,142.91sq ft (199.33m²)
Grate area	27.07sq ft (2.51m²)
Boiler pressure	225psi (15.51 bar)
Wheels	
Bogie	3ft 2in (0.96m)
Coupled	6ft 8½in (2.04m)
Trailing	4ft 1½in (1.26m)

Wheelbase (engine)	7ft (2.13m) + 5ft 6in (1.68m) + 7ft (2.13m) + 8ft 3in (2.51m)
Total	27ft 9in (8.45m)
Weights full	
Bogie	17.9 tons (18.19 tonnes)
Leading coupled	19.75 tons (20.12 tonnes)
Trailing coupled	19.75 tons 20.12 tonnes)
Trailing pony truck	17 tons (17.27 tonnes)
Total engine	74.5 tons (75.7 tonnes)
Total tender	40 tons (40.04 tonnes)
Combined total	114.5 tons (116.34 tonnes)
Tractive effort (85%)	25,090lb ft (112kN)
Tender capacity	
Water	3,500 gallons (15,911ltr), water scoop equipped
Coal	6 tons (6.1 tonnes)

The first batch of production Stars, 4001 to 4010 4-6-0s, varied from the prototype no. 40 in wheelbase and weights. A further change was made to the cylinder diameter with 4041–4045 and afterwards to 15in (38cm).

Later on in their careers some engines were fitted with Collett 4,000 gallon (18,184ltr) tenders with the same coal capacity. After World War II some locomotives, including 4062 Malmesbury Abbey, were recorded with Hawksworth 4,000 gallon (18,184ltr), 7 ton (7.1 tonne) flat-sided tenders.

Cylinders (4)	Diameter 14¼in (35.6cm), Stroke 26in (69cm)
Boiler	
Barrel	14ft 10in (4.52m)
Diameter outside	4ft 10¾in (1.5 m) and 5ft 6in (1.68m)
Pitch	8ft 6in (2.51m)
Firebox	
Length from outside	9ft (2.74m)
Tubes	250, diameter 2in (5cm)
Heating surface	
Tubes	1,988.65sq ft (185m²)
Firebox	154.26sq ft (14.33m²)
Total	2,142.91sq ft (199.33m²)
Grate area	27.07sq ft (2.51m²)
Boiler pressure	225psi (15.51 bar)
Wheels	
Bogie	3ft 2in (0.96m)
Coupled	6ft 8½in (2.04m)
Wheelbase (engine)	7ft (2.13m) + 5ft 6in (1.68m) + 7ft (2.13m) + 7ft 9in (2.36m)
Total	27ft 9in (8.3m)
Weights full	
Bogie	20.4 tons (18.19 tonnes)
Leading coupled	18.6 tons (20.12 tonnes)
Middle coupled	18.6 tons 20.12 tonnes)
Trailing coupled	18.2 tons (17.27 tonnes)
Total engine	75.6 tons (75.7 tonnes)
Total tender	40 tons (40.04 tonnes)
Combined total	115.8 tons (tonnes)
Tractive effort (85%)	25,090lb ft (112kN)
with 15in (38cm)	
cylinders (85%)	27,800lb ft (124kN)
Tender capacity	
Water	3,500 gallons (15,911ltr), water scoop equipped
Coal	6 tons (6.1 tonnes)
GWR Power Class	D
Route Availability	RED
BR Power Class	5P
Mileages:	1,250,000–2,035,000 (2,011,680–3,275,015km)

Star Class Locomotive Timeline

Number	Name as built	Date built	Superheated	Steampipes Elbow	Castle	Withdrawn
4000	North Star	4/06	11/09	Rebuilt	Castle	11/29
4001	Dog Star	2/07	1/11		10/30	1/34
4002	Evening Star	3/07	8/09	12/29		3/33
4003	Lode Star	2/07	1/11	3/49		7/51
4004	Morning Star	2/07	1/11	3/46		4/48

(continued)

Number	Name as built	Date built	Superheated	Steampipes		Withdrawn
				Elbow	Castle	
4005	Polar Star	2/07	2/11			11/34
4006	Red Star	4/07	4/11			11/32
4007	Rising Star	4/07	5/11	5/47		9/51
4008	Royal Star	5/07	12/11	7/33		6/35
4009	Shooting Star	5/07	10/12	Rebuilt		4/25
4010	Western Star	5/07	5/07			11/34
4011	Knight of the Garter	3/08	3/08			11/32
4012	Knight of the Thistle	3/08	1/11			10/49
4013	Knight of St. Patrick	3/08	12/10			5/50
4014	Knight of the Bath	3/08	10/10	9/35		6/46
4015	Knight of St. John	3/08	9/10	12/48		2/51
4016	Knight of the Golden Fleece	4/08	11/09	Rebuilt	Castle	10/25
4017	Knight of the Black Eagle	4/08	11/09			11/49
4018	Knight of the Grand Cross	4/08	9/10	5/31		4/51
4019	Knight Templar	5/08	1/10	5/48		10/49
4020	Knight Commander	5/08	11/09	3/49		3/51
4021	King Edward	6/09	6/09	7/48		10/52
4022	King William	6/09	10/10	6/48		2/52
4023	King George	6/09	9/12			7/52
4024	King James	6/09	2/11		2/29	2/35
4025	King Charles	7/09	1/11			8/50
4026	King Richard	9/09	5/13	10/32		2/50
4027	King Henry	9/09	6/12			10/34
4028	King John	9/09	9/11			11/51
4029	King Stephen	10/09	4/11			11/34
4030	King Harold	10/09	1/13			5/50
4031	Queen Mary	10/10	Built	8/48		6/51
4032	Queen Alexandra	10/10	Built	Rebuilt	Castle	4/26
4033	Queen Victoria	11/10	Built	4/40		6/51
4034	Queen Adelaide	11/10	Built	6/32		9/52
4035	Queen Charlotte	11/10	Built		1/31	10/51
4036	Queen Elizabeth	12/10	Built	7/43		3/52
4037	Queen Phillipa	12/10	Built	Rebuilt	Castle	6/26
4038	Queen Berengaria	1/11	Built	8/32		4/52
4039	Queen Matilda	2/11	Built	12/48		11/50
4040	Queen Boudicea	3/11	Built		2/30	6/51
4041	Prince of Wales	6/13	Built	10/47		4/51
4042	Prince Albert	5/13	Built	5/48		11/51
4043	Prince Henry	5/13	Built		10/31	1/52
4044	Prince George	5/13	Built	10/46		2/53
4045	Prince John	6/13	Built	1/46		11/50
4046	Princess Mary	5/14	Built	1/49		11/51
4047	Princess Louise	5/14	Built			7/51
4048	Princess Victoria	5/14	Built	8/32	10/38	1/53
4049	Princess Maud	5/14	Built		2/35	7/53
4050	Princess Alice	6/14	Built	6/46		2/52
4051	Princess Helena	6/14	Built		12/44	10/50
4052	Princess Beatrice	6/14	Built		4/39	6/53
4053	Princess Alexandra	6/14	Built		10/33	7/54
4054	Princess Charlotte	6/14	Built	10/45		2/52

| Number | Name as built | Date built | Superheated | Steampipes | | Withdrawn |
				Elbow	Castle	
4055	Princess Sophia	7/14	Built		5/45	2/51
4056	Princess Margaret	7/14	Built	8/49		10/57
4057	Princess Elizabeth	7/14	Built		4/30	2/52
4058	Princess Augusta	7/14	Built	10/44		4/51
4059	Princess Patricia	7/14	Built			9/52
4060	Princess Eugenie	7/14	Built	12/30	8/44	10/52
4061	Glastonbury Abbey	5/22	Built	7/49		3/57
4062	Malmesbury Abbey	5/22	Built	3/50		11/56
4063	Bath Abbey	11/22	Built			3/37
4064	Reading Abbey	12/22	Built			2/37
4065	Evesham Abbey	12/22	Built			3/39
4066	Malvern Abbey	12/22	Built			12/37
4067	Tintern Abbey	1/23	Built			9/40
4068	Llanthony Abbey	1/23	Built			11/38
4069	Margam Abbey	1/23	Built			4/39
4070	Neath Abbey	2/23	Built	3/37		1/39
4071	Cleeve Abbey	2/23	Built			9/38
4072	Tresco Abbey	2/23	Built			3/38

4073 Castle Class Technical Summary

Cylinders (4)	Diameter 16in (41cm), Stroke 26in (69cm)
Boiler	
Barrel	14ft 10in (4.52m)
Diameter outside	5ft 2in (1.57m) and 5ft 9in (1.75m)
Pitch	8 ft 8½in (2.65m)
Firebox	
Length from outside	10ft (3.05m)
Tubes	201, diameter 2in (5cm)
Flue	14, diameter 5⅛in (13cm)
Superheater	84, diameter 1in (2.5cm)
Heating surface	
Tubes	1,885.62sq ft (175.18m²)
Firebox	163.76sq ft (15.21m²)
Superheater	262.62sq ft (24.4m²)
Total	2,312sq ft (214.8m²)
Grate area	30.28sq ft (2.81m²)
Boiler pressure	225psi (15.51 bar)
Wheels	
Bogie	3ft 2in (0.96m)
Coupled	6ft 8½in (2.04m)
Wheelbase (engine)	7ft (2.13m) + 5ft 6in (1.68m) + 7ft (2.13m) + 7ft 9in (2.36m)
Total	27ft 9in (8.3m)
Weights full	
Bogie	21 tons (21.3 tonnes)

Leading coupled	19.5 tons (19.81 tonnes)
Middle coupled	19.7 tons (20.01 tonnes)
Trailing coupled	19.65 tons (19.96 tonnes)
Total engine	79.85 tons (81.13 tonnes)
Total tender	40 tons (40.04 tonnes)
Combined total	119.85 tons (121.17 tonnes)
Tractive effort (85%)	31,625lb ft (141kN)
Tender capacity (Churchward)	
Water	3,500 gallons (15,911ltr), water scoop equipped
Coal	6 tons (6.1 tonnes)
GWR Power Class:	D
Route Availability:	RED
BR Power Class	6P, 7P from 1 January 1951 onwards
Mileages:	580,346–1,974,461 (933,976–3,177,587km)

Later in their careers some engines were fitted with Collett 4,000 gallon (18,184ltr) tenders with the same coal capacity. Some locomotives were fitted with Hawksworth 4,000 gallon (18,184ltr) 7 ton (7.1 tonne) flat-sided tenders. The earlier Collett and later Hawksworth tenders were swapped around engines as they were overhauled.

4073 Castle Class Locomotive Timeline

No.	Name as built	Renamed	New	Double Chimney	Cond.	Notes
111	Viscount Churchill		9/24		7/53	Rebuilt Great Bear [a]
4000	North Star		11/29		5/57	Rebuilt Star
4009	Shooting Star	Lloyds No. 100 A1	4/25		5/50	Rebuilt Star [b]
4016	Knight of the Golden Fleece	The Somerset Light Infantry (Prince Albert's)	10/25		9/51	Rebuilt Star Renamed Jan 1938
4032	Queen Alexandra		4/26		9/51	Rebuilt Star
4037	Queen Phillipa	The South Wales Borderers	6/26		9/62	Rebuilt Star Renamed March 1937
4073	Caerphilly Castle		8/23		5/60	Preserved Swindon
4074	Caldicot Castle	Initially 'Caldicott'	12/23	4/59	5/60	
4075	Cardiff Castle		1/24		11/61	Hornby Dublo model
4076	Carmarthen Castle		2/24		2/63	
4077	Chepstow Castle		2/24		8/62	
4078	Pembroke Castle		2/24		7/62	
4079	Pendennis Castle		2/24		5/64	Preserved GWS Didcot
4080	Powderham Castle		3/24	8/58	8/64	
4081	Warwick Castle		3/24		1/63	
4082	Windsor Castle	7013 Bristol Castle	4/24		9/64	Name change Feb 1952 [c]
4083	Abbotsbury Castle		5/25		12/61	
4084	Aberystwyth Castle		5/25		10/60	
4085	Berkeley Castle		5/25		5/62	
4086	Builth Castle		6/25		4/62	
4087	Cardigan Castle		6/25	2/58	10/63	
4088	Dartmouth Castle		7/25	5/58	5/64	
4089	Donnington Castle		7/25		9/64	
4090	Dorchester Castle		7/25	7/57	6/63	
4091	Dudley Castle		7/25		1/59	First new withdrawal
4092	Dunraven Castle		8/25		12/61	
4093	Dunster Castle		5/26	12/57	9/64	
4094	Dynevor Castle		5/26		3/62	
4095	Harlech Castle		6/26		12/62	
4096	Highclere Castle		6/26		1/63	
4097	Kenilworth Castle		6/26	6/58	5/60	
4098	Kidwelly Castle		7/26		12/63	
4099	Kilgerran Castle		8/26		9/62	
5000	Launceston Castle		9/26		10/64	LMS Trials 1926
5001	Llandovery Castle		9/26	6/61	2/64	
5002	Ludlow Castle		9/26		9/64	Hornby Dublo model
5003	Lulworth Castle		5/27		8/62	
5004	Llanstephan Castle		6/27		4/62	
5005	Manorbier Castle		6/27		2/60	Streamlined
5006	Tregenna Castle		6/27		9/62	World record holder
5007	Rougemont Castle		6/27		9/62	
5008	Raglan Castle		6/27	3/61	9/62	
5009	Shrewsbury Castle		6/27		10/60	
5010	Restormel Castle		7/27		10/59	
5011	Tintagel Castle		7/27		9/62	
5012	Berry Pomeroy Castle		7/27		4/62	

No.	Name as built	Renamed	New	Double Chimney	Cond.	Notes
5013	Abergavenny Castle		6/32		7/62	
5014	Goodrich Castle		6/32		2/65	
5015	Kingswear Castle		7/32		4/63	
5016	Montgomery Castle		7/32	2/60	9/62	
5017	St. Donat's Castle	The Gloucestershire Regiment 28th 61st	7/32		9/62	Renamed April 1954 [d]
5018	St. Mawes Castle		7/32		3/64	
5019	Treago Castle		7/32	2/61	9/62	
5020	Trematon Castle		7/32		11/62	
5021	Whittington Castle		8/32		9/62	
5022	Wigmore Castle		8/32	2/59	6/63	
5023	Brecon Castle		4/34		2/63	
5024	Carew Castle		4/34		5/62	
5025	Chirk Castle		4/34		11/63	
5026	Criccieth Castle		4/34	10/59	11/64	
5027	Farleigh Castle		4/34	4/61	11/62	
5028	Llantilio Castle		5/34		5/60	
5029	Nunney Castle		5/34		12/63	Preserved Tyseley
5030	Shirburn Castle		5/34		9/62	
5031	Totnes Castle		5/34	6/59	10/63	
5032	Usk Castle		5/34	5/59	9/62	
5033	Broughton Castle		5/35	10/60	9/62	
5034	Corfe Castle		5/35	2/60	9/62	
5035	Coity Castle		5/35		5/62	
5036	Lyonshall Castle		5/35	12/60	9/62	
5037	Monmouth Castle		5/35		3/64	
5038	Morlais Castle		6/35		9/63	
5039	Rhuddlan Castle		6/35		6/64	
5040	Stokesay Castle		6/35		10/63	
5041	Tiverton Castle		7/35		12/63	
5042	Winchester Castle		7/35		12/63	
5043	Barbury Castle	Earl of Mount Edgcumbe	3/36	10/56	12/63	Preserved Tyseley Renamed Sep 1937
5044	Beverston Castle	Earl of Dunraven	3/36		4/62	Renamed Sep 1937
5045	Bridgwater Castle	Earl of Dudley	3/36		9/62	Renamed Sep 1937
5046	Clifford Castle	Earl Cawdor	4/36		9/62	Renamed Aug 1937
5047	Compton Castle	Earl of Dartmouth	4/36		9/62	Renamed Aug 1937
5048	Cranbrook Castle	Earl of Devon	4/36		8/62	Renamed Aug 1937
5049	Denbigh Castle	Earl of Plymouth	4/36	9/59	3/63	Renamed Aug 1937
5050	Devizes Castle	Earl of St. Germans	5/36		8/63	Renamed Aug 1937
5051	Drysllwyn Castle	Earl Bathurst	5/36		5/63	Renamed Aug 1937 Preserved GWS Didcot
5052	Eastnor Castle	Earl of Radnor	5/36		9/62	Renamed Jul 1937
5053	Bishop's Castle	Earl Cairns	5/36		7/62	Renamed Jul 1937
5054	Lamphey Castle	Earl of Ducie	6/36		11/64	Renamed Sep 1937
5055	Lydford Castle	Earl of Eldon	6/36		10/64	Renamed Aug 1937
5056	Ogmore Castle	Earl of Powis	6/36	10/60	6/62	Renamed Sep 1937
5057	Penrice Castle	Earl Waldegrave	6/36	7/58	3/64	Renamed Oct 1937
5058	Newport Castle	Earl of Clancarty	5/37		3/63	Renamed Sep 1937
5059	Powis Castle	Earl of St Aldwyn	5/37		6/62	Renamed Oct 1937

(continued)

No.	Name as built	Renamed	New	Double Chimney	Cond.	Notes
5060	Sarum Castle	Earl of Berkley	6/37	7/61	4/63	Renamed Oct 1937
5061	Sudeley Castle	Earl of Birkenhead	6/37	9/58	9/62	Renamed Oct 1937
5062	Tenby Castle	Earl of Shaftesbury	6/37		8/62	Renamed Nov 1937
5063	Thornbury Castle	Earl Baldwin	6/37		2/65	Renamed Jul 1937
5064	Tretower Castle	Bishop's Castle	7/37	9/58	9/62	Renamed Sep 1937
5065	Upton Castle	Newport Castle	7/37		1/63	Renamed Sep 1937
5066	Wardour Castle	Sir Felix Pole	7/37	4/59	9/62	Renamed Apr 1956
5067	St Fagan's Castle		7/37		7/62	
5068	Beverston Castle		6/38	7/59	9/62	
5069	Isambard Kingdom Brunel		6/38	11/58	2/62	e
5070	Sir Daniel Gooch		6/38		3/64	
5071	Clifford Castle	Spitfire	6/38	5/59	10/63	Renamed Sep 1940
5072	Compton Castle	Hurricane	6/38		10/62	Renamed Nov 1940
5073	Cranbrook Castle	Blenheim	6/38	7/59	3/64	Renamed Jan 1941
5074	Denbigh Castle	Hampden	6/38	9/61	5/64	Renamed Jan 1941
5075	Devizes Castle	Wellington	6/38		9/62	Renamed Oct 1940
5076	Drysllwyn Castle	Gladiator	8/38		9/64	Renamed Jan 1941
5077	Eastnor Castle	Fairey Battle	8/38		7/62	Renamed Oct 1940
5078	Lamphey Castle	Beaufort	5/39	12/61	11/62	Renamed Jan 1941
5079	Lydford Castle	Lysander	5/39		5/60	Renamed Nov 1940
5080	Ogmore Castle	Defiant	5/39		4/63	Renamed Jan 1941 Preserved Tyseley
5081	Penrice Castle	Lockheed Hudson	5/39		10/63	Renamed Jan 1941
5082	Powis Castle	Swordfish	6/39		7/62	Renamed Jan 1941
5083	Bath Abbey		6/37		1/59	Rebuilt Star 4063
5084	Reading Abbey		4/37	10/58	7/62	Rebuilt Star 4064
5085	Evesham Abbey		7/39		2/64	Rebuilt Star 4065
5086	Viscount Horne		12/37		11/58	Rebuilt Star 4066
5087	Tintern Abbey		11/40		8/63	Rebuilt Star 4067
5088	Llanthony Abbey		2/39	6/58	9/62	Rebuilt Star 4068
5089	Westminster Abbey		10/39		9/64	Rebuilt Star 4069
5090	Neath Abbey		4/39		5/62	Rebuilt Star 4070
5091	Cleeve Abbey		12/38		10/64	Rebuilt Star 4071
5092	Tresco Abbey		4/38	10/61	7/63	Rebuilt Star 4072
5093	Upton Castle		6/39		9/63	
5094	Tretower Castle		6/39	6/60	9/62	
5095	Barbury Castle		6/39	11/58	8/62	
5096	Bridgwater Castle		6/39	1/59	6/64	
5097	Sarum Castle		7/39	6/61	3/63	
5098	Clifford Castle		5/46	1/59	6/64	
5099	Compton Castle		5/46		2/63	
7000	Viscount Portal		5/46		12/63	
7001	Denbigh Castle	Sir James Milne	5/46	9/60	9/63	Renamed Feb 1948
7002	Devizes Castle		6/46	6/61	4/64	
7003	Elmley Castle		6/46	6/60	8/64	
7004	Eastnor Castle		6/46	2/58	1/64	
7005	Lamphey Castle	Sir Edward Elgar	6/46		12/63	Renamed Aug 1957
7006	Lydford Castle		6/46	5/60	12/63	
7007	Ogmore Castle	Great Western	7/46	3/61	2/63	Renamed Jan 1948
7008	Swansea Castle		5/48	6/59	9/64	

No.	Name as built	Renamed	New	Double Chimney	Cond.	Notes
7009	Athelney Castle		5/48		3/63	
7010	Avondale Castle		6/48	10/60	3/64	
7011	Banbury Castle		6/48		2/65	
7012	Barry Castle		6/48		11/64	
7013	Bristol Castle	4082 Windsor Castle	7/48	5/58	2/65	Swapped Feb 1952 Hornby Dublo model
7014	Caerhays Castle		7/48	2/59	2/65	
7015	Carn Brea Castle		7/48	6/59	4/63	
7016	Chester Castle		8/48		11/62	
7017	G.J. Churchward		8/48		2/63	
7018	Drysllwyn Castle		5/49	5/56	9/63	
7019	Fowey Castle		5/49	9/58	9/64	
7020	Gloucester Castle		5/49	2/61	9/63	
7021	Haverfordwest Castle		6/49	11/61	9/63	
7022	Hereford Castle		6/49	1/58	2/65	
7023	Penrice Castle		6/49	5/58	2/65	
7024	Powis Castle		6/49	3/59	2/65	
7025	Sudeley Castle		8/49		9/64	
7026	Tenby Castle		8/49		10/64	
7027	Thornbury Castle		8/49		12/63	Preserved Tyseley
7028	Cadbury Castle		5/50	10/61	12/63	
7029	Clun Castle		5/50	10/59	12/65	Preserved Tyseley
7030	Cranbrook Castle		6/50	7/59	9/63	
7031	Cromwell's Castle		6/50		7/63	
7032	Denbigh Castle		6/50	9/60	9/64	Hornby Dublo model
7033	Hartlebury Castle		7/50	7/59	1/63	
7034	Ince Castle		8/50	12/59	6/65	
7035	Ogmore Castle		8/50	1/60	8/65	
7036	Taunton Castle		8/50	8/59	9/63	
7037	Swindon		8/50		3/63	

Notes

a   111 rebuilt from Churchward 4-6-2 Pacific locomotive.

b   4009 renamed A1 Lloyds in January 1936. Then in February 1936 the number 100 was added. Bufferbeam designation was 100A1.

c   4082 was the loco driven by King George V in 1924. On his death in 1952, however, the loco was not available to haul his funeral train. 4082 had the name, number plates and commemorative cab plates removed and transferred to 7013, which did haul the funeral train. The identities were never switched back. The commemorative cab interior plates were subsequently removed from the new 4082.

d   5017 was renamed to commemorate the exploits of the 'Glorious Glosters' regiment in the Korean War.

e   5069 was originally built with outsize radius nameplates. These were replaced with standard radius plates in July 1938.

6000 King Class Technical Summary

Cylinders (4)	Diameter 16¼in (41.3cm), Stroke 28in (71cm)
Boiler	
Barrel	16ft (4.8m)
Diameter outside	5ft 6¼in (1.68m) and 6ft (1.83m)
Pitch	8ft 11¼in (2.72m)
Firebox	
Length from outside	11ft 6in (3.5m)
Tubes	171, diameter 2¼in (6.35cm)
Flue	16, diameter 5⅛in (13cm)
Superheater	96, diameter 1in (2.5cm)
Heating surface	
Tubes	2,007.5sq ft (186.5m²)
Firebox	193.5sq ft (18m²)
Superheater	313sq ft (29.1m²)
Total	2,514sq ft (233.6m²)
Grate area	34.3sq ft (3.19m²)
Boiler pressure	250psi (17.23 bar)
Wheels	
Bogie	3ft (0.914m)
Coupled	6ft 6in (1.98m)

Wheelbase (engine)	7ft 8in (2.34m) + 5ft 6in (1.68m) + 8ft (2.43m) + 8ft 3in (2.51m)
Total	29ft 6in (8.96m)
Weights full	
Bogie	21.5 tons (21.84 tonnes)
Leading coupled	22.5 tons (22.86 tonnes)
Middle coupled	22.5 tons (22.86 tonnes)
Trailing coupled	22.5 tons (22.86 tonnes)
Total engine	89 tons (90.4 tonnes)
Total tender	47.7 tons (48.5 tonnes)
Combined total	136.7 tons (138.9 tonnes)
Tractive effort (85%)	40,300lb ft (179kN)
Tender capacity (Churchward)	
Water	4,000 gallons (18,184ltr), water scoop equipped
Coal	6 tons (6.1 tonnes)
GWR Power Class	Special, unclassified
Route Availability	DOUBLE RED
BR Power Class	7P, 8P from 1 January 1951 onwards
Mileages	1,554,201–1,910,424 (2,501,244–3,074,529km)

King Class Locomotive Timeline

No.	Name as Built	Renamed	New	Double Chimney	Cond.	Notes
6000	King George V	a	6/27	12/56	12/62	Preserved STEAM, Swindon
6001	King Edward VII		7/27	2/56	9/62	
6002	King William IV		7/27	3/56	9/62	
6003	King George IV		7/27	7/58	6/62	
6004	King George III		7/27	7/58	6/62	
6005	King George II		7/27	7/56	11/62	
6006	King George I		2/28	6/56	2/62	
6007	King William III	b	3/28	9/56	9/62	
6008	King James II		3/28	12/58	6/62	
6009	King Charles II		3/28	5/56	9/62	
6010	King Charles I		4/28	3/56	6/62	
6011	King James I		4/28	3/56	12/62	
6012	King Edward VI		4/28	2/58	9/62	
6013	King Henry VIII		5/28	6/56	6/62	
6014	King Henry VII		5/28	9/57	9/62	
6015	King Richard III		6/28	9/55	9/62	
6016	King Edward V		6/28	1/58	9/62	
6017	King Edward IV		6/28	12/55	7/62	
6018	King Henry VI		6/28	3/58	12/62	
6019	King Henry V		7/28	4/57	9/62	

No.	Name as Built	Renamed	New	Double Chimney	Cond.	Notes
6020	King Henry IV		5/30	2/56	7/62	
6021	King Richard II		6/30	3/57	9/62	
6022	King Edward III		6/30	5/56	9/62	
6023	King Edward II		6/30	6/57	6/62	Preserved GWS Didcot
6024	King Edward I		6/30	3/57	6/62	Preserved Quainton RS
6025	King Henry III		7/30	3/57	12/62	
6026	King John		7/30	3/58	9/62	
6027	King Richard I		7/30	8/56	9/62	
6028	King Henry II	King George VI	7/30	1/57	11/62	Renamed Jan 1937
6029	King Stephen	King Edward VIII	8/30	12/57	7/62	Renamed May 1936

Notes

a   Part of the National Railway Museum Collection, on loan to STEAM at Swindon.

b   Withdrawn 5 March 1936 after suffering serious damage in the Shrivenham collision. Replaced by new build on 24 March 1936.

ENGINE HEAD LAMP CODES

Reproduced from the GWR Appendix dated 1936 –
Red lamps until 31 December 1936

CLASS OF TRAIN   *CONSISTING OF*
A LAMPS

Express Passenger Train, Express
Newspaper Train or Express
Diesel Car, Breakdown Van
Train going to clear the line
or Light Engine going to assist
disabled train or empty Coaching
stock trained timed at Express
Passenger speed.

B LAMPS

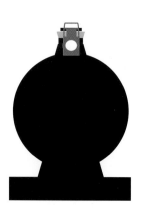

Ordinary Passenger train, Mixed
train or Breakdown train not
going to clear the line.
Branch Passenger train, Autotrain
or Diesel Car.

C LAMPS

Parcels, Fish, Meat, Fruit, Milk,
Horse, Cattle or Perishable train,
composed entirely of Vacuum-
fitted Stock, with the vacuum
pipe connected, also Express
Parcels Diesel Car.

D LAMPS

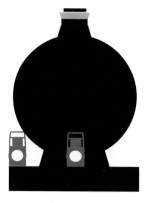

Express Freight or Ballast train
complying with the instructions
in regard to Freight trains
conveying a stipulated number
of vacuum-braked vehicles (not
less than 4) connected by vacuum
pipe to engine and authorised to
run at a maximum speed of 35
mph.
Empty Coaching Stock train not
specially authorised to carry 'A'
head lamps.

E LAMPS

Express Freight, fish, meat, fruit or cattle train (not conveying class 1 traffic, or other traffic specially prohibited) or Ballast train, not running under 'C' or 'D' head lamps conditions, or special train conveying 36-ton Breakdown train not proceeding to an accident.

F LAMPS

Through fast Freight not running under 'C', 'D' or 'E' head lamp conditions, conveying Through load.

G LAMPS

Light Engine or Light Engines coupled together, or Engine and Brake.

H LAMPS

Freight Mineral or Ballast train or train of empties carrying Through load to destination.

J LAMPS

Through Freight, Mineral or Ballast train stopping at intermediate stations.

K LAMPS

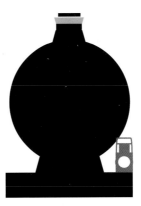

Ordinary Freight, Mineral or Ballast train stopping at local stations, Branch Freight, Pilot trip.

ROYAL TRAINS

The Reigning Monarch is on board.

If no member of the Royal Family is on board then it is usual to display A Lamps on the Royal Train engine.

It was customary in BR days for the crew to receive a gratuity of ten shillings (50 pence) each for a satisfactory Royal Train working.

The Reigning Monarch is not on board but another member of the Royal Family is on board.

ENGINE SHED CODES

This table excludes sub-sheds, except where the original GWR main depot.

Location	GWR 1947	Initial BR	Final BR
Old Oak Common, Paddington	PDN		81A
Slough	SLO		81B
Southall	SHL		81C
Reading	RDG		81D
Didcot	DID		81E
Oxford	OXF		81F
Bristol Bath Road	BRD		82A
Bristol St. Philips Marsh	SPM		82B
Swindon	SDN		82C
Westbury	WES		82D
Yeovil	YEO		82E
Weymouth	WEY		82F
Newton Abbot	NA		83A
Taunton	TN		83B
Exeter	EXE		83C
Laira, Plymouth	LA	83D	84A
St. Blazey	SBZ	83E	84B
Truro	TR	83F	84C
Penzance	PZ	83G	84D
Wolverhampton Stafford Road	SRD	84A	Closed
Oxley, Wolverhampton	OXY	84B	2B
Banbury	BAN	84C	2D
Leamington	LMTN	84D	2L
Tyseley, Birmingham	TYS	84E	2A
Stourbridge	STB	84F	2C
Shrewsbury	SLP (as SALOP)	84G, 89A	6D
Wellington, Shropshire	WLN	84H	2M
Croes Newydd, Wrexham	CNYD	84J, 89B	6C
Birkenhead	BHD	6C	8H
Chester	CHR	84K	6E
Worcester	WOS		85A
Gloucester	GLO		85B
Lydney	LYD sub GLO	Sub 1935	

(continued)

Location	GWR 1947	Initial BR	Final BR
Cheltenham	CHEL sub GLO	Sub 1936	
Hereford	HFD		85C
Kidderminster	KDR		85D
Newport Ebbw Junction	NPT	86A	86B
Newport Pill	PILL	86B	Closed
Cardiff Canton	CDF	86C	88A
Llantrisant	LTS	86D	88G
Severn Tunnel Junction	STJ		86E
Tondu	TDU		86F
Pontypool Road	PPL, PPrd		86G
Aberbeeg	ABeeg	86H	86F
Aberdare	ABDR	86J	88J
Neath (Court Sart)	NEA		87A
Duffryn Yard, Port Talbot	PT & DYD		87B
Danygraig, Swansea	DG		87C
Swansea East Dock	SED		87D
Landore, Swansea	LDR		87E
Llanelly (Llanelli)	LLY		87F
Carmarthen	CARM		87G
Neyland	NEY		87H
Whitland	WTD sub NEY		
Fishguard	FGD		87J
Cardiff (Cathays)	CYS	88A, CAT	88M
Radyr	RYR	88A	
Cardiff East Dock	CED	88B, 88L	88A
Barry	BRY		88C
Merthyr	MTHR		88D
Dowlais (Central)	DLS		Sub 88D
Rhymney	RHY		88D
Treherbert	TRT		88F
Ferndale	FDL		Sub 88F
Abercynon	AYN		88E
Oswestry	OSW	89A, 89D	6E
Brecon	BCN	89B	Sub 88K
Machynlleth	MCH	89C	6F
Aberystwyth	ABH	Sub 89C	

REFERENCES

The reference numbers are derived from the date of the publication's issue. In the case where dates coincide, sub-characters identify specific volumes, such as 'a', 'b', 'c' and so on.

Bibliography

British Railways Pre-Grouping Atlas and Gazetteer, 6th edn (Ian Allan, 2015)

Cooke, R. A., *Atlas of the Great Western Railway: 1947* (Wild Swan, 1988)

Gasson, H., *Firing Days: Reminiscences of a Great Western Fireman* (OPC, 1973)

——, *Footplate Days: More Reminiscences of a Great Western Fireman* (OPC, 1976)

Gradients of the British Main Line Railways (1947) (Ian Allan, 2016)

Great Western Railway Sectional Appendix, 1936

Holden, B. and K. H. Leech, *Portraits of 'Kings'* (Moorland, 1979)

Lyons, E., *An Historical Survey of Great Western Engine Sheds, 1947* (OPC, 1972)

Mount, A. M. L., report to the Ministry of Transport on the accident at Norton Fitzwarren, 4 November 1940, presented 7 December 1940, available at www.railwaysarchive.co.uk

Nock, O. S., *The Great Western Railway in the 20th Century* (Ian Allan, 1964)

——, *History of the Great Western Railway, Volume 3: 1923–1947* (Ian Allan, 1967)

——, *The GWR Stars, Castles and Kings* (Ian Allan, 1980)

——, *Tales of the Great Western Railway* (David & Charles, 1984)

——, *Historic Railway Disasters*, 4th edn (Ian Allan, 1987)

RCTS, *The Locomotives of the Great Western Railway, Part Eight: Modern Passenger Classes* (Railway Correspondence and Travel Society, 1960)

Rowledge, J. W. P., *GWR Locomotive Allocations: First and Last Sheds, 1922–1967* (David & Charles, 1986)

Steam Railway, no. 463 (January 2017)

Thamesdown Museums, *The Great Western Railway Museum Swindon* (OPC, n.d.)

Tuplin, W. A., *Great Western Steam* (Allen and Unwin, 1963)

——, *British Steam since 1900* (David & Charles, 1969)

Vaughan, A., *Obstruction Danger, Significant British Railway Accidents, 1890–1986* (Patrick Stephens, 1989)

Star Class Workings References
(*See* Chapter 3)

The reference numbers are derived from the date of the publication's issue. In cases where dates coincide, sub characters identify specific volumes such as a, b, c and so on.

1970a Earley, M., *The Great Western Scene* (OPC, 1970)

1970b Riley, R. C., *Great Western Album*, Volume 2 (Ian Allan, 1970)

1973a Blenkinsop, R. J., *Shadows of the Great Western* (OPC, 1973)

1973b   Gasson, H., *Firing Days: Reminiscences of a Great Western Fireman* (OPC, 1973)

1973c   *Great Western Steam South of the Severn* (Bradford Barton, 1973)

1975   *Great Western Steam around Bristol* (Bradford Barton, 1975)

1976a   Gasson, H., *Footplate Days: More Reminiscences of a Great Western Fireman* (OPC, 1976)

1976b   *Great Western Steam through the Years* (Bradford Barton, 1976)

1976c   Haresnape, B. and A. Swain, *Churchward Locomotives* (Ian Allan, 1976)

1977   *Great Western Steam Miscellany 2* (Bradford Barton, 1977)

1978a   *Great Western Steam in Close-up* (Bradford Barton, 1978)

1978b   *Great Western Steam through the Years 2* (Bradford Barton, 1978)

1981a   Nicholas, D. and S. J. Montgomery, *100 Years of the Great Western* (OPC, 1981)

1981b   Wainwright, S. D., *Steam in West Cheshire and the North Wales Border* (Ian Allan, 1981)

1983   Beck, K., *The West Midland Lines of the GWR* (Ian Allan, 1983)

1984   Whitehouse, P., *The Great Western in the West Midlands* (OPC, 1984)

1985   Blenkinsop, R. J., *Big Four Cameraman* (OPC, 1985)

1986   Beck, K. M., *The Great Western North of Wolverhampton* (Ian Allan, 1986)

1989   Yarwood, M. F., *Window on the Great Western* (Wild Swan, 1989)

1991   Thomas, D. St. J. and P. Whitehouse, *The Great Days of the GWR* (Atlantic, 1991)

1996   Woodley, R., *The Day of the Holiday Express* (Ian Allan, 1996)

2000a   Copsey, J., 'Stars in Traffic', *Great Western Railway Journal*, 33 (Winter 2000); 34 (Spring 2000), pp. 89–97 [Star general arrangement drawings]; 35 (Summer 2000), pp. 161–9; 'Castles in Traffic', 98 (Spring 2016), pp. 63–77; 99 (Summer 2016), pp. 122–41; 100 (Autumn 2016), pp. 219–45; 102 (Spring 2017), pp. 347–65; 103 (November 2017), pp. 371–81

2000b   Vaughan, A., *Western Signalman (Glory Days)* (Ian Allan, 2000)

2006   Sterndale, S., *Great Western Pictorial No 3: The Tony Sterndale Collection* (Wild Swan, 2006)

2011   Hodge, J., *The North & West Route, Volume 3B: Abergavenny Brecon Road to Maindee Junction* (Wild Swan, 2011)

Websites

Building a Star Class Locomotive, 4041 Prince of Wales, Swindon, 1912 www.youtube.com/watch?v=oyUaBzuAUYs

Building a Castle Class locomotive, 7033 Hartlebury Castle, Swindon, 1950 www.youtube.com/watch?v=meEJG8M3qAw

5028: Llantilio Castle www.llantiliocastle.co.uk

'Railway Roundabout', BBC TV, 1958. The programme features 5043 and 7018 on the Bristolian. A King is also shown on the heavier Friday service. www.youtube.com/watch?v=zkNpaAqrdnk

'6000 King George V', Preserved British Steam Locomotives https://preservedbritishsteamlocomotives.com/6000-king-george-v/

The other preserved Kings are also represented.

6000 and 6023 together at Bristol Temple Meads in 1985. www.flickr.com/photos/16622848@N02/6254930170

David Hey, 'Memories of BR Steam Days' www.davidheyscollection.com/

For GWR and WR reporting numbers on smokeboxes.

INDEX

Those entries that have been abbreviated have also been included in the index, for example British Railways and BR appear as an aggregated whole. Entries for GWR locomotives do not reference the tables for which every subject engine has an entry but rather the body text or photograph caption.